D1596930

CAMBRIDGE STUDIES IN EIGHTEENTH-CENTURY
ENGLISH LITERATURE AND THOUGHT

The Rhetoric of
Berkeley's Philosophy

The works of George Berkeley (1685–1753) have been the object of much philosophical analysis; but philosophers are writers as well as thinkers, and Berkeley was himself positively interested in the functions of language and style. He recognized that words are used not just to convey ideas, but to stir the emotions and influence the behaviour of the hearer or reader. *The Rhetoric of Berkeley's Philosophy*, the first book-length assessment of Berkeley as a writer, offers rhetorical and literary analyses of his four major philosophical texts, *A Treatise concerning the Principles of Human Knowledge, Three Dialogues between Hylas and Philonous, Alciphron* and *Siris*. The Berkeley who emerges from this study is an accomplished stylist, one who builds structures of affective imagery, who creates dramatic voices in his texts, and who masters the range of philosophical genres – the treatise, the dialogue and the essay. Above all, Berkeley's awareness of the rhetorical functions of language is everywhere evident in his own style. His texts persuade as well as prove, enacting a process of inquiry so that the reader may, in the end, grasp Berkeley's truths as his own.

CAMBRIDGE STUDIES IN EIGHTEENTH-CENTURY ENGLISH LITERATURE AND THOUGHT

General Editors: Dr HOWARD ERSKINE-HILL, Litt.D., FBA, Pembroke College, Cambridge and Professor JOHN RICHETTI, University of Pennsylvania

Editorial Board: Morris Brownell, *University of Nevada*
Leopold Damrosch, *Harvard University*
J. Paul Hunter, *University of Chicago*
Isobel Grundy, *Queen Mary College, London*
Lawrence Lipking, *Northwestern University*
Harold Love, *Monash University*
Claude Rawson, *Yale University*
Pat Rogers, *University of South Florida*
James Sambrook, *University of Southampton*

The growth in recent years of eighteenth-century studies has prompted the establishment of this series of books devoted to the period. The series is designed to accommodate monographs and critical studies on authors, works, genres and other aspects of literary culture from the later part of the seventeenth century to the end of the eighteenth.

Since academic engagement with this field has become an increasingly interdisciplinary enterprise, books will be especially encouraged which in some ways stress the cultural context of the literature, or examine it in relation to contemporary art, music, philosophy, historiography, religion, politics, social affairs, and so on. New approaches to the established canon are being tested with increasing frequency, and the series will hope to provide a home for the best of these. The books we choose to publish will be thorough in their methods of literary, historical, or biographical investigation, and will open interesting perspectives on previously closed, or unexplored, or misrepresented areas of eighteenth-century writing and thought. They will reflect the work of both younger and established scholars on either side of the Atlantic and elsewhere.

Titles published
The Transformation of The Decline and Fall of the Roman Empire,
by David Womersley
Women's Place in Pope's World, by Valerie Rumbold
Sterne's Fiction and the Double Principle, by Jonathan Lamb
Warrior Women and Popular Balladry, 1650–1850, by Dianne Dugaw
The Body in Swift and Defoe, by Carol Flynn
The Rhetoric of Berkeley's Philosophy, Peter Walmsley
Space and the Eighteenth-Century English Novel, by Simon Varey

Other titles in preparation
Plots and Counterplots: Politics and Literary Representation, 1660–1730,
by Richard Braverman
The Eighteenth-Century Hymn, by Donald Davie
Richardson's Clarissa and the Eighteenth-Century Reader, by Tom Keymer
*Reason, Grace and Sentiment: A Study of the Language of Religion and Ethics
in England, 1660–1780,* by Isabel Rivers
Defoe's Politics: Parliament, Power, Kingship and Robinson Crusoe, by Manuel Schonhorn

'Georgius Berkeley S.T.P.', 1733; oil on canvas, artist
unknown (reproduced by kind permission of His Grace the
Archbishop of Canterbury: copyright reserved to the
Church Commissioners and the Courtauld Institute of Art)

The Rhetoric of Berkeley's Philosophy

PETER WALMSLEY

Assistant Professor, Department of English
McMaster University

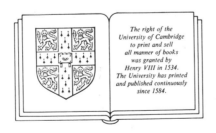

The right of the
University of Cambridge
to print and sell
all manner of books
was granted by
Henry VIII in 1534.
The University has printed
and published continuously
since 1584.

CAMBRIDGE UNIVERSITY PRESS

CAMBRIDGE

NEW YORK   PORT CHESTER   MELBOURNE   SYDNEY

Published by the Press Syndicate of the University of Cambridge
The Pitt Building, Trumpington Street, Cambridge CB2 1RP
40 West 20th Street, New York, NY 10011, USA
10 Stamford Road, Oakleigh, Melbourne 3166, Australia

First published 1990

Printed in Great Britain at the University Press, Cambridge

British Library cataloguing in publication data
Walmsley, Peter
The rhetoric of Berkeley's philosophy. – (Cambridge
studies in eighteenth-century English
literature and thought; 6).
1. Irish philosophy. Berkeley, George, 1685–1753
I. Title
192

Library of Congress cataloging in publication data
Walmsley, Peter
The rhetoric of Berkeley's philosophy / Peter Walmsley.
p.   cm. – (Cambridge studies in eighteenth-century English
literature and thought; 6)
Includes bibliographical references.
ISBN 0-521-37413-8
1. Berkeley, George, 1685–1753 – Literary art. 2. English
language – 18th century – Rhetoric. I. Title. II. Series.
B1348.W35 1990
192 – dc20   89-22385 CIP

ISBN 0 521 37413 8

For Nan and my parents

O vitae Philosophia dux, virtutis indagatrix!

Cicero
(epigraph to Berkeley's *Guardian* 35)

Contents

Acknowledgments

This work was generously supported by the Association of Commonwealth Universities and the Social Sciences and Humanities Research Council of Canada.

I wish here also to express my gratitude to some of those on whose help I have relied. Howard Erskine-Hill first turned me to Berkeley's writings, and I am deeply grateful for his careful criticisms and kind encouragement. Kathleen Wheeler and David Womersley have enlightened me as to my errors and omissions. I am likewise obliged to Patricia Brückmann, whose energy as a teacher and illuminating readings of the eighteenth century have been my inspiration for many years.

Note to the reader

All references to Berkeley's writings appear in the text and indicate the volume and page numbers of *The Works of George Berkeley, Bishop of Cloyne* in nine volumes edited by A. A. Luce and T. E. Jessop (London: Nelson, 1948–57). Luce and Jessop print the latest edition that Berkeley might have revised, indicating the variants of earlier editions at the bottom of the page. Unless otherwise stated, the text reproduced here is that of the first edition of each work. In the case of the notebooks of 1707–8, named by Luce the *Philosophical Commentaries* (hereafter *PC*) and edited by him for Volume I of the *Works*, I cite for convenience the number of the entry.

Note to the reader

Introduction

Elizabeth Montagu, in a letter to Gilbert West of 28 January 1753, reflects on the life and character of George Berkeley, who had died two weeks before. She confirms the testimony of all who knew Berkeley, that he was a man 'eminent in every christian virtue' and was prized as one who 'excelled every one in the arts of conversation'. Montagu's assessment of Berkeley's philosophical writings, however, is less than glowing:

they are some of them too subtile to be even the object of most peoples consideration. He has the hard fate of not convincing any one, tho he cannot be confuted; a judgment of his metaphysical works must be pass'd by superior intelligences, it falls not within the measure of 5 senses.[1]

And thinking, no doubt, of Berkeley's late and extraordinary work, *Siris*, she worries that 'he had an imagination too lively to be trusted to itself'; during his last years of isolation at Cloyne Berkeley worked the rich ore of his imagination into 'bright but useless medals'.

Montagu's letter is typical in its response to Berkeley's work. Almost all his contemporaries found the immaterialism propounded in the *Principles of Human Knowledge* and the *Three Dialogues between Hylas and Philonous* unconvincing, and many chose to dismiss it as 'subtile'. And yet they all conceded that Berkeley 'cannot be confuted', conscious of their own inability to refute any of his premises. This consciousness of the integrity of Berkeley's argument can only be attributed to his lucid and direct exposition of the few, seemingly simple arguments on which his system rests. With his maxim '*esse* is *percipi*', Berkeley asserted that 'ideas' of sense exist only in the perceiving mind and that only minds and their perceptions can be said to exist. He proceeded to explode the conventional distinction between the primary and secondary qualities of objects; figure and motion are as relative to the perceiver as colour and taste. With this and the argument that 'an idea can be like nothing but another idea', he denied the existence of matter. We have no grounds for imagining an unperceived substratum that is somehow like our ideas supporting

[1] Reprinted by G. N. Cantor in 'Two Letters Relating to Berkeley's Social Circle', *Berkeley Newsletter*, 4 (1980), 1–3.

or causing ideas in our minds. And since, obviously, our minds are not
the sources of their own sense experience, then another mind, the all-
seeing mind of God, must be the cause of our sensible world. The world
is a 'language' God speaks to our spirits.

Late in 1712, at the age of twenty-seven, Berkeley completed the *Three
Dialogues*, his last attempt at a full exposition of this simple but radical
epistemology. And at this point he left Ireland for the first time and came
to London. There seem to have been several reasons for this move. His
leaves of absence from Trinity College, Dublin, where he was a junior
fellow, cite improvement of learning and recovery of health, but he certainly also came to London to supervise the publication of the *Three Dialogues* and to see what opportunities the metropolis would afford. On
arrival, Berkeley was told that Richard Steele was eager to make his
acquaintance, and with their first meeting his career took an unexpected
literary turn. Steele had read Berkeley's *Principles* and was obviously
impressed. Writing to his friend Sir John Percival, Berkeley tells how
Steele welcomed him into his own literary circle. Berkeley was soon break-
fasting with Swift and dining with Arbuthnot. Pope presented him with
a copy of *Windsor-Forest*, and Addison found a place for him in his own
box on the opening night of *Cato*. While Berkeley's letters politely protest
that he wishes he were back in Ireland at Percival's fireside, he could not
conceal his pleasure and excitement at these attentions from the wits of
the age. Steele soon took a professional as well as a social interest in his
new friend and invited him to write for *The Guardian*, offering him a
guinea and a supper for each paper. Berkeley contributed more than a
dozen papers, vigorous essays ranging from a devastating lampoon of
Anthony Collins to pious reflections on his own death. Steele and Berkeley also collaborated on *The Ladies Library*, a selection for female readers
from popular books of moral and religious instruction.[2] Finally, Steele
was deep in plans for an edifying entertainment combining poetry readings, music, and painted scenery which he called the Censorium. Berkeley
describes the details of the lavish preparations to Percival, which suggests
that he may have lent a hand in this project as well.

While Berkeley was busy with his new literary tasks, Trinity College
was growing concerned at his protracted absence. In August he solicited
a royal licence permitting him to extend his leave from the college, but
the relative calm of the spring was followed by a politically stormy
summer, and Berkeley found himself having to choose among friends. A
Tory, he stopped contributing to *The Guardian* after Steele's inflammatory
paper on the Dunkirk controversy, and came to rely on Swift's influence.
That autumn Swift introduced Berkeley at Court and helped him secure

[2] See Steven Parks, 'George Berkeley, Sir Richard Steele and *The Ladies Library*', *Scriblerian*,
13 (1980), 1–2.

the chaplaincy in Lord Peterborough's diplomatic mission to Sicily. In October Berkeley left London and the *literati* behind. His employments in the following years show him devoting his energies to education: the second extensive continental tour as tutor to the son of the Bishop of Clogher; the active senior fellowship at Trinity in the early 1720s; and, of course, his campaign to found a college in Bermuda. But in his labours Berkeley never abandons the friendships formed in 1713, particularly his friendship with Pope. In his few surviving letters to Pope, Berkeley presents himself as a man of letters – not just an admirer, but a knowledgeable critic on matters poetical. It seems that Pope accepted Berkeley in this role, showing him a draft of *An Essay on Man* and, at Berkeley's suggestion, striking the apostrophe to Christ.[3] And Berkeley was to turn his own hand to poetry to express his aspirations for the Bermuda project.

> Westward the Course of Empire takes its Way;
> The first four Acts already past,
> A fifth shall close the Drama with the Day;
> Time's noblest Offspring is the last.   (VII.373)

This aspect of Berkeley's biography suggests that the distinction we readily make between the philosopher and the man of letters is misleading. Philosophers *are* writers, and, presumably, what Steele discerned in Berkeley's *Principles* was a prose stylist whose contributions to *The Guardian* could stand beside his own. Berkeley's own philosophical books show him very much aware of his task as a writer. In the course of his work he often stops to reflect on his own method, drawing attention to his diction, for example, or asserting the logical integrity of the particular style of argument he is employing. Berkeley also has much to say about the nature and ends of language. In the Introduction to the *Principles* and in the Seventh Dialogue of *Alciphron* he recognizes the variety and complexity of our responses to language. The simple communication of 'ideas' is not the chief and only function of words for Berkeley. He argues that language is often designed to stir the passions, to encourage certain mental dispositions, or influence the behaviour of the listener. Berkeley was conscious of these functions of language as he composed his own philosophical works. Before writing the *Principles* he made this entry in his notebooks:

The short jejune way in Mathematiques will not do in Metaphysiques & Ethiques, for y^t about Mathematical propositions men have no prejudices, no anticipated opinions to be encounter'd, they not having yet thought on such matters. tis not so in the other 2 mention'd sciences, a man must not onely demonstrate the truth, he must also vindicate it against scruples & establish'd opinions wch contradict it.

---

[3] Joseph Spence, *Observations, Anecdotes, and Characters of Books and Men*, ed. James M. Osborn, 2 vols (Oxford: Clarendon Press, 1966), Vol. I, p. 135.

In short the dry strigose rigid way will not suffice. he must be more ample &
copious, else his demonstration tho never so exact will not go down wth most.

(*PC* 163)

Here, early in his career, Berkeley recognizes that his own philosophical
writing must rely on the suasive powers of language. In order to communicate his ideas, he must, like the rhetorician, consider the disposition
of his audience, anticipate their prejudices and objections, and be copious
in making his case. Moreover the conviction in these lines suggests that
Berkeley would disagree with Montagu regarding the uselessness and
subtlety of his metaphysics.

Berkeley's challenging account of the nature of perception continues
to stimulate philosophical analysis. His works are the subject of much
sophisticated exegesis and paraphrase, and are praised or condemned
for their success or failure to provide an accurate portrait of our sense
experience. Given, however, Berkeley's interest in language and his
apparent concern with the impact of his own writing, it is appropriate to
ask some different questions of his texts. In this study I analyse the style
of Berkeley's four major philosophical writings: the *Principles of Human
Knowledge*, his first full exposition of immaterialism; the *Three Dialogues*,
which reworks this argument in a dramatic form; *Alciphron*, a dialogue of
mid-career devoted to ethics and apology; and *Siris*, an essay in natural
philosophy which displays the shift in Berkeley's late prose style. These
works represent both the breadth of Berkeley's thought and the variety
of rhetorical approaches and genres he adopts. Each will be treated as a
discrete literary venture and the salient features of its style examined,
both the local employment of metaphor, diction, and syntax, and the
larger issues related to the design of the work, such as the choice of
philosophical genre, the development of *personae*, and the arrangement
of arguments.

Several critics have already explored and illuminated Berkeley's language. In particular, Donald Davie has written five essays which discuss
the style of Berkeley's dialogues and consider his attitudes to the metaphoric diction of natural philosophy. And John J. Richetti, like Elizabeth
Montagu, finds in Berkeley's writings evidence of a powerful imagination.
His book *Philosophical Writing: Locke, Berkeley, Hume* shows Berkeley to be
a writer with strong lyric impulses which he restrains in his work, conscious of the dangers of metaphor and the instability of language. I will
address many of the issues explored by Davie and Richetti, but will attend
primarily to the rhetorical concerns Berkeley had expressed in entry
163 of his notebooks: how he plans to dispel 'prejudices' and conciliate
'scruples and establish'd opinions', and how he abjures 'the dry strigose
rigid way' for a more 'ample and copious' expression. By showing how

each text is designed to 'vindicate' the truth and make it convincing and compelling to the reader, I hope ultimately to reveal something of Berkeley's purposes and priorities as a writer.

PART I

The Principles of
Human Knowledge

1

Ideas and the ends of language

Bacon's denunciation of language and its attendant idols of the market became a commonplace in seventeenth-century philosophy. Learned writers repeated his doubts about language's ability to increase our knowledge, and many proposed standards for a new philosophical style. In the *Leviathan* Hobbes calls for 'perspicuous words' to free us from the 'absurdity' of our speech,[1] while Locke devotes a whole book of his *Essay concerning Human Understanding* to a reform of learned language. For Locke, 'Words, without clear and distinct *Ideas*' have to be banished by a careful process of definition in which we keep our simple ideas of sense in view and remind ourselves that words do not stand for things, but ideas of things.[2] Both Locke and Hobbes followed Bacon in rejecting appeals to authority, and both denounced metaphors in philosophical discourse. When writing or speaking the philosopher should keep in mind Locke's three '*ends of Language*':

First, To make known one Man's Thoughts or *Ideas* to another. *Secondly,* To do it with as much ease and *quickness,* as is possible; and *Thirdly,* Thereby *to convey* the *Knowledge* of Things. Language is either abused, or deficient, when it fails in any of these Three.[3]

In concluding his account '*Of the Abuse of Words*' in Book III, Locke warns us to shun the arts of language in philosophy:

if we would speak of Things as they are, we must allow, that all the Art of Rhetorick, besides Order and Clearness, all the artificial and figurative application of Words Eloquence hath invented, are for nothing else but to insinuate wrong *Ideas,* move the Passions, and thereby mislead the Judgment; and so indeed are perfect cheat.[4]

---

[1] *Leviathan*, ed. Michael Oakeshott (Oxford: Blackwell, 1946), chapter 5, p. 29.
[2] *An Essay concerning Human Understanding*, ed. Peter H. Nidditch (Oxford: Clarendon Press, 1975) (III.x.1), p. 490.
[3] *Essay* (III.x.23), p. 504.
[4] *Essay* (III.x.34), p. 34. Wilbur Samuel Howell finds the seeds of a new rhetoric in the *Essay*'s rather spare list of stylistic virtues and its emphasis on communication over persuasion – *Eighteenth-Century British Logic and Rhetoric* (Princeton, N.J.: Princeton University Press, 1971), pp. 490–1.

Order and clarity are the only qualities of prose permitted by Locke's cautious philosophical rhetoric.

In his early writings Berkeley seems to share his predecessors' anxiety about language. His notebooks of 1707 and 1708 reveal an early and apparently enthusiastic reception of Locke's Book III: 'Axiom. No word to be used without an idea' (*PC* 356), and later, 'N.B. Much Complaint about the Imperfection of Language' (*PC* 596). And like Locke he expresses concern that the imprecision of words in common use as well as the cloudiness of most metaphysical jargon threatens to undermine his exposition of an empirical philosophy. These concerns are duly given prominent expression in *An Essay towards a New Theory of Vision* (1709) where Berkeley interrupts his explanation of the heterogeneity of the objects of sight and touch to warn the reader that

> In treating of these things the use of language is apt to occasion some obscurity and confusion, and create in us wrong ideas: For language being accommodated to the common notions and prejudices of men, it is scarce possible to deliver the naked and precise truth without great circumlocution, impropriety, and (to an unwary reader) seeming contradictions.   (I.219)

Berkeley then urges us not to take issue with his inevitably faulty expression, but to strive instead to grasp his meaning and 'consider the bare notions themselves'.

This theme of the inadequacy of language for philosophical discourse is explored in greater depth in the Introduction to *A Treatise concerning the Principles of Human Knowledge* (1710). In the notebooks Berkeley had remarked that Book III of Locke's *Essay* seemed at odds with the argument of the first two books; Locke obviously should have begun his investigations by thinking about words. To avoid the same blunder, Berkeley proposes to discuss 'the nature and abuse of language' in the Introduction to the *Principles* as a subject proper 'to prepare the reader for the easier conceiving what follows' (II.27). But the problems presented by language are, for Berkeley, tied up with the theory of mental abstraction, a theory most recently expounded by Locke. Although Locke strove to tie language and thought to sensory experience, he none the less admitted a scholastic explanation of mental abstraction and condoned a limited use of abstract language. Berkeley's account of language in the *Principles* begins with an objection to Locke's statement that

> Words become general, by being made the signs of general *Ideas*: and *Ideas* become general, by separating from them the circumstances of Time, and Place, and any other Ideas, that may determine them to this or that particular Existence.[5]

A general term is, for Locke, the name of an abstract idea. Berkeley

---

[5] *Essay* (III.iii.6), pp. 410–11.

objects on the grounds that it is only possible to form particular, not abstract ideas. He makes his point by showing the absurdity of an abstract idea of the mode *colour*, trying to frame 'an idea of colour in abstract which is neither red, nor blue, nor white, nor any other determinate colour' (II.28). Abstract ideas of substances prove even more improbable. In an idea of *man* 'there is included stature, but then it is neither tall stature nor low stature, nor yet middle stature, but something abstracted from all these' (II.29). Obviously, another account of the meaning of general terms is needed, and Berkeley proposes that 'A word becomes general by being made the sign, not of an abstract general idea but, of several particular ideas, any one of which it indifferently suggests to the mind' (II.31). Berkeley accepts the multiple reference of general terms as a true and proper function of language, but he fears we frequently find ourselves using abstract terms which, upon examination, have no attendant particular ideas. The assumption that each word has a single determinate idea as its meaning has led us to believe in the existence of abstract general ideas, a belief which Berkeley recognizes as the source of much confusion in philosophical speculations. So his theme in the closing sections of the Introduction is 'that most parts of knowledge have been strangely perplexed and darkened by the abuse of words' (II.38).

On the grounds of these important discoveries, Berkeley is moved to make a pact with the reader at the end of his Introduction. He resolves to be wary of language, and to keep ideas 'bare and naked into my view, keeping out of my thoughts, so far as I am able, those names which long and constant use hath so strictly united with them' (II.38–9). Berkeley does not analyse for us the relation of word to idea in the mind, but instead embodies it in a conventional metaphor of clothing.[6] Ideas are 'naked, undisguised' and must be 'divested of words', while words are 'dress' and a 'curtain' (II.39–40). Above all, abstract ideas are not real ideas but simply words we mistakenly treat as ideas. They are 'a fine and subtle net' (II.39) to the understanding, which when pulled aside reveal empty space. Berkeley enumerates for us the benefits of his stripping away of words from ideas. It will mean that the *Principles*' argument will be free of 'controversies purely verbal' and can thus concentrate on Locke's fundamental process of learning, carefully comparing clear and distinct ideas 'to discern the agreements or disagreements' between them (II.39). In return for his efforts Berkeley asks the reader to

---

[6] Sprat, for example, tells us that ornaments of speech were once employed 'to represent *Truth*, cloth'd with Bodies . . . But now they are generally chang'd to worse uses: They make the *Fancy* disgust the best things, if they come sound, and unadorn'd' – *The History of the Royal Society*, ed. Jackson I. Cope and Harold Whitmore Jones (London: Routledge, 1959), p. 112.

make my words the occasion of his own thinking, and endeavour to attain the same train of thoughts in reading, that I had in writing them . . . He will be out of all danger of being deceived by my words, and I do not see how he can be led into an error by considering his own naked, undisguised ideas.   (II.40)

What this pact fails to elucidate, however, is a technique for extracting Berkeley's particular 'ideas' from the inevitably representative and indeterminate language of the *Principles*.

Despite such ambiguities, Berkeley's Introduction makes one thing clear – that there exists a serious disjunction between language and accurate thought, so that in our reading we must try to lay aside words while collecting the sense of the text. Berkeley does not, however, accept all the consequences of such an attitude. First, he is careful not to join Locke in insisting on a dichotomy between philosophical and ordinary speech.[7] Such an admission would damage Berkeley's frequent appeals to common sense and common usage. Second, his sceptical attitude to language implies that the individual mind is inevitably isolated and that, because of the representative nature of language, private meaning (the determinate idea) and public meaning (the word) will never concur. Indeed, in the surviving draft of the Introduction Berkeley suggested that in the *Principles* he would play a 'solitary philosopher', one who never learned a language and is thus free to contemplate nothing but his 'constant train of particular ideas' (II.141). Berkeley was wise to edit here. That a mind cut off from the concourse of humanity should have a better purchase on truth has unhappy repercussions for ethics and theology, sciences important to the argument of the *Principles*. Moreover the notebooks reveal that Berkeley wondered, on reflection, if his lone thinker would be able to retain any knowledge without the help of language (*PC* 607). Berkeley's revision to the Introduction shows that he was not unaware of the difficulties inherent in his policy of attending to ideas alone, but that he felt at the same time his pact with the reader was a necessary prelude to his argument.

So the reader of the *Principles* is prepared for a rigorous culling of vocabulary and a constant scrutiny of language. Berkeley is true to his word. At several points of Part I we are reminded to take care lest we be 'imposed on by words' (II.59) and warned, when tenacious of our abstractions, to 'annex a meaning to our words' (II.79). But it turns out that only one family of abstract words is made the object of all this scrutiny, words relating to matter. The tenet that objects exist apart from our perception of them is, in Berkeley's eyes, the greatest delusion foisted on mankind by the doctrine of abstraction, and he repeatedly insists that propositions claiming the external existence of objects 'have no meaning

---

[7] *Essay* (III.iv.3), p. 476.

in them' (II.64). More specifically, in his *a priori* arguments Berkeley analyses the common vocabulary of matter. Here he isolates the terms *substance* and *substratum* and considers the idea they evoke: that matter somehow supports primary qualitites. His immediate recourse is to a determinate mental image. 'It is evident', he tells us, '*support* cannot here be taken in its usual or literal sense, as when we say that pillars support a building: in what sense therefore must it be taken?' (II.47). *Substance* and *substratum* thus tumble into the dustbin of abstractions. Later, in the refutations which form the middle section of the *Principles*, this argument is given a more dramatic elaboration. Here the reader is forced to take up the defence of *matter*. Berkeley first points out to us that no positive quality can be attributed to matter. 'But, say you, it is the *unknown occasion*, at the presence of which, ideas are excited in us by the will of God' (II.70–1). Berkeley replies that an 'occasion' is either an agent or an accompaniment, and that matter, inert and imperceptible, can be neither of these (II.71). He then rejects for a second time the proffered notion of matter as substance or support of ideas (II.74). Finally the reader suggests matter might be defined as a '*quiddity*, *entity*, or *existence*', or even as 'an unknown *somewhat*', all of which Berkeley dismisses as abstract ideas: 'I do not find that there is any kind of effect or impression made on my mind, different from what is excited by the term *nothing*' (II.75). In these elaborate processes of linguistic scrutiny, the reader is placed in the uncomfortable position of violating the pact of the Introduction by not imitating Berkeley's train of ideas. Embarrassingly, we seem to be forcing him to strip our language for us. Berkeley either explodes the metaphor behind our philosophical terms, or appeals to their vulgar rather than their philosophical usage. It is always the failure of a word to evoke a clear picture in the mind – a Berkeleian 'idea' – that leads to its damnation as empty talk.

Ian Hacking has argued that the language theories expounded by seventeenth- and eighteenth-century philosophers are 'applied'. Hobbes, Locke, and Berkeley are interested in language, and discuss it in their works, only in so far as it can help them with the problems of 'pure' philosophy they wish to solve.[8] Hacking does not explore, however, the many ways in which Berkeley's strict language pact is a useful, even a necessary prolegomenon to his immaterialist argument. First, the polemic technique of stripping words seems perfectly suited for Berkeley's critique of our notions of matter; Locke himself candidly admitted the impossibility of a sensory knowledge of corporeal substance. But it lays the ground for immaterialism in a second way. By inculcating a Lockian scientific language, Berkeley can invoke as well the empiricist's theories

[8] *Why Does Language Matter to Philosophy?* (Cambridge: Cambridge University Press, 1975), pp. 2 and 43.

of thought. While Locke warned that words named ideas, not things, he strove all the harder for a language that was tied to our original sensory experiences, and he consistently referred to sensations as 'ideas'. By invoking Locke's new empirical system of meaning in his Introduction, Berkeley can easily imply the complementary conception of idea as sensation, a usage he consolidates in this very Lockian passage which opens Part I:

It is evident to any one who takes a survey of the objects of human knowledge, that they are either ideas actually imprinted on the senses, or else such as are perceived by attending to the passions and operations of the mind, or lastly ideas formed by help of memory and imagination, either compounding, dividing, or barely representing those originally perceived in the aforesaid ways.   (II.41)

This limited employment of *idea* was not simply assumed by Berkeley as a consequence of his early immersion in Locke's *Essay*, but was a conscious choice. In the first of his notebooks he acknowledges that *ideas* can mean 'thoughts' as well as 'sensations', only considering 'confining this term to things sensible' in the second (*PC* 490). At entry 685, he reminds himself 'Excuse to be made in the Introduction for the using the Word Idea viz. because it has obtain'd. But a Caution must be added.' The Introduction does not, however, draw our attention to his adoption of the philosophical use of the term, perhaps because a visual testing of 'ideas' as well as words is an important strategy in his argument. In his rejection of the primary *versus* secondary quality distinction, for example, he asks us to 'conceive the extension and motion of a body', while plainly intending we should visualize them: 'I must withal give it some colour' (II.45). And his final *a priori* argument, that we have no 'idea' of how body acts on spirit, plays on the pervasive notion that seeing is knowing. The revolutionary principle itself, '*esse* is *percipi*', can only pertain in a Lockian world where 'ideas' are seen in the mind.

There is, for Berkeley, yet a third useful consequence to the linguistic pact whereby both reader and writer attend only to mental pictures. By insisting that the distinct visual image is the standard of accurate thought, he avoids tactile 'ideas'. Touch is the other sense by which we may be said, erroneously or not, to know objects in space. Although it is clear that Berkeley had formulated his immaterialist thesis by the time he wrote his *New Theory of Vision*, that work did not challenge the view that we can know 'outward objects' by touch. He apologizes for this in the *Principles*: 'it was beside my purpose to examine and refute it in a discourse concerning *vision*' (II.59). But the *Principles* talks little of touch, and when he does raise it, Berkeley still seems unwilling to admit that its 'ideas' are not somehow more real than those of sight. In his critique of Newtonian absolutes near the conclusion of the book, he argues that it is by touch that we know both space and body (II.93). Likewise we are told that ideas of sight are 'marks and prognostics' of those of touch, and

that visible ideas are the language whereby the governing spirit, on whom we depend, informs us what tangible ideas he is about to imprint upon us, in case we excite this or that motion in our own bodies.   (II.58–9)

On the terms of Berkeley's own Introduction a 'language' is of a lesser order of reality than the things it signifies. And Berkeley cannot believe that sight is necessarily temporally prior to touch. He seems still to be paying lip-service to the 'vulgar error' that when we close our hand on a small stone, we are very certain of its existence. Even though Locke remained adamant about the incomprehensibility of matter, he accepted its existence on the basis of just such a tangible test: 'If any one asks me, *What this Solidity is*, I send him to his Senses to inform him: Let him put a Flint, or a Foot-ball between his Hands; and then endeavour to join them, and he will know.'[9] For Locke this idea of solidity or impenetrability 'of all other, seems the *Idea* most intimately connected with, and essential to Body, so as no where else to be found or imagin'd, but only in matter'.[10] Berkeley does not confront an idea so inimical to immaterialism in his *a priori* proofs. Rather he dismisses solidity in a sweeping condemnation of the primary qualities: 'Without extension solidity cannot be conceived; since therefore it has been shewn that extension exists not in an unthinking substance, the same must also be true of solidity' (II.46). Here again the inculcated visual test for words proves valuable. By avoiding touch Berkeley can convincingly tie solidity, an idea of touch, to extension, which has just been dismissed as an invalid abstraction from visual ideas.

Fourth, by comitting both himself and his reader to Locke's crusade against 'words, without clear and distinct *Ideas*', Berkeley makes an emphatic statement about his own project. He asserts that the *Principles* will be an empirical work, for the attack on abstract language was a rallying cry of modern scientific thought. Bacon, in dedicating himself to the task of naming natural objects, rejected the theoretical names applied by scholastics such as 'Primum Mobile' and 'Elementum Ignis'. While he found some names of substances valid, many verbs and names of modes proved the product of 'faulty and unskilful abstraction'.[11] Both Hobbes and Locke were eager to apply Bacon's test of 'thingness' to the names of those abstract Aristotelian conceptions that bore on their studies; 'forms'

[9] *Essay* (II.vi.6), pp. 126–7. Berkeley copied this passage from the *Essay* in his notebooks (*PC* 78).
[10] *Essay* (II.iv.1), p. 123.
[11] *The Philosophical Works of Francis Bacon*, ed. James Spedding *et al.* (London: Longmans, 1857–8), Vol. IV, p. 61.

and 'essences' for Locke, for Hobbes 'incorporeal substances' or 'transubstantiation' – all were banished as insignificant speech. In entry 564 of the notebooks Berkeley recognizes that the main theme of his Introduction was Baconian: 'Doctrine of Abstraction of very evil consequence in all the Sciences. Mem: Bacon's remark. Entirely owing to Language.' So the Introduction establishes an affiliation between the *Principles* and the modern empirical project that will only be broken by the surprising outcome of his *a priori* proof, a proof which, it will be found, is itself essentially *ad hominem*. Only through an extreme empiricism – by being more exacting than Locke in examining our sensory experiences and by doubting primary as well as secondary qualities – can Berkeley produce his vision of a theocentric universe. Confronted with the growing prestige of the work of Locke and Newton, Berkeley saw that they had to be refuted on their own grounds. The linguistic pact of the Introduction is the first step in the *Principles'* process of exposing the great modern materialists as abstract philosophers, men whose words are empty dress, mere signs without things signified.

There is one final reason for beginning the *Principles* with a complaint about language. Berkeley is entering the philosophical forum with a radical proposal, and he naturally worries that opponents to his system might challenge his terminology. In the notebooks he reminds himself 'Mem: to correct my Language & make it as Philosophically nice as possible to avoid giving handle' (*PC* 209). By beginning on the theme that all philosophy is hampered by words, Berkeley disarms the reader who might object to his diction. This strategy is certainly foremost in Berkeley's mind when he complains about verbal obscurity and confusion in the *New Theory of Vision*, asking his reader to be candid and not 'stick in this or that phrase' (I.219). This plea is inserted just as Berkeley is about to defend his most radical proposal: that ideas of sight and ideas of touch are heterogeneous. Not only does he recognize the difficulty of conceiving this point, but he is also aware that the evidence of common usage, in all languages, undermines his doctrine. We call the book we touch and the book we see by the same name. So it is in preparation for a particular violation of everyday speech that Berkeley chooses to instil in the reader a sense of the difficulty of philosophical discourse and the need for a sympathetic reading. Perhaps this same strategy is at work in the Introduction of the *Principles*, where he will insist that *things* are but collections of *ideas*, and that *esse* is *percipi*.

Berkeley's call for a strict philosophical language has been seized on by some critics as an expression of his fundamental attitudes to language and particularly to his own writing. Herbert Rauter,[12] for example, finds

---

[12] ' "The Veil of Words": Sprachauffassung und Dialogform bei George Berkeley', *Anglia*, 79 (1961), 390–1.

Berkeley an insecure writer, and feels Berkeley puts himself at the mercy of the reader in his Introduction when he makes the reader's ideas the ultimate test of the truth of the *Principles*. John J. Richetti also notes the Introduction's 'dramatized relocation of certitude in the reader' and its insistence on a gulf between thought and language. He goes on to characterize Berkeley's writings as betraying a 'reluctant verbalization':

Berkeley's ideal literary situation is thus an exceedingly lively one where the stability and integrity of the text are always in question, where both reader and author are openly critical of its finality and constantly vigilant against 'Gibberish' and 'Jargon'.[13]

While both these critics admirably capture the *Principles'* vigorous engagement with the reader, they tend to slight its confident tone and its unwavering and often persuasive pursuit of its polemical ends. Did Berkeley truly expect his readers to meet the difficult challenge of laying aside his words in reading? Certainly the Introduction's invocation of the reader is, first and foremost, designed to prepare the ground for stripping away materialist language in Part I, a process which is instigated and controlled by the text, not the reader. The simple usefulness of the Introduction's linguistic pact to Berkeley's argument suggests we should proceed cautiously before reading it as a confession of his uncertainty about his role as writer.

But for evidence that Berkeley was not a thorough sceptic regarding language, one need only look more closely at the Introduction itself. For it contains the germ of a second theory of language which is, in many ways, antithetical to the strict Lockian pact of its own conclusion. This second theory grows as Berkeley elaborates his case that a general term does not name a single, abstract idea. He first observes, in section 18 of the Introduction, that definition is different from signification; while the general word '*triangle*' signifies an infinity of possible particular triangles, it may, none the less, be properly defined by the words '*a plain surface comprehended by three right lines*' (II.36). This notion re-emerges later in Part I where Berkeley questions the scholastic discrimination of subject and mode, pointing out that in the proposition 'a die is hard, extended and square' each word does not conjure up its own distinct 'idea' (II.62). Berkeley recognizes that, however troublesome the relations between words and ideas may be, language does have its own valid and often precise internal reference. In section 19 he takes this insight farther:

a little attention will discover, that it is not necessary (even in the strictest reasonings) [that] significant names which stand for ideas should, every time they are used, excite in the understanding the ideas they are made to stand for: in reading

---

[13] *Philosophical Writing: Locke, Berkeley, Hume* (Cambridge, Mass: Harvard University Press, 1983), pp. 129, 152 and 127.

and discoursing, names being for the most part used as letters are in *algebra*, in which though a particular quantity be marked by each letter, yet to proceed right it is not requisite that in every step each letter suggest to your thoughts, that particular quantity it was appointed to stand for.   (II.37)

As in algebra, we need not cash each sign when speaking or listening. Several modern critics have argued that Berkeley's metaphor here marks an important departure from Lockian language theory.[14] Where Locke sees language as a sequence of signs to be accompanied by a correspondent sequence of ideas in the speaker's and, with luck, the listener's mind, Berkeley's 'algebra' recognizes that meaning has to do with a comprehension of relations between signs. Berkeley does not draw these hints together into a coherent formalist linguistic, but he does admit that in normal discourse language need have no immediate reference to ideas.

Berkeley makes one further case against Locke in his Introduction. He stops to show how the principles of rhetoric contradict the notion that each word should have a corresponding idea, beginning section 20 with this direct challenge to Locke's doctrine of the ends of language:

Besides, the communicating of ideas marked by words is not the chief and only end of language, as is commonly supposed. There are other ends, as the raising of some passion, the exciting to, or deterring from an action, the putting the mind in some particular disposition; to which the former is in many cases barely subservient, and sometimes entirely omitted, when these can be obtained without it, as I think does not infrequently happen in familiar use of language. I entreat the reader to reflect with himself, and see if it does not oft happen either in hearing or reading a discourse, that the passions of fear, love, hatred, admiration, disdain etc. arise immediately in his mind upon the perception of certain words, without any ideas coming between.   (II.37)

Berkeley proceeds to explain that some very indeterminate expressions, such as 'danger' or '*good things*', have gained, through experience, large emotional increments:

May we not, for example, be affected with the promise of a *good thing*, though we have not an idea of what it is? Or is not the being threatened with danger sufficient

---

[14] Anthony Flew, in particular, finds a 'revolutionary and historically premature insight', arguing that 'Berkeley had grasped the essential irrelevance to mathematics, and even to language in general, of the occurrence or non-occurrence of any sort of mental imagery.' Berkeley was thus free 'to develop a diametrically opposite theory of meaning. It must start from the public and accessible use of words and expressions, rather than from their private and putative image associations'; see *Hume's Philosophy of Belief: A Study of the First Inquiry* (London: Routledge, 1961), pp. 262–3. Jonathan Bennett admits such Wittgensteinian insights in Berkeley's writings, but is also aware that Berkeley does not abandon Locke's view that a word's meaning is its mental correlate; see *Locke, Berkeley, Hume: Central Themes* (Oxford: Clarendon Press, 1971), pp. 52–3. Berkeley's thoughts on the function and nature of language are placed in their context by Stephen K. Land; see *From Signs to Propositions: The Concept of Form in Eighteenth-Century Semantic Theory* (London: Longmans, 1974), pp. 141–6.

to excite a dread, though we think not of any particular evil likely to befall us, nor yet frame to our selves an idea of danger in abstract?   (II.37–8)

He goes on to a final example of the schoolman who regularly feels submissive on hearing the words '*Aristotle hath said it.*' These examples of emotive meaning are very much condensed from the first draft of the Introduction. There we discover that the '*good things*' are Scriptural; those 'which God hath prepared for them that love him are such as eye hath not seen nor ear heard nor hath it enter'd the heart of man to conceive' (1 Cor. 2.9). Berkeley explains that such seemingly empty words have both a 'good purpose' and 'meaning and design' (II.137). We cannot presume the apostle was trifling; no, he intends by '*good things*' to instil in us a desire and hope for the rewards of heaven.

In all, section 20 expounds a theory of language that is explicitly rhetorical rather than empirical. Berkeley's acknowledgment of the complex suasive intentions of writers, of the emotions that are part of our customary response to language, and of the importance of action as an end of language – these are the central concerns of rhetoric. Moreover, Berkeley, like the rhetorician, assumes the public nature of meaning. Rhetoric depends on the fact that a group of listeners or readers can be counted on to respond as one to certain linguistic strategies. By contrast, seventeenth-century ideation theories of language emphasize that meaning is essentially private, that the ideas we assign to words depend on our individual experiences. Locke warns us not to assume our '*Words to be Marks of the Ideas in the Minds also of other Men*'.[15] Surprisingly, in an Introduction elsewhere so carefully Lockian in its depiction of language, we find none of Locke's disparagement of 'passion' in speech. Consider Berkeley's first two examples of affective language. Our customary responses to Paul's promise of '*good things*' or to a cry of 'danger' are not only appropriate, but necessary, the one for our spiritual, the other for our physical well-being. Even the schoolman's customary reverence on hearing 'Aristotle' is handled with a subdued irony and not the angry contempt that Bacon and Locke had loaded on these bugbears of modern philosophy. Where Locke would condemn such a dangerous 'abuse of words', Berkeley seems genuinely interested in the schoolman's behaviour as a linguistic phenomenon, as another example of how words can function without attendant 'ideas'.

The brief appeal in section 20 to a rhetorical view of language is not entirely forgotten in Part I's busy attack on the language of materialism. Apart from the immediate stimulation of the passions, other ends of language admitted in section 20 are 'the exciting to, or deterring from an action, [and] the putting the mind in some particular disposition'.

---

[15] *Essay* (III.ii.4), p. 406.

These practical effects of language are given vivid and dramatic illustration in Part I's attack on metaphysical notions of time:

Bid your servant meet you at such a *time*, in such a *place*, and he shall never stay to deliberate on the meaning of those words: in conceiving that particular time and place, or the motion by which he is to get thither, he finds not the least difficulty.   (II.83)

Berkeley's point is that we can have no notion of time abstracted from our particular experiences of the passage of ideas in our minds, but the example also pits the appropriate busyness of the servant against the fruitless ponderings of the abstract philosopher. A few pages later Berkeley strikes a somewhat similar note in attacking abstractions in ethics: 'a man may be just and virtuous, without having precise ideas of *justice*, and *virtue*' (II.84). In both these attacks on abstraction, activity is contrasted with ideation as an appropriate response to language. Later, when Berkeley makes his case against the modern mathematicians, he insists that 'use' and 'practice' for 'the benefit of life' are the proper ends of their science (II.95–6). He argues that the mathematician's number system is a kind of language, and, harkening back to the algebra analogy of the Introduction, says that in using this language 'we regard not the *things* but the *signs*, which nevertheless are not regarded for their own sake, but because they direct us how to act with relation to things' (II.97).

All these admissions suggest that Berkeley was fully aware of the limitations of Locke's ideational theory of language, and so cast some doubts on the sincerity of his own statements that words are a veil we must tear aside, and that they somehow stand between us and knowledge. Perhaps *this* claim, made late in the notebooks, better embodies the *Principles'* attitude to words:

Words (by them meaning all sort of signs) are so necessary that instead of being (w^n duly us'd or in their own Nature) prejudicial to the Advancement of knowledge, or an hindrance of knowledge that wthout them there could in Mathematiques themselves be no demonstration.   (*PC* 750)

Certainly, as the *Principles* progresses a revaluation of language, particularly of common speech, occurs. At first, of course, Berkeley's a priori proofs depend on a transformation of common usage and on the institution of a special philosophical language of *ideas*. Notice how Berkeley conveniently slips out of the vernacular in his maxim '*esse* is *percipi*'; *to be is to be perceived* is too obvious a violation of normal thought and language. In this instance he must make it clear he is speaking as a philosopher. And, as we have seen, one term in common use, *matter*, is inadmissable by the strict language pact. On these Lockian grounds again Berkeley can also defend his use of *idea* to mean, ultimately, *thing*, telling us 'I am not for disputing about the propriety, but the truth of the expression' (II.57).

Defending himself as a realist, he says he could have used the word *thing*, but it would have evoked the materialist prejudices of the reader and *thing* includes spirits as well as ideas. But later in the *Principles* Berkeley is also willing to admit, in a number of instances, unphilosophical and indeterminate language. Consider his changing attitude to the word *substance*. We have witnessed his rejection of this word with regard to primary qualities and matter; it is incomprehensible that matter should support ideas 'as pillars support a building'. But he later remarks that it is only the philosophical meaning of *substance* that he dislikes, and is quite willing to maintain 'the vulgar sense' in which substance is 'a combination of sensible qualities' (II.56). And he can talk comfortably of spirit as 'an incorporeal, active substance', stating that 'a spirit has been shown to be the only substance or support, wherein the unthinking beings or ideas can exist' (II.103). Berkeley is, it seems, confident that we will accept *spiritual substance* as a tried theological term denoting spirit's essence or being. But, of course, the unreflective reader brings to *spiritual substance* the vulgar meaning of a solid, real thing, and Berkeley's spiritual world subtly grows more tangible and thus more credible in our minds.

This willingness to reaccept once-rejected diction in new roles is part of a general easing of usage after the *a priori* proofs. In his refutations Berkeley often slips out of his strict language of ideas, as when, in a deferential mood, he gives us permission to speak of natural causes; we may say 'that fire heats' instead of the more correct 'that a spirit heats'. In these matters, Berkeley tells us, 'we ought to *think with the learned, and speak with the vulgar*' (II.62). We may defer in daily discourse to customary usage. While such language may be false in a 'strict and speculative sense', yet 'any phrases may be retained, so long as they excite in us proper sentiments, or dispositions to act in such a manner as is necessary for our well-being' (II.63). Berkeley seems to be actively defending such flawed but effective phrases when he dismisses Newton's account of absolute motion for its violation of 'the propriety of language' (II.92). At the end of the refutations, having appealed at several points to the usual acceptation of words, he proclaims 'that in the tenets we have laid down, there is nothing inconsistent with the right use and significancy of *language*, and that discourse of what kind soever, so far as it is intelligible, remains undisturbed' (II.76–7). This claim is far from the strict diction of the Introduction and *a priori* proofs, where Berkeley was keen to give philosophical accuracy rein over propriety of expression. No doubt Berkeley's gradual relinquishing of his sceptical attitude to language owes something to his need for a more flexible vocabulary in the latter half of the *Principles*, for here he must appeal to the ethical and religious beliefs of the reader. In his notebooks he remarks ''Tis prudent to correct mens mistakes without altering their language. This makes truth glide into their souls insensibly' (*PC* 185). But Berkeley's acceptance of vulgar usage is more than just the sugar coating on the bitter pill of immaterialism. Nor does the *Principles* make a consistent distinction between philosophical and vulgar talk. Too often, as with *substance* and *motion* and *time*, Berkeley finds that the philosopher is wrong and the common speaker is right. As the *Principles* unfolds he grows more and more hesitant in championing a language validated by private sensory experiences, and moves to defend instead the common language which proves so 'necessary for our well-being'.

The Introduction's two uncomplementary views of language are not its only puzzling feature, for its argument keeps returning to a theme that has little apparent relation to either abstraction or language, the theme of the nature of man. It is raised first in section 3, in which Berkeley renounces Locke's essentially sceptical attitude to human knowledge: 'We should believe that God has dealt more bountifully with the sons of men, than to give them a strong desire for that knowledge, which He had placed quite out of their reach' (II.26). We should not doubt our faculties, Berkeley tells us; we should rather doubt the use to which we have put them. This optimistic note is sounded again at the end of the Introduction in a statement almost lyric in its rhythms and imagery:

In vain do we extend our view into the heavens, and pry into the entrails of the earth, in vain do we consult the writings of learned men, and trace the dark footsteps of antiquity; we need only draw the curtain of words, to behold the fairest tree of knowledge, whose fruit is excellent, and within the reach of our hand.

(II.40)

The knell-like anaphora of the opening of this pronouncement expresses the difficulty of the pursuit of knowledge and even suggests a resignation to ignorance, but in mid-sentence Berkeley's message is suddenly transformed into a promise that refreshing truths lie within our grasp.[16]

Together these two expressions of confidence in man's ability to attain knowledge through God's grace frame the Introduction, asking us to reflect on our place in the world. This issue surfaces at several points in the course of the Introduction. In section 9, for example, Berkeley presents this parodic example of a Lockian abstract idea, which must contain only universal characteristics:

[16] This passage seems to echo Cowley's jubilant invitation to the orchard of empirical knowledge in 'To the Royal Society' (iii.18–22), in Sprat, sigs. B1ᵛ–B2ʳ:

> The Orchards open now, and free;
> *Bacon* has broke that Scare-crow Dietie;
> Come, enter, all that will,
> Behold the rip'ned Fruit, come gather now your Fill.

Cowley goes on to explain that the only fruit forbidden man is that which the presumptuous scholastic tries to grasp – knowledge without the use of the senses.

And after this manner it is said we come by the abstract idea of *man* or, if you please, humanity or human nature; wherein it is true, there is included colour, because there is no man but has some colour, but then it can be neither white, nor black, nor any particular colour; because there is no one particular colour wherein all men partake.   (II.28–9)

Berkeley's irony here is double; this abstract idea of man is impossible to frame, but at the same time no physical form, whether abstract or particular, could be a sufficient idea of 'humanity or human nature'. A reliance on sensory criteria leads the empiricist to a reductive, wholly physical conception of man. Likewise, section 11 is devoted to a long and not immediately pertinent joke at Locke's expense. Berkeley quotes at length from Book II of the *Essay*, where Locke suggests that abstraction 'is that which puts a perfect distinction between man and brutes'. Having shown the impossibility of abstract ideas, Berkeley can retort:

I readily agree with this learned author, that the faculties of brutes can by no means attain to *abstraction*. But then if this be made the distinguishing property of that sort of animals, I fear a great many of those that pass for men must be reckoned into their number.   (II.30–1)

Here, as in section 9, Berkeley's irony implies Locke's failure to offer an acceptable account of our rational natures. This difficulty is brought into sharp focus in section 20's description of the schoolman's emotional reaction to the word *Aristotle*, which is so sudden that 'it is impossible any idea either of his person, writings, or reputation should go before' (II.38). But which of these is the appropriate response to *Aristotle*? If we are to play Berkeley's philosophical readers, what 'naked, undisguised idea' should this word, a man's name, generate? Berkeley's raises here an issue that becomes more and more important as the *Principles* progresses – how we can be said to know spirit.

   This issue seems itself chiefly responsible for Berkeley's easing of his rigorous ideation pact. As we have seen, Berkeley's insistence that the only valid idea is a determinate visual image has been most useful in the elimination of *matter*. But *spirit* obviously cannot survive the same scrutiny. While he believes that 'by the word *spirit* we mean only that which thinks, wills, and perceives' (II.104), Berkeley does not mean to suggest that we have anything like a mental picturing of these operations. In planning the *Principles* he shows a deep concern about how he should handle knowledge of spirit. In his notebooks he is dissatisfied with his neat formula for the immaterialist principle because it constricts *mind* to *perceiver and imaginer*: 'Existence is percipi or percipere', he writes, only to insert with a caret 'or velle i:e. agere' (*PC* 429). At entry 878 he notes, 'But in Book 2 I shall at large shew the difference there is betwixt the Soul & Body or Extended being.' But he cannot defer handling this issue; some conception of spirit, however tentative, is necessary for the critical doctrine of immaterialism to become a positive and heuristic system. When Berkeley first considers spirit, he explains that we cannot see or imagine spirit because it is pure activity, and all 'ideas' are inert. We can experience spirit only as a cause of ideas: our own spirit as it creates and manipulates our ideas, and God by the stronger ideas of sense imprinted on our minds. But on Berkeley's chosen terms, *spirit* might join *matter* on the scrap-heap of words for which we can find no ideas. Berkeley repeatedly objects that we can have no idea of spirit; '*inert, fleeting, perishable*' ideas and '*active, indivisible, incorruptible*' spirits inhabit completely different ontological worlds (II.79).

Such assertions help to free the language of spirit from the constraint of his plan to strip away words. Indeed, much of the *Principles*' redemption of language has to do with Berkeley's absolute distinction of idea and spirit as effect and cause, object and agent. Recall that where 'substance' is meaningless when applied to matter, 'spiritual substance' is acceptable to Berkeley. The metaphor of 'support' need not be literalized where no 'idea' is possible. Similarly, Berkeley does not blanch when he admits

so far as I can see, the words *will, understanding, mind, soul, spirit*, do not stand for different ideas, or in truth, for any idea at all, but for something which is very different from ideas, and which being an agent cannot be like unto, or represented by, any idea whatsoever.   (II.52–3)

As Berkeley nears his conclusion he boldly dares us (just, incidentally, as Euphranor dares the free-thinker in *Alciphron*) to reject spirit-words on the grounds that they are attended by nothing like Berkeleian 'ideas':

But it will be objected, that if there is no idea signified by the terms *soul, spirit*, and *substance*, they are wholly insignificant, or have no meaning in them. I answer, those words do mean or signify a real thing, which is neither an idea nor like an idea, but that which perceives ideas, and wills, and reasons about them. What I am my self, that which I denote by the term I, is the same with what is meant by *soul*, or *spiritual substance* . . . In a large sense, indeed, we may be said to have an idea of *spirit*, that is, we understand the meaning of the word, otherwise we could not affirm or deny any thing of it.   (II.104–5)[17]

Berkeley emended this section for the second edition of 1734, suggesting that we have a 'notion' rather than an 'idea' corresponding to the word *spirit*. A.D. Woozley has shown that this is not a radical departure from the sense of these passages as they appeared in the first edition; Berkeley invoked 'notion' simply to differentiate our use of spirit words from words which name ideas. Woozley sees that for Berkeley 'notions are

---

[17] In the surviving manuscript of sections 85 to 145 of Part I – British Museum Add. MS. 39304, pp. 35–104 – this section appears on verso, added as an afterthought. And in the notebooks Berkeley raises this problem of what ideas should be attached to spirit-words (*PC* 523).

needed for a theory of meaning, and for that only. There is no ontological commitment'. Again, 'having a notion of spirit does not *explain* being able to use "spirit" significantly, it is being able to use "spirit" significantly'.[18] But Woozley is none the less disappointed, for he finds that Berkeley does not consistently distinguish between knowing how to use spirit-words, and actually knowing spirit. Without explaining clearly how, Berkeley assures us that we do know mind, and that using spirit-words is somehow evidence of this. Where the notebooks had often complained of the scantiness of language, that we are often at a loss for words to convey our knowledge, Berkeley here appeals to common usage as a guide for discovering what we know and as a tool for bringing that knowledge to light.

In Berkeley's discussion of spirit there is much that undermines his way of ideas, but, at the same time, his Introduction does not leave us unprepared for the tensions that will emerge from his idea/spirit dualism. It instils in us a recognition of the failure of an empirical philosophy to offer an adequate account of humanity. More important, it includes two conceptions of language, one scientific and one rhetorical. While the former is applied strictly to our articulations about the world – to matter-words – the latter permits a language wherein words do not have to be cashed for 'ideas' and where articulations about the life of the spirit, such as Paul's promise of '*good things*', can have a meaning. The Introduction's two attitudes to language prepare us for Berkeley's two ways of talking about the two very distinct beings, idea and spirit, which compose his world.

[18] 'Berkeley's Doctrine of Notions and Theory of Meaning', *Journal of the History of Philosophy*, 14 (1976), 433. M.W. Beal examines Berkeley's discussion of a notion of spirit along with two other instances where Berkeley makes 'meaningfulness in language . . . the final arbiter to be appealed to before accepting something into his ontology or as a proper subject of inquiry'; see 'Berkeley's Linguistic Criterion', *Personalist*, 52 (1971), 505. Beal sees this criterion, however, as a late development in Berkeley's thought. The appeals to vulgar usage in the *Principles*, and Woozley's point that the appeal to 'notions' of spirit-words is evident in the first edition, show that from the start meaningful speech was a criterion for Berkeley. More recently Daniel E. Flage has offered an account of what Berkeley might have meant by 'notions', suggesting that Berkeley believed we have a relative rather than a positive notion of mind. Knowledge of mind involves an 'intentional act' rather than a direct apprehension of an object or idea; see *Berkeley's Doctrine of Notions: A Reconstruction based on his Theory of Meaning* (London: Croom Helm, 1987).

2

Locke, roles, and passion

In section 9 of the Introduction, Berkeley subjects Locke's theory of mental abstraction to irony. He tries, as we have seen, to formulate an abstract idea of *man*, and then attempts the even more general term *animal*:

The constituent parts of the abstract idea of animal are body, life, sense, and spontaneous motion. By body is meant, body without any particular shape or figure, there being no one shape or figure common to all animals, without covering, either of hair or feathers, or scales, &c. nor yet naked: hair, feathers, scales, and nakedness being the distinguishing properties of particular animals, and for that reason left out of the *abstract idea*. Upon the same account the spontaneous motion must be neither walking, nor flying, nor creeping, it is nevertheless a motion, but what that motion is, it is not easy to conceive.   (II.29)

As section 9 unfolds, the absurdity of Locke's proposition reveals itself. In the draft of the Introduction, this passage was much less subtle and its irony, consequently, much less effective. There, between his examples of the abstract man and the abstract animal, Berkeley included some openly critical comments made in the first person:

Suppose now I should ask you whether you comprehended, in this your abstract idea of man, the ideas of eyes, or ears, or nose, or legs, or arms this might perhaps put you to a stand for an answer, for it must needs make an odd & frightfull figure, the idea of a man without all these.   (II.123–4)

And Berkeley originally ended with an attempt to picture an abstract line, an example which lacked the comic incongruity and some of the impossibility of his attempt to imagine the spontaneous motion of an abstract animal. In erasing these Berkeley leaves abstraction to damn itself without himself obtruding on the scene or letting his explicit criticisms interrupt the growing comic confusion. In the final version of section 9 we are presented with nothing but the drama of a mind struggling and ultimately failing to attain Locke's abstractions.

Having finished this ironic *exposé* with its appropriately convoluted prose, Berkeley returns to a very different style in section 10, where he renounces abstract thought:

Whether others have this wonderful faculty of *abstracting their ideas*, they best can

26

tell: for my self I dare be confident I have it not. I have indeed a faculty of imagining, or representing to my self the ideas of those particular things I have perceived and of variously compounding and dividing them. I can imagine a man with two heads or the upper parts of a man joined to the body of a horse. I can consider the hand, the eye, the nose, each by it self abstracted or separated from the rest of the body. But then whatever hand or eye I imagine, it must have some particular shape and colour. (II.29)

Here Berkeley resumes his customary lucid, almost curt style. Notice how the passive constructions of the ironic critique of Locke give way to clear, active expression. The 'I' which he carefully suppressed in section 9 is now the subject and opens most of the sentences followed by the main verb: 'I have', 'I can imagine', 'I can consider'. In the stylistic contrasts between these two juxtaposed sections Berkeley begins to make us attuned to the true voice of the *Principles*, the voice to which Berkeley most readily attaches 'I'. This voice, free from the perplexities of philosophical abstraction, is direct and confident as it tells us what ideas it *can* have.

In such passages as this Berkeley develops the plain style's most powerful qualitites, intimacy and immediacy. Easy and informal expression lacks the distance created by a heavily-ornamented, periodic style, which seems self-conscious and emphatically public. The plain language of section 10 is the language of ordinary conversation, and the impression of conversation is heightened by the ubiquitous 'I' of the *Principles*. Berkeley's *persona* constantly evaluates his own argument, appealing to his own perspicuous ideas and laying the workings of his own mind before the reader. The effect of these initial revelations is to develop the reader's trust. Reading first- rather than third-person reflections we always feel in the presence of a truth of a higher order; when people talk about themselves, they speak with concern and authority. At the same time such excursions present us with an intimate view of the *persona*'s mind as he asks us to compare his thoughts with our own. It is inevitable that from this process of mutual self-revelation a complex and fuller character should grow in the reader's mind and with it, feelings of affinity.

Berkeley clearly recognized this power of the plain style to make the reader confident, comfortable, and so receptive. As we have seen, he often rejects the vocabulary of philosophy and celebrates simple diction, taking words in their 'vulgar acceptation' and admitting colloquial expressions from time to time. He even draws attention to this admirable quality of his prose, noting at the end of his *a priori* proofs that his immaterialism 'hath been premised in the plainest terms I could think of' (II.56). And after his refutations, he fairly points out that the objections were posed 'in the clearest light' and with 'all the force and weight I could' (II.77). Similarly, to support his arguments he often appeals *ad populum*, either to the experience of the reader or to the beliefs of 'the generality of men' (II.30). A favourite phrase is 'it is agreed on all hands' (II.27). His examples are drawn from the realm of daily experience, appealing to our experience of an apple (II.41) or of arranging a meeting with a servant (II.83). While all these techniques make for a lucid exposition, they also achieve a powerful *ethos*. Our natural response to any piece of language is to presume a speaker and to create, where possible, a character for the voice. Indeed, our determination of the speaker's intentions is an integral part of our interpretation of his meaning, a point recognized by Aristotle when he lists *ethos* before all the other topics as the most effective means of proof in deliberative discourse.[1] With his plain style Berkeley begins to adumbrate for us the *persona* of the *Principles*, one who is interested in communicating the truth, a clear thinker, and above all a man of common experience and common sense.

The notebooks show Berkeley at work, consciously refining and developing this *persona*. He had no illusions about the probable reception of immaterialism, knowing full well that it violated much of contemporary learning; he notes in particular that he will be opposed by the 'mighty sect' of 'Mathematicians & Natural Philosophers' (*PC* 406). Realizing that his best hope of a sympathetic hearing lay with the unphilosophical reader, he reminds himself 'I side in all things with the Mob' (*PC* 405). And he uses the notebooks to practise the appeals to common sense that he applies so liberally throughout the *Principles* – 'I know it by experience, I am but one of common sense, and I etc' (*PC* 368). He even contemplates styling himself the laconic Irishman, dubious of the sublime notions of the modern men of learning: 'There are men who say there are insensible extensions, there are others who say the Wall is not white, the fire is not hot &c We Irish men cannot attain to these truths' (*PC* 392). If Berkeley reins in this particular irony, it would not be an extraordinary articulation from the *persona* of the *Principles*, who prides himself on offering plain truth in plain language. There is of course nothing new in Berkeley's strategy here. Socrates had set the precedent for playing the philosophical *ingénu*, and many of Berkeley's immediate predecessors strove to evade the stereotype of the professional philosopher by championing common sense. Locke, for example, was quite capable of playing the populist in the *genus humile*:

When it is considered, what a pudder is made about *Essences*, and how much all sorts of Knowledge, Discourse, and Conversation, are pester'd and disorder'd by the careless, and confused Use and Application of Words, it will, perhaps, be thought worth while throughly to lay it open.[2]

Here the colloquial 'pudder' and 'pester'd', the interjected 'perhaps', and

[1] *Rhetorica*, I.ii.4
[2] *Essay* (III.v.16), p. 438.

the idiomatic 'lay it open' all encourage the reader's confidence. We are reassured by this familiar voice dismissing the abstruse tenets of the schoolmen. More often, however, Locke depicts himself as the virtuoso rather than the plain man in his attempt to avoid the taint of scholasticism. He makes it clear in the *Essay*'s Epistle Dedicatory that he is the Earl of Pembroke's valued protégé and friend, just as he reveals his intimacy with the 'Master-Builders' of the Royal Society. There is an impressive *sprezzatura* about the inception of the *Essay* itself: no sweaty grubbing amidst musty tomes, but the casual offshoot of a philosophical discussion amongst friends. And Locke's digressions and examples display a virtuoso's love of curiosities – the cassowaries in St. James's Park and the diverting story of Prince Maurice's 'reasonable' parrot. In these scattered hints Locke gives us the impression of a man of wit and the world, one who wears his learning lightly. Even Locke's scepticism speaks an elegant detachment from the argument of the *Essay*.

Search as one might, one could discover no hint of the virtuoso's detachment in the *Principles*. Berkeley never approaches the admissions of uncertainty permitted the more worldly voice of Locke's *Essay*. Even the conventional gesture of humility Berkeley felt obliged to include in his Introduction, while it apologizes that the *Principles* will be a 'close and narrow survey', is none the less sure the book can stand beside the large views of the 'great and extraordinary men' who have gone before (II.26–7). The *Principles*' brevity, its forthright exposition, and freedom from digression all argue Berkeley's commitment and confidence. These prominent qualities find further expression in affirmative phrases throughout the text: 'to this I cannot assent' (II.31), 'I dare be confident' (II.29), 'all which seems very plain' (II.34), 'this is too obvious to need being insisted on' (II.79), and 'this to me seems very evident' (II.91). From these phrases, and from his stern handling of the errors of philosophers and schoolmen, Berkeley creates an earnest and assured character. Again, the notebooks reveal the extent of Berkeley's concern with tone, and his full awareness of the effect he wants to achieve:

If I speak positively & with the air of a Mathematician in things of which I am certain. tis to avoid Disputes to make Men careful to think before they censure. To Discuss my Arguments before they go to refute them. I would by no means injure truth & Certainty by an affected modesty & submission to Better Judgements.   (*PC* 532)

Here Berkeley recognizes above all that reading is a sympathetic act and that confidence in the voice of the writer, if subtly managed, will be communicated to the mind of the reader.[3]

---

[3] At entries 468 and 543 of the notebooks Berkeley offers similar defences of his positive tone. John Ward, in *A System of Oratory, Delivered in a Course of Lectures*, 2 vols (London: J. Ward, 1759), Vol. I, p. 147, makes Berkeley's point: 'firmness and resolution is as neces-

In all his anxiety to convey something of his own conviction, Berkeley recognized as well the danger of excess: 'No mention of fears & jealousies, nothing like a party' (*PC* 789), and 'N.B. to rein in y^r Satyrical nature' (*PC* 634). Too much indignation or a lapse into anger would destroy the rational integrity of his argument. Unlike Descartes's introspective *Meditations*, in which the confessional author becomes the sympathetic focus for the emotional developments of the argument, the *Principles*, in its eventual handling of the more heated and public issues of morality and religion, must become rhetorical and suasive. Where Descartes dramatizes his acquisition of truth, Berkeley tries to show us a man secure in the possession of it. He must strike a balance between the candour of the plain man examining his own thoughts and the authority of the churchman and moralist. In revising the *Principles* for its second edition, Berkeley eliminated almost all of those confident affirmative phrases, such as 'this is too obvious to need being insisted on'. He felt, no doubt, that the *persona* of the first edition spoke too much *ex cathedra* at such points. This problem of philosophical tone is, perhaps, not entirely resolved for Berkeley until *Alciphron*, where he chooses two characters to argue his case: the reflective and open Euphranor, and Crito, the angry moralist.

Berkeley's belief that his greatest support lay with the simple notions of 'the mob' stemmed from his conviction that immaterialism would be but coldly received by the learned. So as he strives to align himself with 'the vulgar' in the Introduction, he moves to undermine the authority of those whose principles clash with his own. The Introduction, as we have seen, is an extended *ad hominem* critique of Locke's theory of abstraction and a considerable modification of his views on language. Irony plays a large role here, as in Berkeley's attempts to form abstract ideas of man and animal or in his joke on Locke's failure to distinguish man from brutes. This ironic *exposé* is strategic, not only because it undermines an influential materialist authority, but because it helps to establish Berkeley's own *ethos* by contrast. Locke himself employs just this strategy when he devotes the first of his *Two Treatises of Government* to an exhaustive and humiliating attack on Filmer, or when he pits himself against the proponents of innate ideas in Book I of the *Essay*. In creating such anti-authorities an author is able to display his wit for the reader and win admiration for boldness and originality. Moreover the irony with which

---

sary as modesty, that he [the speaker] may appear to confide in the justice and truth of his cause'. Hume, on the other hand, felt obliged to apologize to the readers of his treatise for using 'such terms as these, *'tis evident, 'tis certain, 'tis undeniable'*. He explains that 'such expressions were extorted from me by the present view of the object, and imply no dogmatical spirit'; see *A Treatise of Human Nature*, ed. L. A. Selby-Bigge, 2nd ed., rev. P. H. Nidditch (Oxford: Clarendon Press, 1980), (I.iv.7), p. 274.

Berkeley handles Locke in the Introduction establishes a special community of author and reader. Irony works by the implicit and indirect evocation of the reader's knowledge, bringing the reader into collusion with the author.

Having proved himself against Locke in the Introduction, Berkeley expands his ironic technique to encompass the other materialist authorities who might detract from immaterialism. In his *a posteriori* arguments Berkeley shows how immaterialism clears up many difficult points in both natural philosophy and mathematics, and in so doing he exposes the folly of their practitioners. The relative motion propounded by Newton, 'a philosopher of a neighbouring nation whom all the world admire' (II.89), Berkeley derides as nonsensical: 'now I ask any one, whether in his sense of motion as he walks along the streets, the stones he passes over may be said to *move*, because they change distance with his feet?' (II.91). The mathematicians fare even worse. Far from practising the purest and most exact of sciences, they are, it seems, 'jejune and trifling' (II.96). While this use of irony and satire entertains, it also reassures the reader by undermining his admiration for the new materialist doctrines. But the caricature of the abstruse philosopher that emerges from the pages of the *Principles* gains a rather sinister dimension as Berkeley makes a number of subtle insinuations about the religion of the modern thinker. Here for example Berkeley associates philosophy with atheism:

The only thing whose existence we deny, is that which philosophers call matter or corporeal substance. And in doing of this, there is no damage done to the rest of mankind, who, I dare say, will never miss it. The atheist indeed will want the colour of an empty name to support his impiety; and the philosophers may possibly find, they have lost a great handle for trifling and disputation.   (II.55)

In the course of the *Principles*, Berkeley manages unobtrusively to juxtapose 'philosophers' with Hobbists, epicureans, Socinians, Manicheans, fatalists, and idolaters. At the same time he depicts the modern philosophers' tenets as irrational and even mystical, citing their belief in the existence of an invisible, powerful matter, or in the 'mighty *mysteries* involved in numbers' (II.95). As they show themselves 'fond and tenacious' (II.99) of their doctrines, philosophers become like proselytizing papists: 'And it is impossible it [the idea of infinity] should ever gain the assent of any reasonable creature, who is not brought to it by gentle and slow degrees, as a pagan convert to the belief of *transubstantiation*' (II.98). These insinuations of irreligion are designed to make Berkeley's opponents not only wrong, but contemptible.

In casting these aspersions, Berkeley is drawing on the account he gives at the very opening of the Introduction of the plight of the learned man:

Philosophy being nothing else but the study of wisdom and truth, it may with reason be expected, that those who have spent most time and pains in it should enjoy a greater calm and serenity of mind, a greater clearness and evidence of knowledge, and be less disturbed with doubts and difficulties than other men. Yet so it is we see the illiterate bulk of mankind that walk the high-road of plain, common sense, and are governed by the dictates of Nature, for the most part easy and undisturbed. To them nothing that's familiar appears unaccountable or difficult to comprehend. They complain not of any want of evidence in their senses, and are out of all danger of becoming *sceptics*. But no sooner do we depart from sense and instinct to follow the light of a superior principle, to reason, meditate and reflect on the nature of things, but a thousand scruples spring up in our minds, concerning those things which before we seemed fully to comprehend. Prejudices and errors of sense do from all parts discover themselves to our view; and endeavouring to correct these by reason we are insensibly drawn into uncouth paradoxes, difficulties, and inconsistences, which multiply and grow upon us as we advance in speculation; till at length, having wander'd through many intricate mazes, we find our selves just where we were, or which is worse, sit down in a forlorn scepticism.   (II.25)

As the reader stumbles through the imitative maze of Berkeley's syntax, he is threatened with entrapment and despair. When Berkeley proceeds to criticize Locke in the following pages, he is but giving us a striking example of the philosopher 'drawn into uncouth paradoxes'. Needless to say, Berkeley's image of the philosopher was a popular one. In *To the Royal Society* Cowley's 'wand'ring' schoolmen 'like th'old *Hebrews* many years did stray/In Desarts but of small extent', and Dryden's epicureans in *Religio Laici* with '*anxious Thoughts* in *endless Circles* roul,/Without a *Centre* where to fix the *Soul:*/In this wilde Maze their vain Endeavours end.' Likewise Milton's philosophical devils

>   reasoned high
> Of providence, foreknowledge, will and fate,
> Fixt fate, free will, foreknowledge absolute,
> And found no end, in wandering mazes lost.[4]

So in the *Principles'* initial portrait of philosophical pursuits Berkeley seems to be evoking and reinforcing a common suspicion that philosophy is futile and even dangerous, leading not to wisdom but to doubts, confusion, and sorrow.

    Berkeley's philosopher, tainted by irreligion and scepticism, becomes a powerful emotive object for the reader of the *Principles*, a lesson in the personal consequences of materialism. Nor is it a lesson we can ignore. Berkeley forces our involvement in the text, demanding that we choose

---

[4] Cowley, *To the Royal Society* (v.3–5), in Sprat, sig. B2ʳ; Dryden, *Religio Laici* (36–8), in *The Poems of John Dryden*, ed. James Kinsley, 4 vols (Oxford: Clarendon Press, 1958), Vol. I, p. 312; Milton, *Paradise Lost* (II.558–61), in *The Poems of John Milton*, ed. John Carey and Alastair Fowler, 2nd ed. (London: Longmans, 1968), pp. 533–4.

between the evidence of our senses and the uncouth paradoxes of the stumbling philosopher. As readers we are not observers but participants, and find ourselves milling in the *Principles'* forum, a place already crowded with a disconcertingly high proportion of Hobbists, Socinians, and idolaters. Our role as reader is given considerable prominence, and we have little opportunity to disentangle ourselves from the personal ethical and religious implications of the argument. In the preface we are asked to be reasonable and fair, not to prove 'weak men' by responding to novel arguments with 'hasty censures'. The Introduction's concluding pact, by stressing the dangers of language, the confusion of modern philosophy, and the great effort with which Berkeley has freed his mind from abstractions, binds us morally to a sympathetic reading of the *Principles*. We are committed to recreating Berkeley's 'same train of thoughts' (II.40) and he makes sure to remind us of this commitment. At a number of points in Part I he apologizes for having to repeat or clarify certain arguments, as here at the beginning of the refutations: 'if I seem too prolix to those of quick apprehensions, I hope it may be pardoned, since all men do not equally apprehend things of this nature; and I am willing to be understood by every one' (II.55). There is a sustained pressure on the reader of the *Principles* to renounce doubt. Berkeley reminds us of the obvious truth of his *dicta* and the easiness of his argument, which he insists should be evident 'to anyone that is capable of the least inquiry' (II.50). Each point is qualified with 'It is very obvious' or 'A little attention will discover' (II.51), making any hesitation on our part seem evidence of stupidity.

One of the chief ways in which Berkeley develops and controls the reader's role in the *Principles* is through the prominence and activity of the first person. As 'I' implies a privileged hearer, we as readers gain a special status; every 'I' seems to imply a 'you'. This conversational quality to his prose is heightened by Berkeley's constant recourse to questions, some of which he answers himself and others which he leaves open to the reader, as here:

But why should we trouble ourselves any farther, in discussing this material *substratum* or support of figure and motion, and other sensible qualities? Does it not suppose they have an existence without the mind? And is not this a direct repugnancy, and altogether inconceivable? (II.48)

The rhetorical question perfectly exemplifies Berkeley's manipulation of the reader's opinion, demanding his participation yet subtly limiting his response. This management of our thoughts gives Berkeley a concomitant control over our emotional response to the argument. Having set us on his 'high road of plain, common sense', he threatens to divert us into the mazes of the philosopher. Here, for example, he gives us an unwanted vocal role in the text by making the 'you' explicit and forcing us into dialogue:

But say you, though the ideas themselves do not exist without the mind, yet there may be things like them whereof they are copies or resemblances, which things exist without the mind, in an unthinking substance. I answer, an idea can be like nothing but an idea; a colour or figure can be like nothing but another colour or figure. If we look but ever so little into our thoughts, we shall find it impossible for us to conceive a likeness except only between our ideas. Again, I ask whether those supposed originals or external things, of which our ideas are the pictures or representations, be themselves perceivable or no? If they are, then they are ideas, and we have gained our point; but if you say they are not, I appeal to anyone whether it be sense, to assert a colour is like something which is invisible; hard or soft, like something which is intangible; and so on of the rest.   (II.44)

Here we find ourselves forcing Berkeley to repeat himself, and in his emphatic repetitions he seems to grow a little frustrated. Later, in apparent desperation, he challenges the recalcitrant reader to prove even 'the bare possibility of your opinion's being true' (II.50). Berkeley's *prolepsis*, by casting the reader in the role of the sceptic, isolates him, threatening to dissolve the intimate pact. Where the Introduction manoeuvred to pull us in, Berkeley now threatens to cast us out, making us long all the more for the fold of truth. When Berkeley appeals 'to anyone', he separates us from the crowd and seems ready to abandon our case. Perhaps he manages this most effectively in the refutations which extend from sections 34 to 84 of Part I. Here the reader must voice sixteen objections to Berkeley's *a priori* proof. Each is refuted in turn, but the objections are so dogged that the reader, in the role of the materialist, ultimately becomes the object of Berkeley's scorn and is accused of 'downright repugnancy and trifling with words' (II.76). These complex strategies of dialogue, strategies which Berkeley will perfect in the *Three Dialogues* and *Alciphron*, draw us into the world of immaterialism, making us confront dramatically and personally the moral consequences of retaining a belief in matter.

The great danger of such strategies is, of course, that the reader may become conscious of them. But few readers are vigilant about rhetoric, and all these strategies are woven into Berkeley's argument, never obviously obtruding on the philosophical business at hand. Consider again what has proved one of Berkeley's most prominent and powerful rhetorical tools – *prolepsis*. To the reader who recognizes it, it gives the impression not of emotional manipulation, but of the utmost candour. In raising and forcefully presenting all our objections to his thesis, Berkeley seems at his most disinterested, reflective, and philosophically impartial. John Ward, Gresham College's Professor of Rhetoric from 1720 to 1759, recommended *prolepsis* as 'it serves to conciliate the audience, while the speaker appears desirous to represent matters fairly, and not to conceal any objection, which may be made against him'.[5] But even if a reflective reader should manage to identify Berkeley's rhetorical plans, such dangers are outweighed by the need for an emotional lever in the *Principles*. Berkeley shows himself particularly sensitive to the complexity of our attachments to the notion of 'matter' and clearly gauges our initial reaction to his claim that it does not exist. The first refutation, which follows hard on his concise proof of immaterialism, acts as a pressure-valve through which the reader's insecurities are given vent: 'What therefore becomes of the sun, moon, and stars? What must we think of houses, rivers, mountains, trees, stones; nay, even of our own bodies? Are all these but so many chimeras and illusions of the fancy?' (II.55). These questions, with their urgency, exclamatory brevity, and particularity, provide a much-needed outlet for the reader's *malaise*. In fact most of the refutations are designed to comfort the reader, assuring him that 'things' are just as knowable, even more knowable, than before: 'Whatever we see, feel, hear, or any wise conceive or understand, remains as secure as ever, and is as real as ever' (II.55). Berkeley uses this calm, firm voice to assert the reality of our sensations, the usefulness of our language, and the regularity of nature. These assurances are essential, for by the end of the *a priori* arguments we do feel unstable, even vulnerable, without matter. Such feelings stem from the fact that we, like Locke, associate matter with touch and solidity. It is the tangible stuff of our world, and we turn to touch for a reassurance of our control of the world around us. Berkeley realizes that reason alone is hardly sufficient to overcome our complex attachments to touch, solidity, and, by extension, matter, so his satire of philosophers and his own ethical appeal encourage a contrary affective response.

[5] Ward, *System of Oratory*, Vol. II, p. 66.

3

The ends of morality and religion

While the refutations of the *Principles* are the height of Berkeley's direct engagement of the reader, in a sense the whole text is devoted to refutation. When Berkeley is not confronting the reader's probable objections to immaterialism, he is grappling with those authorities who would undermine his case. But each of Berkeley's vigorous attacks is followed by some sort of concession: abstract ideas are impossible, but we discover we have general terms to fill the gap; sensations are 'in the mind', but prove just as real as before; we can no longer look for second causes in nature, but can find there instead 'the grandeur, wisdom, and beneficence of the Creator' (II.89). Berkeley seems always to be pushing us too far, only to retreat half the distance. When he is most disconcerting, we suddenly find him conceding to our concerns. This seems to be the pattern Berkeley has chosen for the *Principles* as a whole. While his *a priori* section offers startling epistemological propositions, the refutations help to clarify Berkeley's stand and quell our initial confusion. With his *a posteriori* arguments we are led back into the comfortable world of conservative Christianity. Even within each of the three main divisions of Part I we witness a movement from a discussion of matter and ideas, to spirit, and ultimately to God, finding in faith the certainty that we fear we are deprived of in our senses.

So at the same time as Berkeley offers striking challenges to our conception of the world, he can claim that he is 'guilty of no innovation' (II.80). In the notebooks he admits the novelty of his principle and that he will be perceived by many as something of an upstart (*PC* 465). But as we have seen Berkeley also acknowledges that 'a man must not onely demonstrate the truth, he must also vindicate it against scruples & establish'd opinions wch contradict it . . . he must be more ample & copious, else his demonstration tho never so exact will not go down wth most' (*PC* 163). Berkeley is concerned to play the vindicator as much as the upstart critic, and so his aggressive refutation involves both the evocation of and a concession to the reader's knowledge. Berkeley's role as a vindicator of principles becomes most evident when we compare the form of the *Principles* to the two works which most influenced his early thought, Locke's

Essay and Malebranche's *Recherche*. Both of these books are ostensibly descriptive rather than argumentative as they map and anatomize the operations of the mind. Each proceeds by dividing its subject, human knowledge, into several appropriate categories and then handling each in turn. Both books are, as a consequence, long. Malebranche in particular is prone to digression and tries to be exhaustive in his presentation of examples. Similarly, Locke's *Essay*, in the words of Gilbert Ryle, is a 'revolutionary re-charting of the fields of human knowledge and opinion'; its message lies in its choice of divisions as Locke teaches 'us to distinguish the types of our inquiries'.[1]

The form of the *Principles* could not be more unlike that of the *Essay* or the *Recherche* with their expansive epistemological schemes. It is brief, concerted, does not digress, in short shows nothing of Berkeley's predecessors' obsession with division and classification. The *Principles* does not sketch a system or describe a subject in its various aspects. Instead it argues, relentlessly, in defence of a single thesis, *esse* is *percipi*. In choosing the form of the *Principles* Berkeley turned not to the anatomy, but to rhetoric's guidelines for the arrangement of arguments. The book falls roughly into the conventional 'parts' of discourse established by centuries of rhetorical handbooks. It has, for example, a distinct *exordium* or introduction, one of whose purposes is, as we have seen, to establish Berkeley's *ethos*.[2] And the last section of Part I makes a brief but appropriately hortative *peroratio*. Berkeley obviously also shares the rhetorician's sense of the importance of including a distinct and extensive passage of refutation. The place of the *refutatio* was considered a matter of choice, and Berkeley ingeniously uses it to divide the *a priori* from the *a posteriori* arguments of his *amplificatio* or positive proof, thus managing to dispel the reader's doubts before completing his case. This classical oratorical format is essentially forensic, aimed at influencing the reader's or listener's judgment. Each part of the discourse is designed to plead, in a different way, for the one presiding thesis.

Berkeley was conscious of a need for the kind of concerted, suasive argument he ultimately achieves in the *Principles*. In entry 379 of the

---

[1] 'John Locke on the Human Understanding', in *John Locke: Tercentenary Addresses* (London: Oxford University Press, 1933), pp. 25 and 38. John Yolton, in *Locke and the Compass of Human Understanding* (Cambridge: Cambridge University Press, 1970), p. 14, explores the ways in which the *Essay* is 'descriptive, not justificatory'. And Coleridge was obviously refreshed by Berkeley's precise and orderly argument during his intense philosophical investigations in 1801. He wrote to Josiah Wedgewood that 'Des Cartes system is a *drossy* Berkeleianism', while Locke's *Essay* is 'a prolix Paraphrase on Des Cartes with foolish Interpolations'; see *Collected Letters of Samuel Taylor Coleridge*, ed. Earl Leslie Griggs, 6 vols, Vol. II: 1801–6 (Oxford: Clarendon Press, 1956), p. 384.

[2] Quintilian, *Institutio Oratoria*, IV.i.7–10; Aristotle, *Rhetorica*, III.xiv.7.

notebooks, after sketching three logical demonstrations of immaterialism, he notes simply:

N.B. Other arguments innumerable both a priori & a posteriori drawn from all the sciences, from the clearest plainest most obvious truths whereby to Demonstrate the Principle i.e. that neither our Ideas nor any thing like our ideas can possibly be in an unperceiving thing.

Part I is devoted to communicating both the plenty and variety of these proofs to the reader. His *a priori* proofs demonstrate the non-existence of matter in a sequence of concise arguments ranging from the clear maxim that 'an idea can be like nothing but another idea' to the observation that matter violates the principle of God's efficiency. After the refutations, Berkeley's *a posteriori* proofs argue the probable beneficial consequences of his principle in eliminating problems and confusions in mathematics, natural philosophy, and religion. While Berkeley admits these latter arguments do not infallibly prove that *esse* is *percipi*, they serve at least to make Berkeley's principle more plausible and more attractive. By providing a wealth of both kinds of arguments Berkeley is satisfying his perceived need to be 'ample and copious', to be thorough in substantiating a truth which challenges so many of our preconceptions about the world.[3] By arranging these in the extremely suasive form of the classical oration, he does his utmost to win our favourable judgment on that truth.

To understand the method of the *Principles*, we must recognize not only Berkeley's undivided attention to '*esse* is *percipi*', but also his perception of the status of that articulation. In his notebooks he always refers to it simply as 'the Principle'. It is for him one of the first and fundamental truths from which all reasoning should proceed. Conventional metaphysical principles were not, however, in particularly high esteem in Berkeley's day. Elsewhere in the notebooks Berkeley himself joins Locke in rejecting all the tautologous axioms of the schoolman, such as 'A stone is a stone' or 'The whole is equal to its' Parts' (*PC* 592). Like Descartes's *cogito*, Berkeley's principle is not simply a truism of logic, but a far-reaching account of human experience, and, as the *Principles* makes abundantly clear, it is itself capable of empirical proof. But while Berkeley demonstrates its truth to us, he seems to admit that *esse* is *percipi* might also be appreciated by an act of intuitive apprehension:

Some truths there are so near and obvious to the mind, that a man need only

---

[3] In pitting 'dry' against 'copious' exposition in entry 163 of the notebooks, Berkeley may be invoking a conventional way of talking not just about style in general, but more specifically about the invention of arguments. Ernesto Grassi, in *Rhetoric as Philosophy* (London: Pennsylvania State University Press, 1980), p. 44, cites Vico distinguishing between the topical mind as 'copiosi' and the critical, deductive mind as 'asciutti'. Likewise Ward, in *System of Oratory*, Vol. I, p. 25, distinguishes logic's 'short and concise way of reasoning from the fluency and copiousness of oratory'.

open his eyes to see them. Such I take this important one to be, to wit, that all the choir of heaven and furniture of the earth, in a word all those bodies which compose the mighty frame of the world, have not any subsistence without a mind, that their *esse* is to be perceived or known . . . To make this appear with all the light and evidence of an axiom, it seems sufficient if I can but awaken the reflexion of the reader, that he may take an impartial view of his own meaning, and turn his thoughts upon the subject it self, free and disengaged from all embarras of words and prepossession in favour of received mistakes.   (II.43)

Berkeley, relying on the metaphor of sight, suggests that his principle may be grasped certainly and immediately by the mind.

While his book attempts to compensate in its tightly focused argument for our past neglect of *esse* is *percipi*, as his title suggests, Berkeley is concerned with a number of principles. In his Introduction he promises 'a strict inquiry concerning the first principles of *human knowledge*' (II.26), and when he turns to spiritual matters, he speaks of 'fruitful principles' (II.202) of which he gives us this sample in his conclusion:

We ought therefore earnestly to meditate and dwell on those important points; that so we may attain conviction without all scruple, *that the eyes of the Lord are in every place beholding the evil and the good; that he is with us and keepeth us in all places whither we go, and giveth us bread to eat, and raiment to put on*; that he is present and conscious to our innermost thoughts; in fine, that we have a most absolute and immediate dependence on Him. A clear view of which great truths cannot choose but fill our hearts with an awful circumspection and holy fear, which is the strongest incentive to *virtue*, and the best guard against *vice*.   (II.112–13)

As with '*esse* is *percipi*', Berkeley is asking us to strive for 'a clear view' and directing our attention to the truths themselves that we may attain a profound and immediate conviction. There is, however, in this latter case no warning about the 'embarras of words'. Indeed, what Berkeley is here asking us to 'meditate and dwell' upon are verses of Scripture. Once again, Berkeley's discussion of spirit belies the Introduction's empirical linguistic. Each of Berkeley's cherished principles of knowledge, whether '*esse* is *percipi*' or '*the eyes of the Lord are in every place*', is not an 'idea' but a piece of language. Moreover Berkeley makes these articulations the foci of our attention because he believes that in themselves they embody fundamental and comprehensive truths.

The methodological implications of Berkeley's celebration of principles are extensive. The title of the *Principles* aligns it with the work of Descartes and Newton who, in their respective *Principia*, brought to their own fields of study something of the deductive certainty of mathematics. The notebooks show that while Berkeley was aware that the reader's prejudices about metaphysical matters meant that he could not proceed in a dry 'Geometrical way', he was still convinced that, just as in mathematics, there can be certainty and logical proof in ethics and metaphysics (*PC* 239 and 336). Berkeley initially felt that his Introduction should deal, not with language and abstraction, but with his own chosen method:

I shall Demonstrate all my Doctrines. the Nature of Demonstration to be set forth & insisted on in the Introduction. In that I must needs differ from Locke forasmuch as he makes all Demonstration to be about abstract Ideas wch I say we have not nor can have.   (*PC* 586)

Near the end of the notebooks he changes his mind, fearing that his initial promises of demonstration might raise the reader's expectations too high, or spoil his *ethos* by making him seem too proud (*PC* 858). Neither does he want to seem too scholastic in his aims, a prevailing concern in the later entries and a pertinent one, for clearly what Berkeley seems to mean by a demonstration is not far from the scholastic's syllogism. Consider the shortest of the three 'demonstrations' of the principle he sketches at entry 378:

16   Two things cannot be said to be alike or unlike till
        they have been compar'd
17   Comparing is the viewing two ideas together, & marking
        w^t they agree in & w^t they disagree in.
18   The mind can compare nothing but its' own ideas.   17.
19   Nothing like an idea can be in an ūperceiving
        thing.   11.16.18.

Here Berkeley reveals how deeply his method differs from that of Locke's *Essay*. Although Locke admitted the importance of but never attempted demonstration in ethics, most of the *Essay* is stridently informalist. Locke renounces disputation in any form and scorns conventional maxims and syllogisms.[4] For Locke the apprehension of truth is always prior to its formal expression in language and is, in effect, nothing so much as a sort of mental collation whereby we note the 'agreements and disagreements' between our ideas. The great irony of Berkeley's entry 378 is that it makes Locke's own informalist doctrine into a premise of the immaterialist chain syllogism: 'Comparing is the viewing two ideas together.' Whatever Berkeley's reasons for deciding not to advertise his skill at demonstration in the Introduction, Part I provides ample evidence that he proceeds along the lines of traditional logic just the same. Berkeley's rejection of Locke's informalism is, of course, at the root of the profound contrasts between the forms of the *Principles* and the *Essay*. Where the latter is inductive and descriptive, the former displays a persistent recourse to principles and a vindication of logical proof. Its aggressive, often syllogistic arguing is

---

[4] Yolton, *Compass of Human Understanding*, p. 91. Howell, in *Logical and Rhetoric*, p. 280, makes Locke the champion of 'the new logic' who sets logic 'free . . . from its traditional association with the humanistic enterprise of transmitting ideas'.

Berkeley's clearest renunciation of Locke's division of thought from language.

Berkeley first planned the *Principles* as a work in several volumes. In the notebooks he refers several times to a second volume devoted to morality and metaphysics that would complement the epistemological discussion we find in Part I. T. E. Jessop finds further suggestions in the notebooks that Berkeley conceived of a third volume handling principles of natural philosophy and even a fourth on mathematics (II.5–6). Berkeley still clung to this scheme, or at least wanted to keep his options open, when the first edition of the *Principles* was published in 1710 with 'Part I' on both the title-page and the running heads throughout the book. Part II never appeared, and when in 1729 the American philosopher Samuel Johnson asked after it in a letter, Berkeley complained: 'I had made a considerable progress in it; but the manuscript was lost about fourteen years ago, during my travels in Italy, and I never had leisure since to do so disagreeable a thing as writing twice on the same subject' (II.282). This is all the explanation Berkeley ever offers for his abandonment of the project. But at the same time Part I does not read like the first instalment of a larger work. It seems formally complete and coherent in its vigorous proof of immaterialism. The emphatic and hortative conclusion implicitly denies any need for a sequel to elaborate Berkeley's case. Above all, Berkeley seems to make no attempt in Part I to marshal his material by reserving certain topics for fuller, future discussion. The *a posteriori* proofs pursue the implications of the new principle for natural philosophy (sections 101 to 117) and mathematics (sections 118 to 132), the purported themes of Parts III and IV. Moreover the end of the *Principles* (sections 135 to 156) is devoted to the repercussions of *esse* is *percipi* for religion and metaphysics, inevitably revealing much of what should be handled in Part II. It seems that in writing Part I Berkeley found himself writing the whole of the *Principles*.

Perhaps Berkeley recognized something of this situation even in 1710, when he writes to his friend John Percival of his dissatisfaction with the *New Theory of Vision* and hopes for the *Principles*:

There still remains one objection with regard to the uselessness of that book [the *New Theory of Vision*]: but in a little time I hope to make what is there laid down appear subservient to the ends of morality and religion in a treatise I have now in the press, the design of which is to demonstrate the existence and attributes of God, the immortality of the soul, the reconciliation of God's foreknowledge with freedom of men, and by shewing the emptiness and falseness of several parts of the speculative sciences, to reduce men to the study of religion and things useful.
(VIII.31)

The 'treatise I have now in the press' is only Part I, and yet Berkeley gives no hint of its immaterialist principle, being more concerned with the

religious consequences elucidated in its conclusion. With the exception
of the issue of God's foreknowledge, all the religious principles Berkeley
here identifies for Percival are handled in the *Principles*. Section 141, for
example, shows that immaterialism preserves the difference between soul
as cause and body as perishable effect and thus helps prove that '*the soul
of man is naturally immortal*' (II.106). As for the attributes of God, Berkeley
finds ample evidence of His benevolence and wisdom in the marvellous
contrivance and regularity of the language of nature. And the *Principles*
offers a novel demonstration of the existence of a God who is 'not far
from any one of us'. Indeed, this is the most striking direct consequence of
immaterialism, which makes our every sensory experience an immediate
communication from the divine mind.

But, perhaps, the union of epistemology and religion in the *Principles*
is inevitable given Berkeley's convictions about knowledge itself. Consider
his defence of *a posteriori* arguments:

it is plain that very numerous and important errors have taken their rise from
those false principles, which were impugned in the foregoing parts of this treatise.
And the opposites of those erroneous tenets at the same time appear to be most
fruitful principles, from whence do flow innumerable consequences highly
advantageous to true philosophy as well as to religion.   (II.102)

Berkeley believes that truth leads to truth and error to error. Furthermore, his *a posteriori* arguments assume that truth is necessarily beneficial
to man; true principles naturally lead us to salvation and false principles
to despair. Reflecting upon his own precious *esse* is *percipi* he notes that
'The Reverse of the Principle' has been the source of scepticism and
idolatry, and even 'of that shameful immorality that turns us into Beasts'
(*PC* 411). True principles naturally reveal and evoke other principles
which also tend to the good of mankind. Perhaps this is why Berkeley
found himself, in defending *esse* is *percipi*, turning to the principles of
morality and religion.

Berkeley's conviction that the *Principles* serves the ends of morality and
religion directed many of his stylistic choices. Such a book should have a
broad and immediate appeal, and it does attempt to achieve that with its
brevity and clarity. Similarly it avoids any exceedingly technical arguments or speculations pursued for their own sakes. In a letter to Percival
of 1710, Berkeley dismisses the more intricate ruminations of
Malebranche and Norris, 'whose writings are thought too fine spun to be
of any great use to mankind . . . Fine spun metaphysics are what I on all
occasions declare against, and if anyone shall show me anything of that
sort in my "Treatise" I will willingly correct it' (VIII.41). But the universal
importance and utility of the religious truths that enter the argument

of the *Principles* permit, even demand, more than just clarity in their expression. Plain, logical prose is not the only style it exhibits:

But if we attentively consider the constant regularity, order, and concatenation of natural things, the surprising magnificence, beauty, and perfection of the larger, and the exquisite contrivance of the smaller parts of creation, together with the exact harmony and correspondence of the whole, but above all, the never enough admired laws of pain and pleasure, and the instincts or natural inclinations, appetites, and passions of animals; I say if we consider all these things, and at the same time attend to the meaning and import of the attributes, one, eternal, infinitely wise, good, and perfect, we shall clearly perceive that they belong to the aforesaid spirit, *who works all in all*, and *by whom all things consist*.

(II.108)

Notice how Berkeley is careful to balance his words in both number of syllables and order: 'the constant regularity, order, and concatenation' is echoed by 'the surprising magnificence, beauty, and perfection'. Similarly he knits his language together with repeated sounds: 'consider', 'constant', 'concatenation', and 'contrivance'. Yet at the same time he suspends the principal clause of this long sentence until the end. We strive to maintain our sense of the initial 'if' clause through the first long catalogue, only to have our anticipation heightened by an interjected repetition of this clause with an emphatic 'I say'. Berkeley then staves off the truth with a second catalogue of divine attributes, before finally resolving our confusion in the simplicity and authority of Scripture. The balance of phrase in the catalogues, working against the stops and turns of the syntax, imitates the harmonious confusion of the natural order he is describing. Throughout this passage Berkeley shows his mastery of the arts of language, making a complex appeal to our reasons and our emotions. On reading such passages one is reminded of the Introduction's admission of the rhetorical ends of language and its ultimate refusal to offer a clear distinction between the ways in which language affects our thoughts, passions, and actions.

If, however, we accept the effectiveness of the *Principles'* rhetoric, we must somehow account for the disturbing fact that it was almost completely ignored in its own day. Twenty-four years elapsed between the first edition and the second. The third did not appear until 1776, twenty-two years after Berkeley's death. Harry Bracken's study, *The Early Reception of Berkeley's Immaterialism*, confirms 'that those first two decades after the *Principles* were extremely hard on Berkeley'; no serious review appeared in England and only one in a French journal.[5] John Valdimir

5 *The Early Reception of Berkeley's Immaterialism: 1710–1737*, rev. ed. (The Hague: M. Nijhoff, 1965), p. 38. David Berman argues that it was not until Berkeley had won a prominent moral reputation with his Bermuda project that his philosophical works received a more sympathetic reading; see 'Berkeley's Philosophical Reception after America', *Archiv für Geschichte der Philosophie*, 62 (1980), 311–20.

Price has offered several possible explanations as to why the *Principles* was still-born. He first suggests that Berkeley may have disconcerted his readers by marrying the secular and the theological in his argument, but later concedes that 'the connection of philosophy and religion had been traditional, and readers in the eighteenth century might reasonably have expected to find a good deal more piety in philosophical works than they did'.[6] Second, Price wonders if Berkeley might not have bored his readers by offering them too little of 'real life':

> Very few of Berkeley's comments or arguments seemed to have a direct bearing on one's life, and in pursuing his immaterialist line of thought Berkeley left readers with little to do except expostulate. He devoted much of his analysis to objects in the external world, if only to prove that they weren't 'really' there. In contrast, Locke and Hume were far more interested in the contents of the mind, in discovering how it worked, how knowledge was acquired, how experience enabled us to make inferences, and how we were affected by our perceptions and our reflections derived from these perceptions.[7]

Price is right when he sees that immaterialism is disconcerting at first, but surely no one who reads the *Principles* through could assert that Berkeley 'proves' that objects are not 'really' there. Nor is it fair to say that the *Principles* fails to offer a relevant account of the operations of the mind. Both the Introduction and the *a priori* proofs give detailed descriptions of sense experience and the nature of ideation, descriptions as accurate and lively as any in Locke's *Essay*. As for Hume's engaging empiricism, Price himself admits that it too failed at first to win the public's admiration. And surely Berkeley's first readers would have found something with 'a direct bearing on one's life' in his discussion of the practical principles of religion. Price's third scenario is based on a comment by Hume, an as yet unsubstantiated story that the Rankenian Club corresponded with Berkeley, and a remark by Adam Smith on the *New Theory of Vision*. From these he argues that 'Berkeley appealed almost exclusively to professional philosophers and to those interested in what the general reader might reasonably regard as the minutiae of philosophy'.[8] Yet Berkeley consistently condemned the tendency of modern philosophy to the abstract and the hypothetical, and, as I have tried to show, consistently appeals to the experience and concerns of the ordinary reader. As Price's rather short

---

[6] 'The Reading of Philosophical Literature', in *Books and their Readers in Eighteenth-Century England*, ed. Isabel Rivers (Leicester: Leicester University Press, 1982), pp. 168 and 192–3.

[7] 'Reading', pp. 169–70.

[8] 'Reading', p. 170. M. A. Stewart has been able to document a general interest in Berkeley amongst the Rankenians, but has not uncovered any hard evidence of their alleged correspondence. Stewart goes on to show that one Rankenian, William Wishart, was in fact the author of a satire on *Alciphron*. See 'Berkeley and the Rankenian Club', in *George Berkeley: Essays and Replies*, ed. David Berman (Dublin: Irish Academic Press, 1986), pp. 25–45.

list tends to show, 'professional philosophers' did not have a great deal to say about the *Principles*. In fact Berkeley, using Percival as an intermediary, pressed both Clarke and Whiston for their criticisms of the book, but both persisted in showing little interest in discussing immaterialism.[9]

Of course there need be no good reason for the public failure of the *Principles*. Perhaps it was simply a victim of the vagaries of the reading public, never receiving that initial modicum of attention needed to catapult it to popularity. Or perhaps it fell to some idiosyncrasy of the book trade. It is salutary to remember that Locke's *Essay* may well be indebted to Wynne's abridgement for its ultimate reputation.[10] Berkeley himself was convinced that his London bookseller, John Churchill, refused to push the *Principles* because it was printed in Dublin. Dublin publishers were exempt from the copyright act of 1709 and generally posed a threat to the monopoly of the London conger, of which Churchill was a member. But the twenty-year silence that followed the *Principles* is ominous, so much so that one is tempted to join Price in the search for some cause. Berkeley had predicted in his notebooks that its reception would be troubled, but not because it denied the reality of experience, nor because its argument was too academic. He was worried because immaterialism flies in the face of the modern 'Mathematicians & Natural Philosophers (I mean only the Hypothetical Gentlemen)' (*PC* 406). Berkeley is acknowledging here, as he does in the *Principles* itself, the enormous authority of Newton's work. With its successful applications of mathematical method to natural philosophy, the *Principia* had made mathematical exactness, as Berkeley elsewhere styles it, the 'Darling of the Age' (*PC* 313). Matter was a key component of the formulae by which Newton plotted the motions of the universe, and recent Newton scholarship leaves

[9] Percival wrote to Berkeley that Clarke and Whiston had read the *Principles* and rejected its argument. Whiston records how 'After we had both perused it, I went to Dr. *Clarke*, and discoursed with him about it, to this Effect: "That I [being not a Metaphysician] was not able to answer Mr. *Berkeley's* [subtile] *Premises*; though I did not at all believe his [absurd] *Conclusion*. I therefore desired that he, who was deep in such Subtilties, but did not appear to believe Mr. *Berkeley's* Conclusion, would answer him:" Which task he declined'; see *Historical Memoirs of the Life of Dr. Samuel Clarke*, 2nd ed. (London: F. Gyles and J. Roberts, 1730), p. 81. On 27 November 1710, Berkeley wrote back to Percival enclosing letters to be forwarded to each philosopher (VIII.40). Berkeley's approach met with little success, as appears from his letter to Percival of January 19, 1711: 'Dr. Clarke's conduct seems a little surprising. That an ingenious and candid person (as I take him to be) should declare I am in error, and at the same time, out of modesty, refuse to shew me where it lies, is something unaccountable' (VIII.43–4). One contemporary philosopher who did show an interest, albeit limited, in Berkeley's work was Leibniz. Jotting in his copy of the *Principles*, Leibniz approves of Berkeley's remarks on Newton and mathematics, but dismisses immaterialism itself as paradoxical, a judgment he conveys in a letter to DesBosses; see André Robinet, 'Leibniz: Lecture du *Treatise* de Berkeley', *Etudes Philosophiques* (1983), pp. 217–23.

[10] Howell, *Logic and Rhetoric*, p. 278.

little doubt that in denying matter Berkeley found himself, as he half expected, fighting one of the most powerful intellectual currents of his day.[11] This seems to be confirmed by Samuel Johnson, who wrote to Berkeley in 1729 of the reception of immaterialism amongst his American acquaintance, reporting that 'The great prejudice that lies against it with some is its repugnancy to and subversion of Sir I. Newton's philosophy in sundry points.' And Johnson himself, who claims to be no slave to authority, confesses 'I have so great a regard for the philosophy of that great man, that I would gladly see as much of it as may be, to obtain in this ideal scheme' (II.272).

There is, however, a second and related reason for the ominous silence that followed the first edition, and Price touches on it when he quotes Chesterfield's response to the book. Chesterfield wrote to his son that Berkeley's

arguments are, strictly speaking, unanswerable; but yet I am so far from being convinced by them, that I am determined to go on to eat and drink, and walk and ride, in order to keep that matter, which I so mistakenly imagine my body at present to consist of, in as good plight as possible.[12]

Like the Scriblerians before him and Dr Johnson after, Chesterfield cannot forbear misrepresenting Berkeley for the sake of a sally of wit. Price's comment on Chesterfield's reaction is suggestive: 'Berkeley's book could not be profitably discussed, because the logic of his argument could not be taken farther'.[13] Berkeley would have taken umbrage at this remark, especially given his insistence that there is some urgent rethinking to be done in natural philosophy. But the feeling shared by Price and Chesterfield that the *Principles* is somehow unanswerable is a common reaction, notably the reaction of Pembroke, Leibniz and Elizabeth Montagu, as well as Clarke and Whiston.[14] Boswell too felt tongue-tied: 'though we are satisfied his doctrine is not true, it is impossible to refute it'.[15] Hume was moved to make this analysis of his feelings on reading Berkeley's work:

[11] G. S. Rousseau claims, in 'Science Books and their Readers in the Eighteenth-Century', in *Books and their Readers*, p. 215, 'Abundant evidence exists to support the contention that from roughly 1680 to 1750 science, or natural philosophy, *meant* Newton.'

[12] 'Reading', p. 172.

[13] 'Reading', p. 173.

[14] As with Whiston and Clarke, Berkeley used Percival to deliver a letter to Lord Pembroke which was intended 'to give him to understand by the most gentle and couched intimation possible that I should gladly know the particular grounds of his dissent from me in the point of matter's existence, or the faults he finds in the arguments on that head' (VIII.45). Percival seems to have made the delivery (VIII.47), but surviving correspondence gives us no indication that Pembroke was ever drawn into dialogue.

[15] *Boswell's Life of Johnson*, ed. George Birkbeck Hill, rev. L.F. Powell (Oxford: Clarendon Press, 1934), Vol. I, p. 471.

that all his arguments, though otherwise intended, are, in reality, merely sceptical, appears from this, *that they admit of no answer and produce no conviction.* Their only effect is to cause that momentary amazement and irresolution and confusion, which is the result of scepticism.[16]

Amongst these contemporary critics there is a consensus that Berkeley should be refuted, that some sort of answer is demanded by the *Principles*. This feeling is, no doubt, a product of Berkeley's aggressive rhetoric; he keeps demanding that we think, that we substantiate our disagreements. He demands, in fact, a refutation that we cannot formulate. The classical forensic structure of the *Principles* presses us for a judgment on '*esse* is *percipi*', while our prominent role in the text forbids any casual relation to this theme. By contrast, no reader feels constrained to confute Locke's *Essay*; its descriptive, expansive, and frequently self-contradictory account does not demand a response. The reader can remain an observer rather than a participant. But in the *Principles* we are given two options only; we side either with the sceptical philosopher or with the vulgar, accepting matter or rejecting it, all in full knowledge of the consequences of our decision. Berkeley was dismissed because he had denied Newton's matter, but also because he had to be either accepted or dismissed, nothing in between. No doubt Berkeley's first readers were silent because he had forced them into the embarrassing, even disturbing situation of being unable to justify their belief that matter exists. Perhaps it is significant that there is an undercurrent of hostility in many of these responses to the *Principles*. Many are moved to make a joke of immaterialism, to misrepresent Berkeley as a dreamer, or, as in Hume's footnote, as a sceptic. If this scenario is right, the silence of Berkeley's reading public is not, as Price would have it, the silence of the bored, but the silence of the irresolute and the confounded. Perhaps, then, the early reception of the *Principles* was not such a failure. The fact that it was not discussed and so never attained anything like the *Essay*'s public profile may well indicate that it succeeded all too well in putting a serious and disturbing challenge to its individual readers.

---

[16] *Enquiries concerning Human Understanding and concerning the Principles of Morals*, ed. L.A. Selby-Bigge, 3rd ed., rev. P.H. Nidditch (Oxford: Clarendon Press, 1975) (*HU*.xii.i), p. 155. Donald Davie, responding to a paper by Bonamy Dobrée ('Berkeley as a Man of Letters', *Hermathena*, 82 (1953), 75) said that Berkeley 'aimed to be provocative, but was only provoking'.

4

Metaphor and the evidence of things not seen

When Berkeley's predecessors formulated their strictures on language, their mistrust focused chiefly on metaphor. Hobbes accounted it an 'abuse of speech' to 'use words metaphorically; that is, in other sense than that they are ordained for; and thereby deceive others'.[1] Locke's objections were more fundamental and just as damning. He makes an absolute distinction between judgment, the process by which we distinguish ideas so that we may better reason about them, and wit, which is devoted to 'the assemblage of *Ideas*'. Metaphor for Locke is the prime manifestation of wit, and though it may please, it cannot withstand scrutiny 'by the severe Rules of Truth'.[2] These observations did not hinder either philosopher from a free use of metaphor in his own writings, but the theoretical bases of their objections are clear. In metaphor the mind exercises its ability to find likeness between apparently unlike sensible ideas. Unless our sensory experiences – our pristine, determinate ideas – are granted a higher order of reality than the products of reflection or fancy, the empiricist's claim on truth crumbles. For this very reason Berkeley should have joined the refrain against metaphor. He maintains a qualitative distinction between the 'real', God-given ideas of sense and the faint, chimerical creations of the imagination.

Berkeley does not renounce metaphor in the course of his Introduction's examination of language, but he does make this stern pronouncement late in Part I:

But nothing seems more to have contributed towards engaging men in controversies and mistakes, with regard to the nature and operations of the mind, than the being used to speak of those things, in terms borrowed from sensible ideas. For example, the will is termed the *motion* of the soul: this infuses a belief, that the mind of man is as a ball in motion, impelled and determined by the objects of sense, as necessarily as that is by the stroke of a racket. Hence arise endless scruples and errors of dangerous consequence in morality.   (II.107)[3]

---

[1] *Leviathan* (chapter 4), p. 19.   [2] *Essay* (II.xi.2), pp. 156–7.

[3] This issue is also raised in entries 176, 176a, and 544 of the notebooks. William H. McGowan has shown that only in *Alciphron* does Berkeley admit the heuristic powers of

This statement is a natural development from Berkeley's beliefs that we have no 'idea' of spirit and that spirit cannot be divided into distinct mental faculties. It is specifically modern mechanistic metaphors of mind, the kind that feature in the physiological excursions of Descartes and Malebranche, that Berkeley is objecting to here. He worries that these metaphors equate first and second causes.

Richetti finds evidence of Berkeley's general attitude to metaphor in this passage, and he argues that Berkeley embarks on a programme of literalizing metaphor throughout the *Principles*.[4] 'Berkeley is a sort of philosophical lyric poet who is forced to restrain his powers', and Richetti shows him striking from the first section of the draft Introduction a sentence rich in images in which Berkeley condemns the sceptical philosopher who would find 'dark sides' to 'every drop of water, every grain of sand'.[5] Indeed, the tropes employed in the printed version of the *Principles* tend to be quite unobtrusive. We find nothing like Locke's entertaining similes or Hobbes's extended analogies of body to machine or state to body. Berkeley's figurative usage is more subtle. Rather than similes and analogies, he uses metaphors hidden in the flow of plain language. They seem not unlike the simple examples – the house, the tree, the apple – with which he illuminates his argument. The rhetoricians John Ward and Hugh Blair advise that metaphor in particular is the appropriate trope of the plain style and, consequently, the philosophical essay. The latter finds that metaphor 'insinuates itself even into familiar conversation; and, unsought, rises up of its own accord in the mind'.[6] Ward cautions the plain-stylist, however, to use only the most unobtrusive tropes 'such as are very common, and by time have either come into the place of proper words, or at least are equally plain and clear'.[7] Berkeley, like Ward, recognizes that the most effective metaphor is that which does not advertise its 'untruth'. He heightens the effectiveness of his figurative language by using only a few images, but these repeatedly. The most obvious end to which he manages these strains of imagery is his emotional appeal. Metaphor plays an important role in transforming the insecurity of immaterialism into a disdain for philosophers and their matter.

metaphor; see 'George Berkeley's American Declaration of Independence', *Studies in Eighteenth-Century Culture*, 12 (1983), 105–13.

[4] *Philosophical Writing*, p. 157.

[5] *Philosophical Writing*, p. 142.

[6] Blair, *Lectures on Rhetoric and Belles Lettres*, 2 vols (London: W. Strahan, 1783), Vol. I, p. 296. Similarly, Morris W. Croll in ' "Attic Prose" in the Seventeenth Century', in *Style, Rhetoric, and Rhythm: Essays by Morris W. Croll*, ed. J. Max Patrick et al. (Princeton, N.J.: Princeton University Press, 1966), p. 90, finds the stoic style of the seventeenth century dependent on metaphor: 'It is the greatest of all figures by which literature may interpret the exact realities of experience; and is as much the characteristic possession of the essay style as the musical phrase is of the oratorical.' This essay first appeared in 1921.

[7] *System of Oratory*, Vol. II, p. 144.

Take, for example, Berkeley's management of images of entrapment. In earlier philosophical writings these were a favourite choice for describing the state of a man caught up in difficult learned disputes. The philosopher without precise definitions 'will find himself entangled in words', says Hobbes, 'as a bird in lime twigs, the more he struggles, the more belimed'. Glanvill depicts philosophers' minds 'illaqueated or lime-twigged, as it were, with the Ideas and Properties of corporeal things'. And Locke notes how syllogism abducts the reason, 'and forcing it upon some remote Difficulty, holds it fast there, intangled perhaps, and as it were, manacled in the Chain of Syllogisms'.[8] 'Perhaps', 'as it were', 'as' – in each case the writer is careful to advertise that the similitude he is suggesting is only partial, even fanciful, an embellishment rather than an argument. The peculiarity of these images make them stand out in their argumentative context; it is hard to imagine a lime-twigged philosopher or a mind manacled by syllogisms. Turning again to the opening of the Introduction we find Berkeley employing the trope much more subtly:

> But no sooner do we depart from sense and instinct to follow the light of a superior principle, to reason, meditate, and reflect on the nature of things, but a thousand scruples spring up in our minds, concerning those things which before we seemed fully to comprehend. Prejudices and errors of sense do from all parts discover themselves to our view; and endeavouring to correct these by reason we are insensibly drawn into uncouth paradoxes, difficulties, and inconsistences, which multiply and grow upon us as we advance in speculation; till at length, having wander'd through many intricate mazes, we find our selves just where we were, or, which is worse, sit down in a forlorn scepticism.   (II.25)

That he uses metaphor not simile, that he develops the common and accepted metaphor of thought as journey, and that we can actually imagine ourselves in a maze – all these show that we have here more than a merely ornamental feature. The image is an integrated aspect of Berkeley's expression, not easily detached from his description of the growth of scepticism. Intellectual doubt is given a very particular and powerful correlative as the passage evokes in us a maze's disturbing feelings of claustrophobia and dislocation. Berkeley does not leave this image behind; verbs and nouns suggesting entrapment are part of the regular vocabulary of the *Principles*. He speaks of the 'lets and difficulties' which have 'blocked up the way to knowledge' (II.26). We learn that the 'fine and subtle net of *abstract ideas*' has

> miserably perplexed and entangled the minds of men, and that with this peculiar circumstance, that by how much the finer and more curious was the wit of any man, by so much the deeper was he like to be ensnared, and faster held therein.   (II.26)

---

[8] Hobbes, *Leviathan* (chapter 4), p. 21; Glanvill, *Saducismus Triumphatus* (London: J. Collins and S. Lownds, 1681), p. 148; Locke, *Essay* (IV.xvii.5), p. 678.

Furthermore, Berkeley invokes us to be 'free and disengaged from all embarrass of words' (II.43), warns us that the mind which accepts matter would 'screen it self from the providence of God' (II.73), and confesses that when called upon to frame a Newtonian idea of time, he finds himself 'lost and embrangled in inextricable difficulties' (II.83). In each of these images only a word or two is needed to evoke feelings of entrapment in relation to materialist thought. By constant, subtle repetition, these feelings become ingrained in our minds as we read the *Principles*.

Berkeley's attitude to metaphor is neatly encapsulated in his handling of the word 'support'. As we have seen, he repeatedly dismissed Locke's assertion that matter is somehow a substance or support for primary qualities simply by exploding the metaphor; we have no idea how matter could literally support qualitites 'as when we say that pillars support a building' (II.83). This impresses the reader as a laudable instance of clear thought and a helpful stripping away of subversive language, but Berkeley revives the metaphor near the end of the *Principles*, turning it to his own ends:

For as we have shewn the doctrine of matter or corporeal substance, to have been the main pillar and support of *scepticism*, so likewise upon the same foundation have been raised all the impious schemes of *atheism* and irreligion . . . All their monstrous systems have so visible and necessary a dependence on it, that when this corner-stone is once removed, the whole fabric cannot choose but fall to the ground.   (II.81)

This clever manipulation helps to effect that emotional transference Berkeley wants to achieve in the *Principles*. Our dependence on matter springs from a belief that somehow it supports things with its solidity. Without it we fear we should spend our lives falling through air and clutching at empty fancies. But here Berkeley shows matter to be a support of hateful things, and worse, the support of a structure that is about to tumble about our ears. The substance we believed would buoy us up will crush us. This vision of the crumbling edifice invokes the images of confinement that have pervaded the book and accrues some of their emotional force as well. Here matter is again depicted as a maze or a trap.

Berkeley's own argument is thoroughly dependent on a metaphor, but a metaphor so accepted and pervasive in our language that we hardly recognize it as such. Much of Berkeley's rejection of corporeal substance is based on a visual test – that we have no 'idea' of matter either supporting primary qualities or acting on spirit. This test is in turn founded on a rejection of Locke's abstract ideas. The only true 'ideas' are either sense data or determinate visual images created in the mind. To win us over to this rather reductive definition Berkeley solicits the aid of the metaphor that thought is sight. Ironically, Locke himself drew attention to this metaphor in his discussion of clear ideas:

The Perception of the Mind, being most aptly explained by Words relating to the Sight, we shall best understand what is meant by *Clear*, and *Obscure* in our *Ideas*, by reflecting on what we call *Clear* and *Obscure* in the Objects of Sight.[9]

Berkeley is less frank about his use of this metaphor than Locke, perhaps because his argument is so dependent upon it. In refuting Locke's abstractions he appeals to 'the idea I have in view' (II.34), and, in a higher pitch, he chides us for 'looking for ideas, where there are none to be had' (II.40). When Berkeley makes his notorious equation of seeing and imagining the books in the closet, he has his favourite metaphor to hand: 'do not you your self perceive or think of them all the while?' (II.50).

All this suggests that Berkeley was by no means ignorant of the nature and powers of metaphor, and that he realized its usefulness even though he rejected the application of physical terms to spirit. But elsewhere in the *Principles* he actually seems to give metaphor a significant role in describing spirit and its operations. This is most evident in his quotation of Scripture. The *Principles'* last pages are an extensive appeal to biblical authority in which Berkeley's tenet that God is immediately present in all our perceptions is given dramatic confirmation. As these texts cap his argument, so do they strikingly complete the strains of imagery and metaphor he has developed. Evoking the Second Epistle to the Corinthians, for example, he assures us that our spirit 'should survive the ruin of the tabernacle' (II.105). This plays on his own thread of architectural imagery, most particularly on his metaphoric description of materialism whose 'whole fabric cannot choose but fall to the ground' (II.81). Again, he gives his predominant light imagery – that matter is a 'screen', 'dust', and 'darkness' – final credence when he speaks of God as 'pure and clear light' (II.108). In these allusions Berkeley makes his own metaphors and images more explicit, and yet more authoritative. The 'darkness' and 'decay' of materialism grow much more threatening when we are reminded of their origins in the word of God. This celebratory revelation of scriptural imagery shows that Berkeley finds at least certain metaphors are a valid means of conveying the truth about our spiritual condition.

The importance of Scripture, both to the logic and the rhetoric of the *Principles*, has been consistently ignored. 'There is nothing', Berkeley comforts himself, 'in Scripture that can possibly be wrested to make against me, but, perhaps, many things for me' (*PC* 281). The combination of concern and conviction expressed in this note makes itself heard in the *Principles*. In the last of his refutations Berkeley strives to make it clear that immaterialism *does* distinguish between the real and the imaginary, and so in no way detracts from the facts of biblical narrative or the impact of Christ's miracles. Berkeley's closing words claim that the purpose of

[9] *Essay* (II.xxix.2), p. 363.

his book is to dispose the learned 'to reverence and embrace the salutary truths of the Gospel, which to know and to practise, is the highest perfection of human nature' (II.113). Such gestures of deference to biblical authority cannot be dismissed as simply conventional. Locke's *Essay*, for example, cited Scripture in the most tentative fashion, and chose texts which suggest Scripture's inability to communicate to our fallen natures: 'thou knowest not the works of God, who maketh all things'.[10] Locke insisted that revelation must be subject always to reason and warns that all traditional revelation is 'liable to the common and natural obscurities and difficulties incident to Words'.[11]

Berkeley's text shows none of these scruples. As the conclusion of the *Principles* passes from metaphysics to apology and exhortation, Berkeley reveals the text that was, no doubt, the inspiration of immaterialism:

> It is therefore plain, that nothing can be more evident to any one that is capable of the least reflexion, than the existence of God, or a spirit who is intimately present to our minds, producing in them all that variety of ideas or sensations, which continually affect us, on whom we have an absolute and entire dependence, in short, *in whom we live, and move, and have our being.*   (II.109)

Berkeley's habit of working biblical allusions smoothly into his prose emphasizes how well their messages sort with his own. And he is using his texts very pointedly here. Both this and the text in the next section – '*he be not far from every one of us*' – come from Acts 17, in which Paul chastises the Athenians for worshipping 'the unknown God'. Berkeley has been keen to point out that modern philosophers, by busying themselves with second causes, have, like the idolatrous Athenians, cut themselves off from a knowledge of God. Moreover, '*in whom we live, and move, and have our being*' had a certain celebrity among philosophers, featuring in the work of Locke, Malebranche, Bentley, and even Spinoza.[12] Berkeley reflects on this in his notebooks:

> Spinosa (vid: Pref. oper: Posthum:) will Have God to be Omnium Rerum Causa immanens & to countenance this produced that of St. Paul, in him we live etc. Now this of St. Paul may be explain'd by my Doctrine as well as Spinosa's or Locke's or Hobbs' or Raphson's etc.   (*PC* 827)

[10] From the title-page epigraph added to the fourth and subsequent editions of the *Essay*.
[11] *Essay* (III.ix.23), p. 490.
[12] Locke used what was to become Berkeley's favourite text to imply that God might be real space, a notion Berkeley found very dangerous; see *Essay* (II.xiii.26), p. 179. Bentley made it the text for his first five Boyle lectures. And it closes the most famous chapter, on seeing all things in God, of Malebranche's *Recherche*, translated into English by Thomas Taylor; see *Father Malebranche His Treatise concerning the Search after Truth*, 2nd ed. (1694; rpt. London: W. Boyer, 1700), p. 122. A. A. Luce, in *Berkeley and Malebranche: A Study in the Origins of Berkeley's Thought* (London: Oxford University Press, 1934), p. 4, and Charles J. McCracken, in *Malebranche and British Philosophy* (Oxford: Clarendon Press, 1983), p. 209, agree that Berkeley probably first read Malebranche in this translation.

Berkeley's specific application of this text in a context in which its precise truth is revealed manages to wrest it from the hands of those materialists who tend to make God a distant first cause in our lives. Indeed a reflective reader would surely notice that many of the texts Berkeley uses in his conclusion celebrate the divinity of Christ and so are stock in trade against the Socinians (Heb. 1.3, Col. 1.17, 1 Cor. 12.6). Many others are from Old Testament diatribes against idolatry (Jer. 10.13, Amos 5.8, Isa. 45.15). Both of these heresies Berkeley has associated with materialism because it attributes agency to things other than God. But most important, Berkeley's citation of Scripture in the conclusion of the *Principles* is fully integrated with his argument. His exposition of immaterialism, by discovering God to be the immediate author of all our sensory experiences, prompts a rereading of the verses of Scripture he presents to us. It now seems literally true that God is '*upholding all things by the Word of his Power*' (II.108) and that '*he be not far from every one of us*' (II.110). Berkeley had, in his notebooks, expressed a belief that though '*Principles* may be founded in Faith yet this hinders not but that legitimate Demonstrations might be built thereon' (*PC* 584). As we have seen, from Berkeley's *esse* is *percipi* there grows an epistemology which confirms as it draws upon the revealed principles of Christianity.

Scripture is, of course, unabashedly metaphorical. 'In their Similitudes and Allusions,' Addison writes of the biblical authors, 'provided there was a Likeness, they did not much trouble themselves about the Decency of the Comparison'.[13] But more than this, Scripture is unabashedly metaphorical in describing spirit. Surprisingly, Berkeley does nothing to evade this uncomfortable fact in the *Principles* and, in his search for a language of spirit, even turns to the Bible for guidance. In section 151 Berkeley concentrates on the moot issue of the knowledge of spirit. Berkeley admits that God hides himself from our eyes, but for a purpose: 'the finger of God is not so conspicuous to the resolv'd and careless sinner, which gives him an opportunity to harden in his impiety, and grow ripe for vengeance' (II.110). In the stock biblical metaphors Berkeley chooses here, spiritual conditions and events are given very specific physical correlatives: 'the finger of God', 'harden in impiety', 'ripe for vengeance'. Berkeley goes on to explain that though invisible, God is 'plainly legible' in the world to the 'unbiased and attentive mind'. The apprehension of this 'legible' God involves interpretation. It is like reading rather than simply seeing. It depends on sensible ideas the way reading depends on letters, ultimately transcending them. The biblical metaphors Berkeley employs

---

[13] *The Spectator*, ed. Donald F. Bond (Oxford: Clarendon Press, 1965), Vol. II, p. 127.

have something to do with this method of 'reading' God in the world in that they effect a disintegration of mundane seeing. Unlike Berkeley's own metaphors, they are obtrusive, advertising both their violation of common language and their privileged scriptural origins. In the penultimate section of the book, that in which Berkeley asks us to meditate on the 'important points' from Scripture, he lights again on this paradoxical seeing. He tells us that God's existence is at once the most 'evident and momentous truth', and yet one which many, 'through a supine and dreadful negligence', have ignored and even doubted. In the decay of modern morality Berkeley finds ample evidence that mankind has failed to grasp the central principle of Christianity, 'Since it is downright impossible, that a soul pierced and enlightened with a thorough sense of the omnipresence, holiness, and justice of that *Almighty Spirit*, should persist in a remorseless violation of his laws' (II.112). Again, Berkeley appeals to a striking scriptural metaphor, here to account for how spirit knows spirit. 'Pierce', a disturbing image, suggests that the way to knowledge of God need not be the laborious way of ideas. It implies that revealed principles are themselves powerful and that to know them we need only make our minds susceptible to their power. 'Pierce' also sends us to the Epistle to the Hebrews:

For the word of God is quick, and powerful, and sharper than any twoedged sword, piercing even to the dividing asunder of soul and spirit, and of the joints and marrow, and is a discerner of the thoughts and intents of the heart.
(Heb. 4.12)

In questions of spirit, knowledge may be attained by a submission to the power of language, through a meditation on revealed principles, as much as by that analysis of sensory ideas with which the *Principles* began. In their intense particularity, Berkeley's metaphors appeal to the powerful evidence of the senses, but in their evocative displacement of such evidence, they testify to the mind's power to transcend and transform the world.

Berkeley's appeals to Scripture in the closing pages of the *Principles* go far to qualify his initial castigation of language as a hindrance to learning. In fact, Berkeley explicitly argues here that human communication is necessarily dependent on God's will. Our every word or gesture, if it is to be heard or seen by another spirit, must be an idea produced by God: 'He alone it is who *upholding all things by the Word of his Power*, maintains that intercourse between spirits' (II.108). Language, like nature, is a testament of God's beneficence and wisdom. By quoting the beginning of Hebrews in this context, Berkeley reminds us of God's special relation to language, for here Paul tells us that God had 'spoken unto us by his Son'. This speaking is not just Christ's words in the gospels, but His very historical presence among us. Paul is saying that Christ upholds all things by the power of God's word, evoking John's account of Christ as word made flesh. For God, word and idea are one. Hebrews is also significant for Berkeley as a probing examination of faith:

Now faith is the substance of things hoped for, the evidence of things not seen. For by it the elders obtained a good report. Through faith we understand that the worlds were framed by the word of God, so that things which are seen were not made of things which do appear.   (Heb. 11.1–3)

In these verses we find the essentials of immaterialism: the immediate agency of God in our perceptions; the strong distinction of spirit from idea; and the rejection of material causes. Berkeley is not willing to leave these truths the objects of faith alone, but makes them a focus for the convergence of faith and reason, of empirical and revealed principles.

Throughout the *Principles* Berkeley has explained the nature of ideas by reviving the ancient metaphor that the world is God's book: 'that visible ideas are the language whereby the governing spirit, on whom we depend, informs us what tangible ideas he is about to imprint upon us' (II.59). Ideas of sense are divine language, 'marks or signs for our information' (II.59), and writings in the volume of nature.[14] The system of language and the system of ideas are truly of a kind for Berkeley. Indeed, if we invert his metaphor we can discover at least one important aspect of Berkeley's theory of language. Berkeley claims in the opening of Part I that each sensory object has an attendant passion 'of love, hatred, joy, grief, etc.' (II.41). This echoes the rhetorical linguistic expounded a few pages earlier in the Introduction, where Berkeley argues that often, on either 'hearing or reading a discourse, the passions of fear, love, hatred, admiration, disdain, etc. arise' (II.37). So much of the rhetoric of the *Principles* is a struggle to transform, through the affective powers of language, the emotional attachments we have to a materialist world. The conclusion of the *Principles*, in its celebration of the divine word, reveals that the same principles of human knowledge may be attained through language as through sense. Metaphorical,

[14] There is disagreement as to the philosophical value of Berkeley's metaphor for sense perception. Colin Murray Turbayne, in *The Myth of Metaphor*, 2nd ed. (Columbia, S.C.: University of South Carolina Press, 1970), vigorously promotes Berkeley's *New Theory of Vision*. The Cartesian mechanical model of vision is 'dead' because we take it literally, and Berkeley's linguistic model, in its strange newness, will remind us that it is only a model. But Alan R. White, in 'A Linguistic Approach to Berkeley's Philosophy', *Philosophy and Phenomenological Research*, 16 (1955–6), 187, is more sceptical: 'Whatever the advantages the new descriptions have over the ordinary . . . they have the great disadvantage that they are utterly misleading, and give, and have given, rise to the whole edifice of paradoxical theory and myth.'

indeterminate, affecting our emotions with our reasons, the word of God is still for Berkeley the vehicle of truth.

PART II

Three Dialogues between
Hylas and Philonous

5

The opportunities of dialogue

In Dublin, late in the spring of 1710, Jeremy Pepyat published the first edition of the *Principles*. By July, a shipment of the book was under way to London, there to be sold at the Churchills' shop in Paternoster Row. Berkeley felt he had managed, in conversation, to convince many of his Dublin friends, but he knew that London remained the test of his difficult thesis, and so took all practical steps to ease its reception. He arranged for two copies of his book to be sent to Percival, with the request that he present one of these to the Earl of Pembroke, the book's dedicatee. Berkeley also urged Percival to pass his own copy amongst his 'ingenious acquaintances' in London (VIII.35). Percival complied, but had to report to Dublin that the capital remained unperturbedly materialist:

'Tis incredible what prejudices can work on the best geniuses, nay and even on the lovers of novelty, for I did but name the subject matter of your book to some ingenious friends of mine and they immediately treated it with ridicule, at the same time refusing to read it, which I have not yet got one to do, and indeed I have not yet been able to discourse myself on it because I had it so lately, neither when I set about it may I be able to understand it thoroughly for want of having studied philosophy more. A physician of my acquaintance undertook to describe your person, and argued you must needs be mad, and that you ought to take remedies. A Bishop pitied you that a desire and vanity of starting something new should put you on such an undertaking . . . Another told me an ingenious man ought not to be discouraged from exercising his wit, and said Erasmus was not the worse thought of for writing in praise of folly.[1]

While perhaps a little blunt, this candid letter accurately predicts the disappointing reception of the *Principles*. The correspondence of the next six months shows Berkeley pressing Percival to publicize his work, and particularly, as we have seen, to elicit criticisms from Clarke, Whiston, and Pembroke. Although Percival was diligent in his friend's service, his good offices were to no avail. Disappointment did not, however, lead Berkeley to repudiate or even qualify immaterialism. He had been ignored, not refuted. His problems were problems of presentation not of

---

[1] Benjamin Rand, *Berkeley and Percival* (Cambridge: Cambridge University Press, 1914), p. 80.

proof, and could be remedied with a more convincing, more involving appeal.

Less than three years after the first appearance of the *Principles*, Berkeley left Ireland for the first time in his life, carrying with him the manuscript of the *Three Dialogues*. In one sense it differs little from the *Principles*. A paraphrase of its argument would reveal the *a priori* proofs essentially unchanged: the same ingenious attack on primary qualities, the same critiques of ancient and modern theories of matter, the same insistence on the agency of the divine mind in perception. Its form, however, is radically different. Obviously, Berkeley felt that dialogue had the potential to capture a readership for immaterialism where the treatise had failed. But in choosing the dialogue, Berkeley drew heavily on his experiences of planning and writing the *Principles*. This classical form offered Berkeley the opportunity to develop and intensify appeals and strategies that were inchoate in the *Principles'* form and style.

One such rhetorical strategy was drawn to his attention by Percival's letter. Berkeley's reply was prompt:

whatever doctrine contradicts vulgar and settled opinion had need been introduced with great caution into the world. For this reason it was I omitted all mention of the non-existence of matter in the title-page, dedication, preface, and introduction, that so the notion might steal unawares on the reader, who possibly would never have meddled with a book that he had known contained such paradoxes. If, therefore, it shall at any time lie in your way to discourse with your friends on the subject of my book, I entreat you not to take notice to them I deny the being of matter in it, but only that it is a treatise of the *Principles of Human Knowledge* designed to promote true knowledge and religion.   (VIII.36)

Percival's mistake was that he had named the subject matter of the *Principles*, a subject matter so improbable that his friends refused to read it. With this in mind, Berkeley saw fit to intensify in the *Three Dialogues* those initial deceits of presentation which might attract the reluctant reader. As with the *Principles*, he begins with a title-page which is as evasive as it is appealing:

THREE

DIALOGUES

BETWEEN

Hylas and *Philonous*

The Design of which

Is plainly to demonstrate the Reality and
Perfection of Humane Knowledge, the
Incorporeal Nature of the Soul, and
the Immediate Providence of a DEITY:
In Opposition to
SCEPTICS and ATHEISTS.
ALSO,
To open a METHOD for rendering the SCIENCES
more easy, useful, and compendious.

Far from hinting at immaterialism or even epistemology, this promises a work of popular apologetics.[2] There is nothing here to frighten those who, like Percival, are reticent and uncomfortable philosophers. But the sort of gentle insinuation Berkeley hoped to effect in the *Principles* was hampered to some extent by the conventions of its treatise form. In pondering the advantages of dialogue Hume observes that in the treatise it is customary for the philosopher to explain 'immediately, without preparation . . . the point at which he aims; and thence proceed, without interruption, to deduce the proofs, on which it is established'.[3] Berkeley is constrained by this convention in the *Principles*. Even though he manages to avoid the immaterialist thesis throughout his long introduction, Part I does begin with a concise and direct exposition of his philosophy. Dialogue frees Berkeley entirely from these demands about the order of exposition, and he makes the most of this flexibility, gradually unfolding his argument. The immaterialist system, we shall see, is not fully constructed until well into the second dialogue, by which time the reader finds himself committed to Berkeley's argument.

The dialogue's flexibility and openness serves Berkeley in other ways, for it also permits repetition, which is a natural feature of extended spoken argument. In the *Three Dialogues* we find Philonous free to return, again and again, to the two main confusions that impede the acceptance

---

[2] More specifically, Berkeley's title-page places the work in a growing body of dialogues which mix apology with lay metaphysics. These included Charleton's *Immortality of the Human Soul* (1657), More's *Divine Dialogues* (1668), and Malebranche's *Conversations Crétiennes* (1676). By 1711 Shaftesbury was moved to complain at the plethora of books 'by our new orthodox Dialogists', whose satires on infidelity result in 'Burlesque-Divinity'; see *Characteristicks of Men, Manners, Opinions, Times*, 2nd ed. (n.p., 1714), Vol. III, pp. 291–2. Prominent among the High Church dialogues of the period were Jeremy Collier's *Essays upon Several Moral Subjects* (1697–1709) and Charles Leslie's *Truth of Christianity Demonstrated* (1711).

[3] *Hume's Dialogues Concerning Natural Religion*, ed. Norman Kemp Smith, 2nd ed. (London: Nelson, 1947), p. 127.

of his case. It is the business of the first dialogue to remove the first of these obstacles – our failure to distinguish between immediate or sensory and mediate or reasoned perception. We all assume, like Hylas, that *matter* is a universal term for the stuff of the world, and that in its myriad manifestations it can be touched, tasted, smelt, and seen. For the philosopher, however, matter is mediately perceived, reasoned to be the cause beneath the sensible qualitites of objects. To this essential distinction Berkeley returns at least five times in the course of the *Three Dialogues* (II.183, 191, 221, 222–3 and 244). Berkeley's second essential point, which comes into play at the beginning of the second dialogue, is that a denial of matter does not entail a denial of the reality of the sensible world. Hylas, like Yeats, assumes that Philonous is making the whole world a dream. So again Philonous must repeat that our sense-data are real, regular, and sufficient, and that it is instead the philosopher who cuts us off from reality by insisting on a mysterious insensible matter (II.228, 244 and 261). While Hylas' slowness to grasp Philonous' arguments is the ostensible reason for a frequent return to these two themes, these constant reminders are much needed by the reader. Philonous offers this defence of the reiterative tendency of their conversation:

And though a demonstration be never so well grounded and fairly proposed, yet if there is withal a stain of prejudice, or a wrong bias on the understanding, can it be expected on a sudden to perceive clearly and adhere firmly to the truth? No, there is a need of time and pains: the attention must be awakened and detained by a frequent repetition of the same thing placed oft in the same, oft in different lights.   (II.223)

Obviously Berkeley has reconsidered the opinion he expressed in the *Principles*: that a clear view and impartial inspection of '*esse* is *percipi*' could evoke an immediate assent in the reasonable reader. The method of the *Three Dialogues* recognizes that prejudice is not so readily vanquished nor demonstration so powerful as Berkeley once believed. By inculcating the premises of the materialist proof again and again in the changing contexts of the dialogue, Berkeley hopes with time to bring us to a clear apprehension of his principles. A further advantage of the dialogue's open form is that it permits Berkeley an easy modulation of tone. By convention, only the *peroratio* of the treatise is appropriate for affective and hortative writing, and, indeed, only in the latter pages of the *Principles* can Berkeley achieve a fuller, more affective style. But in the changing tones and tempers of the dialogue's interlocutors, in the constantly shifting pattern of confrontation and conciliation, Berkeley creates a much more sustained management of the affective implications of the issues he handles.

At the same time, the question and answer format of the dialogue facilitates the presentation and refutation of objections. Many late seventeenth-century dialogues were intensely polemical, more interested in destroying another philosophical system than expounding their own. John Eachard, for instance, chooses the dialogue for his broadly satiric attacks on Hobbes's philosophy. Similarly, More's *Divine Dialogues* (1668) include a running caricature of Descartes in the figure of Cacophone, an 'airy and sophistical' thinker.[4] In both More and Eachard, one character proposes the ideas of the philosopher in question so that another character may ridicule and refute them. This feature of dialogue would appeal to Berkeley, whose early writings show a strong polemical tendency. The style of the *Principles* reveals the extent to which immaterialism is a critical doctrine, bent on undermining the theories of Locke and Newton. The refutation section of Part I engages in *prolepsis*, and becomes through Berkeley's use of the first and second persons an incipient dialogue with the materialist reader.[5] *Passive Obedience*, published one year before the *Three Dialogues*, is likewise devoted to a direct engagement with the reader's prejudices and a tireless anticipation of his doubts. Berkeley spends half of *Passive Obedience* in an inquiry 'into the grounds and reasons of the contrary opinion' and a consideration of 'the objections drawn from the pretended consequences of non-resistance' (VI.17). In fact all Berkeley's writings strive to create for themselves a controversial environment in which positive exposition may grow out of the confutation of error.

In the *Three Dialogues*, Hylas, whose name means matter, is a commonsense proponent of modern materialist thought. The dialogue is devoted to dissecting Hylas's assumptions, answering his doubts, and correcting his misinterpretations. This wary, aggressive method makes the *Three Dialogues* convincing. Percival, who had remained politely non-committal about his friend's ideas, confesses that he not only managed to read this book, but that he found its case impressive:

I can now tell you I have read your last book through and through, and I think with as much application as I ever did any. The new method you took by way of dialogue, I am satisfied has made your meaning much easier understood, and was the properest course you could use in such an argument, where prejudice against the novelty of it was sure to raise numberless objections that could not

---

[4] *Divine Dialogues* (London: J. Flesher, 1668), Vol. I, sig. B4ᵛ. In Eachard's delightful *Mr. Hobbs's State of Nature Considered* (London: N. Brooke, 1672) and *Some Opinions of Mr. Hobbs* (London: W. Kettilby, 1673), Hobbes is caricatured as 'the most wary, mistrustful and suspicious creature, now living upon the face of the whole earth'.
[5] Rauter, in ' "Veil of Words" ', p. 395, sees incipient dialogue in the *Principles'* extensive use of questions, and A. A. Luce remarks how 'the entries of Berkeley's notebooks are almost entirely conversational', recording a dialectic of hypothesis and doubt in which 'Berkeley is questioning his other self'; see *The Dialectic of Berkeley's Immaterialism: An Account of the Making of Berkeley's Principles* (London: Hodder and Stoughton, 1963), p. 26.

anyway so easy as by dialogue be either made or answered . . . I declare I am much more of your opinion than I was before.[6]

From start to finish the *Three Dialogues* addresses the preconceptions and doubts of readers like Percival. Its success lies in Berkeley's ability to put himself in the place of one struggling to conceive and ultimately accept immaterialism. At the same time, Berkeley had been ranked with Malebranche by Clarke and Whiston, and the dialogue form easily permits a rejection of this categorization.[7] In the Second Dialogue, Hylas raises the apparent similarity between Philonous' statements and Malebranche's thesis of '*seeing all things in God*' (II.213). Philonous responds that Malebranche, unlike himself, believes in an inanimate archetype for ideas and fails to distinguish the natures of ideas and spirits (II.213–14). It is only in these careful criticisms of Malebranche, however, that Berkeley's immaterialist theories are fully revealed. Again Berkeley waits to expound his thoughts until he has the check of an antithesis, the reassurance that, even with its faults, immaterialism is at least a better proposal than its predecessors. This need for a critical environment is admirably satisfied by the dialogue, with its natural pattern of challenge and reply. At the same time the genre helps Berkeley avoid a pedantic *ethos*. In dialogue the author does not seem to appear at all, and Percival is impressed by the apparent ingenuousness of Berkeley's method. By playing the critic he avoids censure as the pedant or projector blind to any but his own system.

Another immediate advantage of dialogue is the wide opportunity it gives Berkeley to illustrate his argument. The genre presents itself as a record of the conversation of particular people in an actual setting. Berkeley's thesis, which attends to matters of perception, may thus easily prove itself in specific sensory experiences. We 'see' Hylas and Philonous test their hypotheses on the world around them: 'But to fix on some particular thing; is it not a sufficient evidence to me of the existence of this *glove*, that I see it, and feel it, and wear it?' (II.224). Being able 'to fix on some particular thing' not only helps tie an otherwise abstract argument to common experience, but is especially useful to Berkeley, who must insist, against appearances, on the realism of his thesis. Moreover, these appeals to sense help Berkeley dispel the impression that his theory of perception is solipsistic. Immaterialism denies the shared material archetypes of our sensory ideas, replacing them with a direct communication from the divine mind. It appears that while he brings us closer to God, Berkeley threatens to isolate us from our fellow man. The *Three Dialogues* explicitly denies this tendency. Hylas asks: 'Doth it not therefore

[6] Rand, *Berkeley and Percival*, pp. 120–1.
[7] Rand, *Berkeley and Percival*, p. 87.

follow from your principles, that no two can see the same thing?' (II.247). Philonous replies that the same objection may be made of modern materialist theories of perception, but he is understandably hesitant about speculating on the extent to which divine ideas may serve as archetypes for several perceivers. Instead, he turns to the world before them: 'I see this *cherry*, I feel it, I taste it' (II.249). We watch Hylas and Philonous share a single sensory object, an ostensive proof that, although we may not strictly say they are the *same*, God so forms the sensory ideas of different perceivers that they are co-ordinate.

Dialogue also permits Berkeley to develop a rich strain of literal imagery. On the first page, Philonous describes the conversation's setting, a college garden:

Can there be a pleasanter time of the day, or a more delightful season of the year? That purple sky, these wild but sweet notes of birds, the fragrant bloom upon the trees and flowers, the gentle influence of the rising sun, these and a thousand nameless beauties of nature inspire the soul with secret transports; its faculties too being at this time fresh and lively, are fit for those meditations, which the solitude of a garden and tranquillity of the morning naturally dispose us to.

(II.171)

There is a tension in this account between the garden's privacy and nature's busy solicitation of our senses with 'a thousand nameless beauties'. The *milieu* itself is identified as an interlocutor in the debate. In the course of the *Three Dialogues* the friends gaze at 'the beautiful red and purple we see on yonder clouds' (II.184), pluck a tulip (II.196), admire a cherry tree (II.234), and consider the fountain playing in the lawn (II.262–3). While these images bring a pleasure of their own to the dialogue, they also subtly substantiate Berkeley's peculiar version of the cosmological argument – that God is the immediate source of all our sensory ideas. Berkeley's reader would be accustomed to think of nature as the expression of God's love and wisdom. By choosing his illustrations from nature, then, and particularly from the beautiful in nature, Berkeley helps us imagine a more direct communication between our minds and God's. The glory of a sunrise in June seems a particularly appropriate example of a divine idea.

In these lyric moments Berkeley provides the one literary quality in which dialogue, of all philosophical forms, excels. Dialogue offers the reader the hope that the burden of the argument will be somewhat relieved by the entertaining interplay of characters and description of setting. So the dialogue, as a pleasant as well as familiar genre, helps Berkeley attract the unphilosophical reader to immaterialism.

6

The character of the elenchus

There were, then, several characteristics of dialogue that made it particularly suitable for the kind of argument Berkeley wanted to make. He came to the form with an epistemological proof best made in a fully realized setting, and with methodological and stylistic proclivities which the dialogue could easily accommodate. Above all, Berkeley wanted to win an audience and hoped he could do so with dialogue's promise of instruction mingled with delight. But however much the conventions of the genre satisfy Berkeley's rhetorical demands, he is far from complacent in employing the genre. The style of the *Three Dialogues* is strikingly unlike that of other dialogues of his time. In general, Ciceronian models prevailed, such as the formal debate of *De natura deorum*, where one character presents all his view on an issue at length before another, with opposing views, replies. This seems to be the form adopted in Dryden's *Of Dramatick Poesie* with its extended speeches. A more popular style of dialogue was that of Cicero's *De republica*, in which a character who holds a mistaken opinion is corrected at length by an opponent, but is permitted to interrupt now and again with objections or demands for clarification. Such is the method of Boyle's *Discourse of Things Above Reason*, More's *Divine Dialogues*, and Charles Leslie's *The Truth of Christianity Demonstrated*. Likewise, in Walter Charleton's *Immortality of the Human Soul* the objections raised by the materialist Lucretius are merely occasions for Athanasius's further elaboration of his case for the incorporeity of the soul. The repartee of the first and second of the *Three Dialogues* sets it apart from these more discursive debates. Berkeley depicts a tight, logical wrangling: not a placing of a right opinion against a wrong one, but a relentless questioning. Hylas' statements are carefully scrutinized for their meaning and consequences. The model for this style of dialogue is itself ancient, its chief practitioner and apologist being, of course, Plato.[1]

[1] In his Introduction Jessop mentions that the *Three Dialogues* are more like Plato's dialogues than Malebranche's or Shaftesbury's, but fails to say why (II.155–6). Michael Morrisroe, in 'Ciceronian, Platonic, and Neo-Classical Dialogues: Forms in Berkeley and Hume', *Enlightenment Essays*, 3 (1972), 156–7, briefly identifies Berkeley's dialogues as Platonic on the grounds of the pace of the argument and the fact that Philonous, like Socrates, is a sceptical mentor figure. He offers no account of the elenchus or of the impact of Platonic

In the notes on her husband's life, Anne Berkeley recalls that 'As to authors, Plato and Hooker were two of his principal favourites.'[2] A fascination with Plato's writings can be traced throughout Berkeley's career. In 1709, we find him earnestly advising Percival to consult Plato's thoughts on politics and suicide (VIII.23 and 29). Likewise his *Guardian* essay No. 120 quotes at length from the *Gorgias* on justice and the future state. In 1738, Berkeley was to give a Greek font, the first in Ireland, to Trinity College's new press. The font's first use was in printing an edition of Plato's dialogues, and it is not unlikely that the donor influenced this choice. And one of Berkeley's last letters asks Thomas Prior to encourage the subscription to a new edition of Plato's dialogues being proposed by a Glasgow printer (VIII.305). Plato's influence on Berkeley's philosophy is, however, not so easy to determine. Despite the Neoplatonic overtones of *Siris*, Berkeley's early insistence on the reality and value of the sense-data sets him at odds with Plato. Perhaps the only unquestionable legacy is the style of dialogue known as 'elenchus'.

For the ancients, elenchus was primarily an exercise for students in logic and definition. Its technique was developed in the teaching practices of Socrates and the sophists, and its rules were later laid down by Aristotle at the Academy. These are, briefly, as follows. One student, who accepts the role of answerer, states a thesis. Another then attempts to refute this thesis, not by direct argument or evidence, but by asking a series of simple questions. To each question the answerer may only reply 'yes' or 'no'. The questioner's aim is to force the answerer to contradict his initial statement. This idiosyncratic form of debate entails several constraints. The initial thesis must be of a form that permits analysis: a maxim or a definition rather than a plain statement of fact. In both the *Gorgias* and the *Theaetetus* Socrates has difficulty eliciting a general statement so that he may attack with contradictory instances; neither Gorgias' expansive speeches nor Theaetetus' particular examples will do. Similarly, the progress of elenctic dialogue depends on the answerer's ability to resist the temptation to qualify his answers. In the *Protagoras*, for example, Socrates strives in vain to convince the sophist that short answers are called for. Finally, it is essential to successful elenchus that the answerer speak his mind. Plato shows how the dispute can become mired when an evasive answerer, such as Euthydemus, pretends to hold ridiculous but consistent views, rather

---

dispute. In Malebranche's dialogue, *Conversations Crétiennes*, translated anonymously as *Christian Conferences* (London: J. Whitlock, 1695), Theodore advises Aristarchus to apply the elenchus to the conversion of free-thinkers; he should 'ask them questions with art and ingenious plainness' and make them adhere to their answers (p. 42). Although Malebranche was praised as the Plato of France in his day, in this dialogue the attempt to depict elenchus dissipates after a few brief exchanges.

[2] 'Corrigenda and Addenda to the Second Volume', *Biographia Britannica*, 2nd ed., Vol. III (London: J. Rivington, 1784).

than admit self-contradiction. In the eyes of Plato and Aristotle such dishonest thinkers played not elenchus, but 'eristic', which term seemed to designate nothing but the disputants' failure to commit themselves to the pursuit of truth.

As Berkeley was preparing the *Three Dialogues* for publication he was appointed Junior Greek Lecturer at Trinity College, Dublin, and his duties may well have included reading aloud from the works of Plato and then quizzing the undergraduates on what he had read. But even apart from the works of Plato, the elenchus was very much alive at Trinity. As at Oxford and Cambridge, disputations were a central feature of Trinity's curriculum in Berkeley's day, enshrined both in the College's Laudian statutes and in the *Regulae* drawn up by the fellows.[3] The standard procedure for these exercises was essentially Socratic, consisting of a close confrontation between an answerer and a questioner. First, a respondent proposes and briefly elaborates as many as three theses. All attention then focuses on the first thesis, which is challenged by two or more opponents or questioners, who raise objections in the form of syllogisms. The respondent is responsible for answering each challenge as it arises, the usual technique being to repeat the opponent's syllogism, and then attempt to dismiss it either by denying a premise or by qualifying one of the terms. William T. Costello, in his study of disputations at Cambridge early in the seventeenth century, reveals the elenctic style of the questions: 'In every case, the opponent follows a carefully plotted line of syllogisms designed to trap the answerer into a position where he may be forced, step by step into admitting the exact opposite of his thesis.'[4] After a fixed period the moderator who regulates the performance calls a halt and asks the respondent to propound his second thesis, and the dispute recommences in the same fashion. At Trinity there were three disputations every week on the lecture material of each class with each student taking his turn. These contests involved four or five students at a time, and the moderator would sometimes demand that they dispute '*more Socratico*'.[5] Each prospective BA was obliged to participate in six disputations, twice as respondent and four times as opponent, and Laud imposed a fine of

[3] See Robert Bolton's *A Translation of the Charter and Statutes of Trinity-College, Dublin* (Dublin: R. Bolton, 1749). For accounts of the disputations at Trinity, see John William Stubbs, *The History of the University of Dublin from its Foundation to the End of the Eighteenth Century* (Dublin: Hodges, 1889), pp. 140–1 and 202–3; Constantia Maxwell, *A History of Trinity College Dublin 1591–1892* (Dublin: University Press (Trinity College), 1946), p. 52; and R. B. McDowell and D. A. Webb, *Trinity College Dublin 1592–1952: An Academic History* (Cambridge: Cambridge University Press, 1982), p. 5.
[4] *The Scholastic Curriculum at Early Seventeenth-Century Cambridge* (Cambridge, Mass.: Harvard University Press, 1958), p. 20.
[5] Maxwell, *History*, p. 52.

one penny on any undergraduate who failed to attend, sixpence if the student was to have disputed that day.

In all, Berkeley would have spent a good deal of time in the years preceding the publication of *Three Dialogues* first participating in and then probably moderating Socratic disputations. This practical, first-hand experience reveals itself in the opening pages of the *Three Dialogues*, where, appropriately, the setting is a college garden and the interlocutors are scholars.[6] Hylas has heard a rumour that Philonous doubts the existence of matter, which Hylas claims is a 'manifest piece of scepticism'. Philonous takes this thesis and sets to work:

PHILONOUS. Pray, Hylas, what do you mean by a *sceptic*?

HYLAS. I mean what all men mean, one that doubts of every thing.

PHILONOUS. He then who entertains no doubt concerning some particular point, with regard to that point cannot be thought a *sceptic*.

HYLAS. I agree with you.

PHILONOUS. Whether doth doubting consist in embracing the affirmative or negative side of a question?

HYLAS. In neither; for whoever understands English, cannot but know that *doubting* signifies a suspense between both.

PHILONOUS. He then that denieth any point, can no more be said to doubt of it, than he who affirmeth it with the same degree of assurance.

HYLAS. True.

PHILONOUS. And consequently, for such his denial is no more to be esteemed a *sceptic* than the other.

HYLAS. I acknowledge it.

PHILONOUS. How cometh it then, Hylas, that you pronounce me a *sceptic*, because I deny what you affirm, to wit, the existence of matter? Since, for ought you can tell, I am as peremptory in my denial, as you in your affirmation.

(II.173)

Here we find both the logical scrutiny and the customary progress to contradiction that distinguish the elenchus. Philonous attacks one of the terms of Hylas' thesis, proving that Hylas' own sense of the word *sceptic* is at odds with his original use of it.[7] Like the questioner in a disputation,

---

[6] The theses debated in the *Three Dialogues* are of the sort defended in the schools. In fact, in 1708 a Cambridge undergraduate 'kept an act in ye Schools upon these Questions. Philosophia non tendit in atheismum. Materia non potest cogitare. Materia est divisibilis.' In 1782 and again in 1790 scholars at Cambridge, no doubt availing themselves of the ready-made replies found in the *Three Dialogues*, chose 'to defend Berkeley's immaterial system'; see Christopher Wordsworth, *Scholae Academicae* (1877; rpt. London: Frank Cuss, 1968), pp. 301, 376 and 321.

[7] Rauter, in ' "Veil of Words" ', pp. 392–4, sees Berkeley's choice of dialogue as a result of the scepticism about language expressed at the end of the Introduction to the *Principles*. The ambiguity of words and the tenuous connections between words and ideas meant Berkeley wanted to use language casually and suggestively rather than precisely, and the informality of the dialogue permits this looseness. There is, however, considerable complexity in the *Principles'* statements on language. And the *Three Dialogues*, like the *Principles*, not only concentrates on establishing the meanings of words by appealing to

Philonous adopts a line of questioning that is essentially syllogistic, although his premises are protracted over several questions rather than given all at once. Here also are the very simple questions and terse replies of the elenchus. Philonous' short statements are effective questions, as he waits for Hylas' response before proceeding, ensuring Hylas' acquiescence at every point.

Again, the goal of the elenchus is to lure the respondent into a self-contradictory reply, and often Philonous concludes a bout with a painfully clear account of his success:

Since therefore you are in the very perception of light and colours altogether passive, what is become of that action you were speaking of, as an ingredient in every sensation? And doth it not follow from your own concessions, that the perception of light and colours, including no action in it, may exist in an unperceiving substance? And is not this a plain contradiction?   (II.197)

The logical law of non-contradiction is the chief rule of the elenchus. In fact, the first purpose of the elenchus in both the ancient and modern academies was to teach logic. Two late seventeenth-century champions of traditional education, René Rapin and Obadiah Walker, defended the disputation because it successfully fulfilled this role in the curriculum. Walker's *Of Education*, which made six editions between 1673 and 1699, argues that disputation 'discovers the very Center and Knot of the Difficulty' and puts the scholars 'upon a continual *stretch* of their Wits to defend their Cause'.[8] Rapin, defending the universities against Ramist reformers, pleads that disputation must not be done away with:

Because after all, it imprints upon the Mind a Character of Order and Regularity, and a Justness of Thought; it teaches us to reduce the Subjects we treat of to certain *Principles*; and consequently to discourse upon them by Rule and Method: It exercises younger Wits, by the Subtilties of Logick and Metaphysics.[9]

It was precisely because of their intimate relation with formal logic that Locke dismisses 'captious Logical Disputes' in *Some Thoughts concerning Education*: 'Truth is to be found and supported by a mature and due

---

common usages, but the elenchus's logical preoccupations involve a careful refining of the meanings of words like *sceptic* and *gravity*. Dacier described Socratic dialectic as 'a Science which teaches to define what everything is' and which aims at 'a right application of words'; see *The Works of Plato Abridg'd* (London: A. Bell, 1701), Vol. I, p. 146.

[8] *Of Education*, 6th ed. (London: R. Wellington, 1699), p. 120.

[9] *The Whole Critical Works of Monsieur Rapin*, trans. Basil Kennet *et al.*, 2nd ed. (London: R. Bonwicke *et al.*, 1716), Vol. II, p. 405. Kennet's *Rapin* made three editions between 1706 and 1731, and Berkeley included a copy in his gift of books to Yale in 1733. According to Joseph Stock, Berkeley met Kennet in Leghorn in 1714, where the latter was serving as chaplain to the English factory; see *Memoirs of George Berkeley, D.D. Late Bishop of Cloyne in Ireland*, 2nd ed. (London: J. Murray and R. Fauldner, 1784), p.7.

Consideration of Things themselves, and not by artificial Terms and Ways of Arguing.'[10]

In contrast to Locke, Berkeley seems to celebrate the disputation's logical precision. In the *Three Dialogues* the rules of logic order the debate, and dialogue educates the reader, not just in immaterialism, but in the method of demonstration so influential in the composition of the *Principles*. In his Preface to the *Three Dialogues* Berkeley promises 'it has been my endeavour strictly to observe the most rigid laws of reasoning'. He goes on to contrast his own 'close and methodical application of thought', a method that leads to God, to 'that loose, rambling way, not altogether improperly termed *free-thinking*' (II.168). Orderly reasoning is of prime importance for Berkeley. He makes here the same point that he makes at length in *Alciphron*. The deist's error is not that he trusts too much in reason unaided by faith, but that he has not learned to apply the rules of reason. The free-thinker 'can no more endure the restraints of *logic*, than those of *religion*, or *government*' (II.168). Throughout the *Three Dialogues* Philonous elucidates for Hylas, and for us, the fallacies that obstruct the path to truth, and the dialogue often explicitly establishes its own logic. Philonous finds he must frequently remind Hylas to hold to his own premises and definitions, and is finally driven to the point at which he must swear 'by all the laws of disputation I may justly blame you for so frequently changing the signification of the principal term' (II.219). And in the concluding pages, to arm Hylas against any new objections to immaterialism, Philonous lays down three simple logical rules against which any such doubt should be tested. First, Hylas should remember that 'that which bears equally hard on two contradictory opinions, can be a proof against neither' (II.259–60). Philonous explains that if the same objection can be made against materialism, then it is no valid criticism of immaterialism. Second, 'take heed not to argue on a *petitio principii*'. That is, Hylas should be careful not to beg the question by assuming the existence of external substances. And third, 'beware of imposing on your self by that vulgar sophism, which is called *ignoratio elenchi*' (II.260). Here the danger is that of assuming immaterialism denies the reality of sensible objects. Philonous makes it clear in this speech that each of these fallacies had been committed repeatedly by Hylas in the course of the dispute.

Hylas is thus identified, not just as the exponent of a false principle, but as an exemplar of that 'loose, rambling way' of thought that can lead to a dangerous scepticism. No doubt for Berkeley Hylas was also the embodiment of the reader who refused to admit the lucid *a priori* proof of the *Principles*. Notice how, in his final logical assessment of the proceedings of the *Three Dialogues*, Philonous identifies fallacies in which Hylas

---

[10] *The Educational Writings of John Locke*, ed. James L. Axtell (Cambridge: Cambridge University Press, 1968), p. 297.

mistakes the scope of the argument and fails to 'comprehend the state of the question' (II.260). Hylas' problem is that he is forever worrying about matters that do not pertain to the question under analysis. The critical concentration of the elenchus is needed to bring Hylas to the point at which he may apprehend the few simple premises of immaterialism, his prejudices, erroneous assumptions, and misinterpretations cut away. No doubt Berkeley chose the Socratic method for its ability, in Rapin's words, 'to reduce the Subject we treat of to certain *Principles*'. Part I of the *Principles*, with its forensic format, was designed to encourage a sustained attention, on the part of the reader, to the principle *esse* is *percipi*. The *Three Dialogues* is no less committed to a concentrated examination and demonstration of this truth. But the dialogue is also an education for the reader in the philosophical method needed to attain that truth. Through Philonous' constant revelation of errors and inconsistencies in Hylas' thought, we can learn to recognize our own fallacies.[11]

Amongst the Greek thinkers there was much talk of the merits and failings of this dialectic form of debate, but despite differences of opinion, one point was clear: the elenchus was extremely popular. In the *Republic*, Socrates tells Glaucon that the youngest students often become addicts of elenchus, arguing for pleasure and forever contradicting one another,[12] and in many dialogues Socrates himself takes a playful delight in the dispute. At the outset of the *Theaetetus*, for example, Socrates is boisterous, teasing his aging friend Theodorus and eagerly laying down the rules of the debate as if it were a children's game.[13] Socrates' playfulness has its source in the agonistic nature of the elenchus. In a discursive debate one may be contradicted, but Socratic dispute forces the answerer into the embarrassment of self-contradiction. In vain Socrates' answerers try to wrest the role of questioner from his tight grip. The competition becomes so fierce that Plato sometimes characterizes the elenchus as a sparring match and its disputants as pancratiasts.[14]

---

[11] In his essay 'Philosophy as Literature: The Dialogue', in *Philosophy and Rhetoric*, 9 (1976), p. 9, Albert William Levi celebrates Berkeley's ability to create an exciting drama of ideas in his dialogues. Levi proceeds to draw a distinction between philosophy as theory and philosophy as activity, the latter being the object of philosophical dialogue (p. 17): 'the forms of philosophizing which are concerned with proof are by nature the most ponderous and static, and those which aim to clarify, or discover, or make things "shine forth" are the most brilliant, absorbing, and exciting'. The danger of Levi's distinction is that it implies the *Three Dialogues*, in depicting a learning process, is not 'concerned with proof '. This view also implies that treatises are static, an adjective that could hardly be applied to the *Principles*' argument. Is there not a progression in the syllogism itself, something of the narrative of discovery that Levi so admires in the dialogue?

[12] *Republic*, VII.539b.   [13] *Theaetetus*, 146a.

[14] *Euthydemus*, 271c; *Theaetetus*, 169a–c. In general, Plato's later dialogues are less elenctic than the earlier ones, but even these devote much time to a theoretical defence of elenchus as a technique.

In Berkeley's day, the agonistic qualities of the Platonic dialogues received considerable attention, largely, it would seem, because of the influence of Diogenes Laertius' *Lives of the Philosophers*, which classified Plato's dialogues using terminology borrowed from gymnastic contests.[15] These agonistic qualities of elenchus also featured in university disputations, where even serious public exercises for degrees seemed to have encouraged buffoonery amongst the scholars in attendance. Locke, remembering his own university days, condemns disputations for teaching nothing but 'Fallacy, Wrangling and Opiniatrety'. He thought the battle of wits encouraged close-mindedness:

For this in short, is the Way and Perfection of Logical Disputes, That the opponent never take any Answer, nor the respondent ever yield to any Argument. This neither of them must do, whatever becomes of Truth and Knowledge; unless he will pass for a poor baffl'd Wretch, and lie under the Disgrace of not being able to maintain whatever he has once affirm'd, which is the great Aim and Glory in Disputing.[16]

Glanvill agrees: 'the precipitancy of *disputation*, and the stir and noise of Passions, that usually attend it, must need be prejudicial to Verity: its calm insinuations can no more be heard in such a bustle, then a whisper among a croud of Saylors in a storm'.[17] Walker, on the other hand, defends the competitive nature of the disputations, recognizing the practical benefits of a teaching method in which the student finds entertainment:

it makes them [the undergraduates] quick in Replies, intentive upon their Subject: where the *Opponent* useth all means to drive his Adversary from his hold; and the *Answerer* defends himself *sometimes* with the force of Truth, *sometimes* with the subtilty of his Wit; and *sometimes* also he escapes in a mist of Words, and the doubles of a Distinction, whilst he seeks all Holes and Recesses to shelter his persecuted Opinion and Reputation. This properly belongs to the *Disputations*, which are Exercises of young Students, who are by these Velitations, and in this

---

[15] Among Diogenes' types of dialogue 'the PEIRASTIC were, to represent a *Skirmish*, or Trial of Proficiency; the ENDEICTIC were, it seems, likened to the Exhibiting a *Specimen* of Skill; and the ANATREPTIC, to Presenting the Spectacle of a thorough *Defeat*, or sound Drubbing'; see Floyer Sydenham, trans., *The Dialogues of Plato*, 3 vols (London: W. Sandby, 1767–9), i, 9n). Diogenes' work informs the accounts of Plato in both Thomas Stanley's *The History of Philosophy* (London: H. Moseley and T. Dring, 1655) and the anonymous *The Lives of the Ancient Philosophers* (London: J. Nicholson and T. Newborough, 1702), and is, as well, the basis of 'La Vie de Platon' in André Dacier's *Œuvres de Platon* (Paris: J. Anisson, 1699), which made, in translation, four English editions in the eighteenth century. There was a translation of Diogenes in the period: *The Lives, Opinions, and Remarkable Sayings of the Most Famous Ancient Philosophers*, trans. T. Fetherstone *et al.* (London: E. Brewster, 1688).

[16] *Educational Writings*, pp. 205 and 297.

[17] *Scepsis Scientifica*, 2nd ed. (London: H. Eversden, 1665), p. 122.

Palaestra, brought up to a more serious search of Truth. And in them I think it not a fault to *dispute for Victory*, and to endeavour to save their Reputation.[18]

The pleasure and pressure of the fight helped ensure the scholar's commitment to the exercise. This is not just wishful thinking on Walker's part; young scholars genuinely seemed to delight in the battle of wits. John Byrom, answering in the Cambridge Tripos of 1711, was disappointed when he learnt that of his three opponents, one was a sot and another a beau: 'I came off very gloriously, though I wish I had better antagonists.' Likewise, Richard Cumberland at Trinity, Cambridge, records with obvious pleasure how he played the questioner with success, relying, like Socrates, on 'involving consequences' and 'unforeseen confutations'.[19]

Berkeley, like Plato, does not shrink from showing the pains and delights of elenchus. The competition of the *Three Dialogues* is most evident in the interlocutors' tone. Philonous can be very sharp with Hylas, pressing him with strings of rhetorical questions, bluntly pointing out his errors, and charging him with forgetting, or trifling, or jesting, or, and this most often, with being sluggardly in admitting an obvious truth:

If you should say, we differed in our notions; for that you superadded to your idea of the house the simple abstracted idea of identity, whereas I did not; I would tell you I know not what you mean by that *abstracted idea of identity*; and should desire you to look into your own thoughts, and be sure you understood your self – Why so silent Hylas? (II.248)

Here Philonous mocks his friend's slowness, easily predicting the sort of objection Hylas will make and answering it before it is made. And Hylas, while he can be ingenuous in admitting his own confusions and contradictions, is none the less dogged in his defence of matter, providing, in the Third Dialogue, many substantial objections to Philonous' system. Nor does he hesitate to strew Philonous' path with the stumbling-blocks of scholastic jargon in the Second Dialogue.

If Hylas' intellectual weakness seems to make for an unequal match, he has the more plausible and popular thesis as compensation – that matter exists. Furthermore, Berkeley helps keep the competition alive with a sort of intellectual gambling. The presiding wager of the *Three Dialogues* sets, right from the start, a high and very personal stake on the outcome:

Softly, good Hylas. What if it should prove, that you, who hold there is [such a thing as matter], are by virtue of that opinion a greater *sceptic*, and maintain more paradoxes and repugnancies to common sense, than I who believe no such thing? (II.172)

[18] *Of Education*, p. 120.
[19] Wordsworth, *Scholae*, pp. 25 and 28.

The loser of the elenchus is to be branded a sceptic. Lest Hylas' repeated failures and concessions take the edge from the sport, Berkeley has Philonous enliven the game with two winner-take-all bets. In the first dialogue, in the face of Hylas' strong common-sense objection that objects seem to exist at a distance from us, Philonous puts everything at stake:

But (to pass by all that hath been hitherto said, and reckon it for nothing, if you will have it so) I am content to put the whole upon this issue. If you can conceive it possible for any mixture or combination of qualitites, or any sensible object whatever, to exist without the mind, then I will grant it actually to be so.   (II.200)

An appeal to mental images wins Philonous the point. Again in the third dialogue, Philonous seems to take great risks when he bets

Now if you can prove, that any philosopher hath explained the production of any one idea in our minds by the help of *matter*, I shall for ever acquiesce, and look on all that hath been said against it as nothing.   (II.242)

In both instances Philonous promises to free Hylas of the humiliation of all the previous elenctic bouts and risks also admitting that he himself is a sceptic. With this gambling Berkeley keeps us excited by the game-like competition of the *Three Dialogues* and interested in the outcome of its logical wrangling.

Donald Davie is in danger of underestimating these agonistic qualities of the *Three Dialogues* in his essay 'Berkeley and the Style of Dialogue'. While Davie is sensitive to the vigour of the debate, he interprets the whole as an 'exemplification of the virtue of candour'. He shows that for the eighteenth century 'candour' meant more than frankness and open-mindedness; it was a willingness to help another in the search for truth and to give him the benefit of the doubt. Candour was a virtue closely allied to charity itself. For Davie, Hylas is an example of candour, willing to admit error and permitting himself to be ruled by the dictates of logic. Philonous, too, is 'more than fair' in giving Hylas time to grasp the difficult points at issue. But in characterizing the *Three Dialogues* as a model of candid conversation and as 'an example of good manners and disinterested behaviour', Davie casts a serious aspersion on the rhetorical impact of the work, for he believes that 'when candour and civility are achieved in literature, they bore us'.[20] Davie is right when he argues that Berkeley shows us much of the friendship of Hylas and Philonous, and of their mutual concern for the truth, but this need not and does not make the *Three Dialogues* dull. Candour does not forbid the engagement of wits that makes dispute exciting. The embarrassing line of questioning Philonous pursues is, after all, designed to free Hylas from error. Given

[20] In *The English Mind*, ed. H. S. Davies and G. Watson (Cambridge: Cambridge University Press, 1964), p. 103.

the obvious importance of the issues which the dialogue handles, coupled with the obstinacy of Hylas' prejudices, candour, as Davie glosses it, demands that Philonous employ his aggressive argumentative techniques. As Walker pointed out, it is precisely the agonistic qualities of elenchus which make it a valuable teaching instrument, forcing the disputants to commit all their energies to discovering the very knot of the issue. Perhaps the nature and effect of the *Three Dialogues* are best revealed if we consider it, not as model of polite conversation, but as a form of competitive play, even as a kind of comedy.

The answerer's role in the elenchus is inevitably limited. Once he has proposed his thesis he can only answer yes or no, and, at most, object to a question he feels is ambiguous. His only other resort is to scrutinize the progress of the questions in order to determine, if possible, how the questioner plans to force him into contradiction. With this knowledge, he can then decide whether the questioner desires a 'yes' or a 'no' in a specific instance and may be able to thwart the attack by a contrary reply. Hylas is not quick enough to predict Philonous' strategies in this way. At best he only shuffles terms, or gives tentative answers: 'I give up the point for the present, reserving still a right to retract my opinion, in case I shall hereafter discover any false step in my progress to it' (II.190). To frustrate such evasions, the questioner can adopt one of a number of tactics. First, he can ask questions for which only one answer is possible. Philonous proves a master of the constraining question. How could Hylas answer 'yes' to 'Can one and the same thing be at the same time in itself of different dimensions?' (II.189), or 'no' to 'But that one thing may stand under or support another, must it not be extended?' (II.198)? Second, the sequence of questions may be designed to conceal the character of the ultimate refutation, so that the answerer cannot know when to withhold assent. In his *Topics*, Aristotle teaches all the tricks of concealment: how to lose the answerer in a multitude of questions and how to reverse the natural order of an argument to keep the middle term hidden.[21] Such techniques, gleaned from Plato's practice of the dialogue, are everywhere displayed in the *Three Dialogues*.

Consider how Philonous chooses to attack Hylas' belief that whereas the secondary qualities of objects are ideas or modes of mind, primary qualities actually resemble separate external entities. In the *Principles*, Berkeley dismissed this distinction by showing that primary and secondary qualities are inextricably mixed: 'I desire any one to reflect and try, whether he can by any abstraction of thought, conceive the extension and motion of a body, without all other sensible qualities' (II.45). One might expect the *Three Dialogues* to adopt this convincing strategy, but Berkeley

---

[21] *Topica*, 155b–156a.

chooses to reserve this argument. After a long proof of the mind-dependence of secondary qualities, Philonous begins his attack on the primary qualities with this very different line of questioning:

PHILONOUS. Is it your opinion, the very figure and extension which you perceive by sense, exist in the outward object or material substance?

HYLAS. It is.

PHILONOUS. Have all other animals as good grounds to think the same of the figure and extension which they see and feel?

HYLAS. Without doubt, if they have any thought at all.

PHILONOUS. Answer me, Hylas. Think you the senses were bestowed upon all animals for their preservation and well-being in life? or were they given to men alone for this end?

HYLAS. I make no question but they have the same use in all other animals.

PHILONOUS. If so, is it not necessary they should be enabled by them to perceive their own limbs, and those bodies which are capable of harming them?

HYLAS. Certainly.

PHILONOUS. A mite therefore must be supposed to see his own foot, and things equal or even less than it, as bodies of some considerable dimension; though at the same time they appear to you scarce discernible, or at best as so many visible points.

HYLAS. I cannot deny it.

PHILONOUS. And to creatures less than a mite they will seem yet larger.

HYLAS. They will.

PHILONOUS. Insomuch that what you can hardly discern, will to another extremely minute animal appear as some huge mountain.

HYLAS. All this I grant.

PHILONOUS. Can one and the same thing be at the same time in itself of different dimensions?

HYLAS. That were absurd to imagine.

PHILONOUS. But from what you have laid down it follows, that both the extension by you perceived, and that perceived by the mite itself, as likewise all those perceived by lesser animals, are each of them the true extension of the mite's foot, that is to say, by your own principles you are led into an absurdity.

(II.188–9)

This argument from the sensory experience of animals, experience of which we have no immediate knowledge, is perhaps less sound than the *Principles'* succinct challenge. In fact this argument does not appear in the *Principles*, but seems to be adopted straight from the early pages of Malebranche's *Recherche*.[22] Before this exchange, Philonous has already made several similar appeals to animal sensation. To prove the mind-dependence of odours, he has asked if 'filth and ordure affect those brute animals that feed on them out of choice, with the same smells which we perceive in them?' (II.181). Again, a few pages later, he argues that the

---

[22] McCracken, *Malebranche*, p. 218. Richard H. Popkin notes that a form of the argument also appears in Bayle's article on Zeno, remark G, in the *Dictionnaire*; see 'Berkeley and Pyrrhonism', *Review of Metaphysics*, 5 (1951–2), p. 229.

eyes of minute animals must perceive different colours from the ones that we do, just as the colours of objects appear differently to us when we look through a microscope. What is it about this particular argument that attracted Berkeley when writing the *Three Dialogues*, but not the *Principles*? Part of the answer lies in certain qualities which make it especially suitable for elenchus. For one thing it works indirectly, talking innocently about mites' feet when Hylas' thesis was about the existence of figure and extension in objects. The appealing specificity of the mite, its foot, and its perceptual problems helps distract us from the larger, more abstract issues at hand. Philonous takes advantage of the difficulty we have in keeping the particular and the universal in mind at once. This line of argument is further disarming in that it appears at first to agree with the answerer. Philonous begins, not by immediately discounting Hylas' thesis, but apparently by extending its application from human to animal perception. Indirect argument may be modelled simply: 'A therefore B, but not B, therefore not A.'[23] In Philonous' case, he take's Hylas' thesis A – that visually perceived extension is in the object – and derives from it a second thesis B – that an object's dimensions must then appear the same to all observers. But this essential deduction is only clarified in Philonous' conclusion, and while Hylas has been worrying about his A, Philonous has been busy attacking it indirectly in the form of B.

The overall effect of Philonous' deceptive line of questioning is to create suspense as it diverts the answerer with a multitude of questions. This suspense is partly a natural consequence of the indirect argument which requires several concessions from the answerer. But Philonous goes further, indulging in unnecessary elaborations concerning the sense-data of mites and even smaller creatures. In Plato's writings we often feel this suspense when Socrates collects far more examples than are needed to make his point. This combination of circumlocution and concealment delays a conclusion while giving more and more clues as to the final tack of the argument. We join Hylas in attempting to project the path to the inevitable demise of his thesis, speculating at each point as to whether or not we may withhold our assent in the face of the obvious. Our participation in elenctic dialogue as surrogate answerers is further encouraged by the fact that the answerer is defending a thesis we accept. Both Philonous and Socrates share a certain absurdity in our eyes for violating common sense and demanding a radical reappraisal of our experience of the world. But as well as suspense, there is a strong element of surprise in Socratic dialogue. As we read through a dialogue we are confronted, at the conclusion of each round of the elenchus, with a refutation that springs unexpectedly from the involutions of the indirect proof. This

[23] I am indebted here to Richard Robinson's account of Plato's indirect arguments, in *Plato's Earlier Dialectic*, 2nd ed. (Oxford: Clarendon Press, 1953), pp. 23–6.

moment of surprise is coupled with the answerer's self-contradiction, which, as both humiliating and incongruous, is comic. These moments at which paradox is unexpectedly revealed make the dialogue highly entertaining, and Berkeley heightens the comedy by encouraging our participation, tempting us to solve the puzzle of the elenctic process.

7

Comic characters

The dialogue's specific advantages over the treatise, its ability to entertain and engage the reader, depend to a great degree on its depiction of character. An attitude or argumentative stance can find expression in the character of the interlocutor, and the abstract be made concrete, familiar, and accessible to the reader. The reader reluctant to venture into abstruse speculation is thus insensibly drawn into thought, led on, if by nothing else, by a natural curiosity about human nature and behaviour. With its depiction of a mind in action, dialogue provides those 'parallel circumstances, and kindred images' which, in Johnson's opinion, give biography its 'irresistible interest'.[1] Our interest is encouraged to the degree that complex and specific characters emerge from the dialogue, and it has been argued that Berkeley's dialogues fail to attain any such appealing portraiture. Blair judged that 'Bishop Berkeley's Dialogues concerning the existence of matter, do not attempt any display of Characters; but furnish an instance of a very abstract subject, rendered clear and intelligible by means of Conversation properly managed.'[2] In this century Elizabeth Merrill has argued that the intensity of Berkeley's 'thought . . . leaves little room for any consideration of the individual personality', and Michael Morrisroe agrees that 'Berkeley's characters seem to exist less for themselves than for the response that Berkeley needed in order to get across his points.'[3] The assumption implicit in these criticisms is that characterization and argument are two poles between which the dialogue as a form is torn – that the intellectual intensity of the debate precludes drama. It is true that Berkeley's characterization is subtle, but the complexity of his characters enhances the impression of actual conversation, an impression which could easily be destroyed by caricature. Moreover our involvement in the progress of the *Three Dialogues* depends on Hylas being to some extent a universal character, the voice of the average reader

[1] *The Rambler*, ed. W. J. Bate and Albrecht B. Strauss, Vols. III–V of *The Yale Edition of the Works of Samuel Johnson* (New Haven, Conn.: Yale University Press, 1969), Vol. III, p. 319.
[2] *Lectures*, Vol. II, p. 296.
[3] Merrill, *The Dialogue in English Literature*, Yale Studies in English, 42, ed. Albert S. Cook (New York: Henry Holt, 1911), p. 84; Morrisroe, 'Dialogues', p. 157.

in the text. But Hylas and Philonous are, none the less, clearly drawn and individuated characters. What we learn of Hylas and Philonous emerges from their roles in the dispute. We learn the idiosyncracies of their minds through the positions they endorse and their techniques of argument. Likewise they both express emotions, but these arise in response to the turns of the debate. In short, Berkeley effects an integration of philosophy and drama where the play of ideas alone is permitted to engender character.

Sharing a conviction with Hylas in the existence of matter does not prevent us from recognizing the specific shortcomings he displays as answerer. Like Plato's Crito, Hylas is a good friend, but can be a little opaque. He keeps repeating his old mistakes, slow to digest the points Philonous has made clear. And Philonous easily manoeuvres him into some absurd positions, such as the ludicrous thesis that while extreme sensations of heat exist in the mind, mild ones do not (II.177). Again, after relinquishing all claims to know matter, Hylas can still brazenly declare:

But to prevent any farther questions, let me tell you, I at present understand by *matter* neither substance nor accident, thinking nor extended being, neither cause, instrument, nor occasion, but something entirely unknown, distinct from all these. (II.221)

This posture is no more ridiculous, however, than Hylas' sophistical attempts to evade the elenchus by resorting to the mysteries of scholastic diction, or by swearing, in frustration, to give Philonous nothing but negative answers. In the Third Dialogue, we find him relishing the thought of revenge:

Material substance was no more than a hypothesis, and a false and groundless one too. I will no longer spend my breath in defence of it. But whatever hypothesis you advance or whatsoever scheme of things you introduce in its stead, I doubt not it will appear every whit as false: let me but be allowed to question you upon it. That is, suffer me to serve you in your own kind, and I warrant it shall conduct you through as many perplexities and contradictions, to the very same state of scepticism that I my self am in at present. (II.229)

Here Berkeley shows the frustration, confusion, and humiliation of the elenchus turning to resentment. Still reluctant to take responsibility for the logical insubstantiality of his opinions on matter, Hylas blames the elenchus for his present predicament, and assumes that Philonous' thoughts will be just as vulnerable to its sceptical analysis. This is, of course, just one more example of Hylas' folly. His own three brief attempts at elenchus, far from discomfiting Philonous, only serve to elicit careful clarifications of immaterialism. Philonous shows that all Hylas'

objections spring from his failure to grasp the central tenets and consequences of immaterialism.

Berkeley achieves much of the characterization of the *Three Dialogues*
through the subtle contrasts between the tactics of the two disputants.
Davie has accounted the *Three Dialogues* 'the drama of a slow mind and a
quick one'.[4] Truly, our perception of Hylas' particular weaknesses grows
from our sense of Philonous' virtuosity as questioner. Despite his concern
to show Hylas the way to truth, Philonous is very much master of the
game, and appears, like Socrates, to be less than entirely frank in his
strategies. Dissimulation is, to some extent, demanded of the elenctic
questioner, who makes no pretence to knowledge but is none the less full
of criticisms of his opponent's beliefs. Rapin remarks that Socrates wears
'the Disguise of an apparent Simplicity and an unaffected Plainness' in
Plato's dialogues.[5] Philonous adopts just such a misleading posture in the
Three Dialogues. He repeatedly protests, much to Hylas' frustration, that
he is a simple advocate of 'common sense' (II.172), one who finds himself
'obliged to think like other folks' (II.230) – a homely attitude belied by
his radical and rigorous metaphysical scepticism. Berkeley lets us recognize the extent of Philonous' role-playing and the ways in which he
conceals his own opinions in manipulating the debate. The predominant
Socratic irony of the teacher who pretends to be the student pervades the
Three Dialogues.

Just as Socrates always teases his friends, so Philonous uses irony to
prod Hylas along the path of knowledge:

I would therefore fain know, what arguments you can draw from reason for the
existence of what you call *real things* or *material objects*. Or whether you remember
to have seen them formerly as they are in themselves? or if you have heard or
read of any one that did?   (II.204)

But granting matter to be possible, yet upon that account merely it can have no
more claim to existence, than a golden mountain or a centaur.   (II.224)

But then we differ as to the kind of this powerful being. I will have it to be spirit,
you matter, or I know not what (I may add too, you know not what) third nature.
                                                                     (II.240)

This dry condescension becomes acute when Hylas resorts, as does Locke,
to mechanical explanations of sense experience. Hylas learnedly informs
Philonous that what we see and feel is nothing but the shaking of various
nerves running from the sense organs to the soul. Sound, by this account,
'is merely a vibrative or undulatory *motion* in the air'. This comment
prompts Philonous to wonder if 'It is then good to speak of *motion*, as of
a thing that is *loud, sweet, acute,* or *grave?*' (II.182). Berkeley's use of irony

[4] 'The Style of Dialogue', p. 96.
[5] *Critical Works*, Vol. I, p. 337.

here serves several ends. We are entertained by the incongruity of Philonous' dry expression of Hylas' foolish ideas. But more, irony encourages a complicity in its implicit appeal to a shared knowledge; in appreciating Philonous' irony, we come to admire his wit and his reserve. Finally, the butt of his humour is always matter, so irony is another means of helping us to a critical perspective on our own beliefs.

Each of Philonous' ironic comments points out Hylas' failure to consider the implications of his beliefs. As the *Three Dialogues* unfolds, Hylas' mind is slowly exposed as a pastiche of popular opinions. He admits he is a devotee of 'the modern way of explaining things' (II.208) and seems to have accepted many notions on popular authority, without attempting to sift or co-ordinate this divergent material. Again and again, Hylas emits undigested modern learning as if by rote, even reproducing the findings of Boyle's famous vacuum experiments (II.181). His complex mechanical and physiological explanations seem arcane intrusions in the process of elenchus with its concentration on basic issues of perception and its spare vocabulary. And Hylas is disturbed when Philonous implies that 'the natural philosophers have been dreaming all this while' (II.242). In the third dialogue, he worries that microscopes might be rendered useless by immaterialism (II.245). Still, although he has absorbed much of the new science, Hylas is far from a modern philosopher himself. He admits that he was never thoroughly convinced of the distinction between primary and secondary qualities, a distinction at the very heart of materialism. Indeed, many of Philonous' elenctic victories depend on Hylas' absurd blend of materialism and naive realism. Hylas does not doubt his senses. Unlike the philosopher he believes that he sees, touches, and smells matter, and appeals ultimately to the 'common sense of men' in this case (II.234). Each round of the elenchus exposes the contradictions between his principles.

William Charlton has shown how philosophy is essentially an exploration of problems, but that the average reader seldom recognizes the problematic nature of the philosopher's questions and so fails to take them seriously. Charlton argues that 'the philosopher must not only announce that there is a problem, but bring the problem to life'.[6] In the *Three Dialogues* Hylas becomes an exemplification of the problems Berkeley wants to bring to our attention. Berkeley strives to shatter our complacency by drawing the difficult issues of being and perception in the familiar and accessible form of human character and emotion. In Hylas Berkeley establishes a difficult balance. His gullibility, slowness, and confusion are comic. Yet, at the same time, in his confused beliefs Hylas is enough like us to give the elenctic comedy a troubling edge. In

[6] 'Is Philosophy a Form of Literature?', *British Journal of Aesthetics*, 14 (1974), 9.

making Hylas the focus of both our ridicule and our sympathy, Berkeley brings us to a critical perspective on our own logical failings. Like the most effective satire, the ironic method of the *Three Dialogues* seems at points to bring us to laugh at our own folly.

8

Comic form

Throughout his career Plato worried about the utility of Socrates' teaching method. A key difficulty with elenchus is that it concentrates on a proof of ignorance; its successful conclusion is the discovery that the answerer's thesis is wrong. It seems that elenchus cannot teach us what we should believe, but only eliminate one thing we should not. At his most playful, Socrates describes himself as one who has nothing to teach, who 'neither knows nor thinks that he knows', but only sets about to prove that all men share his ignorance.[1] This prevalent scepticism in Plato's work was often attributed to the dialogue form in general. Boyle seems to have chosen the dialogue for *The Sceptical Chymist: or Chymo-Physical Doubts & Paradoxes* because it could best express his reservations about all chemical theory. And Dryden defends the form of his *Of Dramatick Poesie* as 'Sceptical, according to the way of reasoning which was used by *Socrates, Plato,* and all the Academiques of old'.[2] Much later Hurd argued that the dialogue should not be used to discuss important topics, such as religion, because of 'the sceptical inconclusive air, which the decorum of polite dialogue demands', while Hume reveals that he chose dialogue to express his thoughts on religion for this very reason: 'Any question of philosophy . . . which is so *obscure* and *uncertain*, that human reason can reach no fixed determination with regard to it; if it should be treated at all; seems to lead us naturally into the style of dialogue and conversation.'[3]

[1] *Apology*, 21d. The scepticism of the Socratic method was a point of some difficulty for philosophy in the late seventeenth century. There was a tendency to perceive Socrates as a moralist and the pattern of a Christian stoic, and some Neoplatonists even sought to prove that Plato was conversant with Mosaic law. In this context, Socrates' doubts became problematic, and led to some strained, if ingenious, solutions. André Dacier, in *Works of Plato Abridg'd*, I, 10, attributed Socrates' scepticism to a growing intuition of the revelation Christ would bring: 'Thus we see where his Doubts terminated; they led Men to aknowledg the need they had of a God, to assure 'em of the great Blessings for which they hop'd.' Rapin, in *Critical Works*, Vol. II, p. 353, had similar difficulties reconciling Socrates' alleged moral mission with his admissions of *aporia*: 'rational as he was, he too much distrusted his Reason'.
[2] 'A Defense of an Essay of Dramatique Poesie', in *The Indian Emperor*, 2nd ed. (London: H. Herringman, 1668), p. 14.
[3] Richard Hurd, *Moral and Political Dialogues*, 3rd ed., 3 vols (London: A. Millar *et al.*, 1765), Vol. I, p. x; Hume, *Dialogues*, pp. 127–8. Hume once wrote to James Balfour, who had

This point had been made by Shaftesbury, and was to be made again by Blair, who demanded 'a fair and full view of both sides of the argument'. Blair detested an obviously biased performance in dialogue, where one character

personates the Author, a man of learning, no doubt, and of good principles; and the other is a man of straw, set up to propose some trivial objections; over which the first gains a most entire triumph; and leaves his sceptical antagonist at the end much humbled, and generally, convinced of his error.[4]

Blair's point is that men are not readily converted, nor controversial topics easily resolved in conversation. The dialogue, as a mimetic form, is constrained to present a credible exchange. The consensus was, then, that the best dialogues remained inconclusive, unresolved.

That Berkeley should choose this most sceptical of genres in which to recast his neglected immaterialism is perplexing, for he was well aware that his most pressing rhetorical task was to free immaterialism from the taint of scepticism. Even in the notebooks we find him planning to 'take notice that I do not fall in with Sceptics' (_PC_ 79), and the _Principles_ duly protests: 'We are not for having any man turn sceptic . . . nor are there any principles more opposite to scepticism, than those we have laid down' (II.57). Few were impressed by these assurances, as Percival's letter of the reception of the _Principles_ in London confirmed. Berkeley's reply to Percival, which protests at length that immaterialism is not sceptical, shows that Berkeley was now well aware of the tendency to perceive his philosophy in this light. There is, of course, much in Berkeley's thought that does appear sceptical. In his attempt to reconstruct Berkeley's early intellectual development from the notebooks, A. A. Luce has argued that Berkeley's very first philosophical reflections were deeply sceptical explorations of the path cut by Locke, Malebranche and Bayle. Luce proposes that Philonous' claim that he has undergone a 'revolt from metaphysical notions to the plain dictates of Nature and common sense' is a confession of Berkeley's own experience. Berkeley's frequent attacks on scepticism are 'organically connected with

criticized _A Dialogue_, that 'In every dialogue no more than one person can be supposed to represent the author.' This specious claim is cast in some doubt by Hume's appeal to Gilbert Elliot for help with the _Dialogues on Natural Religion_: 'You wou'd perceive by the Sample I have given you, that I make Cleanthes the Hero of the Dialogue. Whatever you can think of, to strengthen that Side of the Argument, will be most acceptable to me. Any Propensity you imagine I have to the other Side, crept in upon me against my Will.' Hume goes on to describe how his first scribblings on religion involved 'a perpetual Struggle of a restless Imagination against Inclination, perhaps against Reason', and he confesses that he is most comfortable in the voice of the sceptical Philo; see _The Letters of David Hume_, ed. J.Y.T. Greig, 2 vols (Oxford: Clarendon Press, 1932), Vol. I, pp. 153–4.

[4] _Lectures_, Vol. II, p. 294. Eugene R. Purpus makes this point in his survey of attitudes toward dialogue, 'The "Plain, Easy, and Familiar Way": The Dialogue in English Literature, 1660–1725', _ELH_, 17 (1950), 50–1.

the evolution of his own philosophy; they spring from a personal contact with continental scepticism, by which he was attracted and repelled, and influenced, first positively and then negatively'.[5] It was only with the discovery of the principle, recorded for us in the notebooks, that Berkeley was able to break free from these doubts and recreate a stable, if immaterial world. Even if immaterialism is, in the end, a philosophy in tune with the beliefs and the language of the common man, there is no question that the process to that philosophy involves a radical doubting of our preconceptions of the natural world.

In the *Three Dialogues* Berkeley does not seem to shrink from the inherent scepticism that seems a convention of the form he has chosen. He works hard to portray a viable intellectual confrontation free from authorial bias and pedantry. If Hylas is ultimately converted to immaterialism, it is only after an intense logical scrutiny of his own materialist opinions. Berkeley's sensitive exploration of Hylas' intellectual dilemma, and the substantiality of the objections Hylas is permitted to voice, help make his conversion credible.[6] But Berkeley has an even more effective strategy for fulfilling the dialogue's demands for doubt. He permits Philonous, the eventual proponent of immaterialism, to indulge in scepticism himself, giving the elenchus free rein in the first half of the work. Our initial experience of Philonous is not as pedant, but as an apparent enemy to the most fundamental truths. To think of him simply as Berkeley's 'mouthpiece' is to forget that for the first half of the *Three Dialogues* Philonous propounds no positive doctrine and establishes no principles. Rather he plays the sceptic with abandon, bringing both Hylas and the reader to a disturbing *aporia*. In choosing Socratic dialogue Berkeley has adopted the form which best expresses the initial scepticism of immaterialism, indeed which openly advertises its radical doubt. But he does so in order to draw our attention to the rhetorically problematic issue of scepticism, just as when he makes the definition of *sceptic* a central issue in the debate. Through elenchus Berkeley is able to show precisely the nature and source of his doubts about the material world.

[5] *Dialectic of Immaterialism*, p. 67.
[6] Such is the openness of the debate that K. M. Wheeler, who finds the argument of the *Three Dialogues* unsatisfactory on a literal level, has presented an impressive case for a thoroughly ironic reading. Philonous's immaterialism and Hylas's materialism are equally untenable: 'Neither is free of the delusion of reason in positing a cause and a support independent to and outside of mind, whether it be called Mind or Matter'; see 'Berkeley's Ironic Method in the *Three Dialogues*', *Philosophy and Literature*, 4 (1980), 26. For Wheeler, Hylas's failure to challenge the flaws in Philonous's case are intentional defects by which Berkeley points us to the insufficiencies of immaterialism and encourages us to formulate our own transcendent position. Richard T. Lambert responds to Wheeler's article, admitting that Berkeley's spirit/idea dualism is troublesome, but arguing that spirit is at least a viable cause for ideas in a way matter is not; see 'The Literal Intent of Berkeley's Dialogues', *Philosophy and Literature*, 6 (1982), 165–71.

The *Three Dialogues* begins in doubt, but if Philonous proves the master of the dialogue, Hylas is clearly its instigator. He is pacing early in the garden because he could not sleep, troubled, it turns out, by the scepticism of learned men and particularly by Philonous' doubts about material substance. These worries about the tendencies of philosophy are foremost in his mind when he meets Philonous, and the dialogue itself is proposed as an expression of his internal debate; Hylas asks Philonous, 'permit me to go on in the same vein . . . for my thoughts always flow more easily in conversation with a friend' (II.171). On this premise, the first dialogue becomes a dramatization of the dilemma that robbed Hylas of his rest, with Philonous playing one of those doubting philosophers who, in Hylas' words, 'entertain suspicions concerning the most important truths' (II.172). And by applying the elenchus Philonous instigates what must be an exploration of Hylas' mind, a calling into language of his thoughts.

In the *Three Dialogues*, even more than in the *Principles*, Berkeley is careful to begin the argument in the realm of the unobtrusive and acceptable. In the initial clenctic passages, Philonous attacks opinions held by Hylas that are popularly perceived as erroneous. In an extended exchange he brings Hylas to the admission that heat is not in objects, but 'in the mind', and then moves on to dismiss the external existence of all the other secondary qualities. Hylas is forced to relinquish his beliefs about the reality of tastes, odours, sounds and colours. These confutations prove nothing new, but simply substantiate arguments most recently expounded by Locke and Malebranche. And Hylas admits that his defence of naive realism was only half-hearted. Truly, he confesses, we must make a distinction between the secondary and the 'real' primary qualities: 'For my part, I have been a long time sensible there was such an opinion current among the philosophers, but was never thoroughly convinced of its truth till now' (II.188). Hylas, and the reader, assume Philonous is simply elucidating the philosophers' theories. Philonous' next step, however, proves more radical. The elenchus proceeds to doubt Hylas' thesis that primary qualities are 'real'; extension, motion and solidity, notions precious to Newtonian formulae and Lockian epistemology, are, each in turn, relegated to the uncertainty of purely mental existence. Yet even in this Philonous seems strangely conventional. He is merely pursuing rigorously that questioning of commonsense assumptions and sensory experience that is fundamental to modern epistemology.

But all convention is abandoned when Philonous turns the elenchus on Hylas' fundamental model of perception – that some objects 'out there' are perceived 'in here' through the activity of both mind and object. First, Philonous uses a tulip to illustrate the fact that the mind is not active in perception; we cannot choose to see a yellow tulip instead of a red one.

Second, Hylas' thesis of a material substance is dealt with, as it was in the *Principles*, by asking for a literal interpretation of the metaphor of substance. Third, Hylas' own query about his ability to conceive an unperceived tree provides immediate evidence of a purely mental visual image. Finally, Philonous elicits from Hylas the admission that depth perception is a mental rather than an external, mechanical process. Together these four elenctic passages move effectively to undermine Hylas' assumption that the world is 'out there', and Philonous drives home the import of Hylas' admissions of ignorance with these aggressive rhetorical questions:

> But how can that which is sensible be like that which is insensible? Can a real thing in itself *invisible* be like a *colour*; or a real thing which is not *audible*, be like a *sound*? In a word, can any thing be like a sensation or idea, but another sensation or idea?
> (II.206)

The last of these questions formulates the challenge with which Berkeley confronted the reader in the beginning of Part I of the *Principles*: that 'an idea can be like nothing but an idea'. By making it here, at the end of the First Dialogue, Berkeley has given himself time to prepare the ground, to ensure that we are in a state of mind to appreciate the full import of this maxim. A few lines later, Hylas can himself admit that '*no idea can exist without the mind*' (II.206). Through the elenchus the external world has been gradually but effectively diminished to the status of dubious hypothesis. Philonous' radical questioning completes the First Dialogue's rapid devolution from philosophical commonplaces to scepticism, a process all the more disarming as it seems a model of modern philosophical procedure. Its emotive impact on the reader is given voice in Hylas' final comments:

> I am at present so amazed to see myself ensnared, and as it were imprisoned in the labyrinths you have drawn me into, that on the sudden it cannot be expected I should find my way out. You must give me time to look about me, and recollect myself.
> (II.207)

Berkeley knows that we, like Hylas, have been caught out by the unprecedented turn of the First Dialogue. We are trapped by the confining demands of the elenchus into such a paradoxical position that we need to 'recollect ourselves'. More than anything else we want, like Hylas, 'to look about' us, to reconstruct a solid sensible 'out there' and re-establish our realist confidence.

Berkeley exploits the rhetorical impact of the elenchus, dramatising in Hylas the emotive consequences of a sceptical line of thought. Hylas, who began the dialogue worried lest his friend Philonous be under the influence of sceptical philosophy, now finds himself a victim of philosophical *aporia*. His plight is as painful as it is ironic, and as in the Introduction to the *Principles*, Berkeley uses the image of the maze to communicate the feelings of confusion and powerlessness that accompany serious doubt. At the beginning of the Second Dialogue Hylas still has reservations about the way in which Philonous has undermined the modern way of explaining things, but Philonous makes short work of these. His victory seems complete with Hylas' admission that 'no sensible things have a real existence' and his confession that he is now willing to call himself 'an arrant *sceptic*' (II.210). But Philonous makes yet another unprecedented move:

Look! are not the fields covered with a delightful verdure? Is there not something in the woods and groves, in the rivers and clear springs that soothes, that softens, that transports the soul? At the prospect of the wide and deep ocean, or some huge mountain whose top is lost in the sky, or of an old gloomy forest, are not our minds filled with a pleasing horror? Even in rocks and deserts, is there not an agreeable wildness? How sincere a pleasure is it to behold the natural beauties of the earth! To preserve and renew our relish for them, is not the veil of night alternately drawn over her face, and doth she not change her dress with the seasons? How aptly are the elements disposed? What variety and use in stones and minerals? What delicacy, what beauty, what contrivance in animal and vegetable bodies? How exquisitely are all things suited, as well to their particular ends, as to constitute apposite parts of the whole! And while they mutually aid and support, do they not also set off and illustrate each other? Raise now your thoughts from this ball of earth, to all those glorious luminaries that adorn the high arch of heaven. The motion and situation of the planets, are they not admirable for use and order? Were those (miscalled *erratic*) globes once known to stray, in their repeated journeys through the pathless void? Do they not measure areas round the sun ever proportioned to the times? So fixed, so immutable are the laws by which the unseen Author of Nature actuates the universe. How vivid and radiant is the lustre of the fixed stars! How magnificent and rich that negligent profusion, with which they appear to be scattered thorow the whole azure vault! Yet if you take the telescope, it brings into your sight a new host of stars that escape the naked eye. Here they seem contiguous and minute, but to a nearer view immense orbs of light at various distances, far sunk in the abyss of space. Now you must call imagination to your aid. The feeble narrow sense cannot descry innumerable worlds revolving round the central fires; and in those worlds the energy of an all-perfect mind displayed in endless forms. But neither sense nor imagination are big enough to comprehend the boundless extent with all its dazzling furniture. Though the labouring mind exert and strain each power to its utmost reach, there still stands out ungrasped a surplusage immeasurable. Yet all the vast bodies that compose this mighty frame, how distant and remote soever, are by some secret mechanism, some divine art and force linked in a mutual dependence and intercourse with each other, even with this earth, which almost slipt from my thoughts, and was lost in the crowd of worlds. Is not the whole system immense, beautiful, glorious beyond expression and beyond thought! What treatment then do those philosophers deserve, who would deprive these noble and delightful scenes of all reality? How should those principles be entertained, that lead us to think all the visible beauty of the creation a false imaginary glare? To be plain,

can you expect this scepticism of yours will not be thought extravagantly absurd
by all men of sense?   (II.210–11)

With his arresting imperative 'Look!', Philonous signals a complete shift
of tone and argument. In place of the tight repartee of the elenchus, we
find an expansive digression of unprecedented length. Indeed, he seems
to answer here Hylas' plea for time to 'look about me'. The issue of
materialism seems suddenly abandoned for sublime landscape description, and the elenchus's appeal to reason lost in an explicit call to the
imagination. Philonous builds a great catalogue of images – 'woods and
groves', a 'huge mountain', the 'high arch of heaven' – each sufficiently
vague and conventional to permit our own free visualizations of the sub-
limities of nature. At the same time Philonous' speech is intensely
emotional in its appeal. He unabashedly asks us to feel a 'pleasing horror'
at the scenes he evokes, and his highly-wrought language expresses his
own apparent excitement. The movement of the prose is extremely ener-
getic, beginning with a sequence of short rhetorical questions and excla-
mations, and including several syntactical inversions:

At the prospect of the wide and deep ocean, or some huge mountain whose top
is lost in the clouds, or of an old gloomy forest, are not our minds filled with a
pleasing horror?

The motion and situation of the planets, are they not admirable for use and
order?

With these questions Berkeley creates the impression of a mind obsessed
with the naming of things and striving to capture the variety of creation.
This impression is enhanced by the combination of asyndeton with
anaphora: 'What delicacy, what beauty, what variety', 'So fixed, so immutable', 'some secret mechanism, some divine art'. The entire effect is of
the spontaneous effusions of one rapt in visionary flight. And, as he
communicates his own intense feelings of awe and exhilaration, Philonous's questions and imperatives demand our participation: 'Now you
must call imagination to your aid.' But at the same time as we cannot help
being caught up in this unexpected lyric excursion, are we not slightly
disconcerted by Philonous' language? Were we not, just moments ago,
mincing terms in the game of elenchus, a game which demanded a constant wariness of the speaker's intentions? Our consciousness of Philonous as a shrewd arguer makes us wonder if Philonous is not aiming for
a specific effect, playing the rhapsodist for Hylas' benefit.
    If there is something unexpected about the style of this passage, its
theme ensures our confusion. In terms of the argument of the previous
dialogue, this is a violent *non sequitur*. Philonous there denied any possible
agency in the world. Matter does not exist. All that we perceive is wholly

mental and we can apprehend no causes for our sensations. Yet now Philonous seems to be saying just the opposite, implying that we know that the world has full existential status: 'Who would deprive these noble and delightful scenes of all reality?' But even within this simple theme there lies a troubling irony. While Philonous appeals to 'men of sense' who admit the reality of the sensible world, the world he describes is, in fact, imaginary. Philonous and Hylas dwell on the fields and woods visible from the garden for only a moment, before leaving the realm of 'feeble narrow sense' to picture in their minds the sea, the mountains, and the turning heavens. We learn, in due course, that 'neither sense nor imagination are big enough to comprehend' the extent of the heavens, and yet Philonous proceeds to describe them none the less. So strong is his fancy that the earth 'almost slipt from my thoughts, and was lost in a crowd of worlds'. So at the very moment that Philonous is explicitly arguing for the reality of the sensible world, he displays his mind's power to create and destroy that world at will.

Philonous' insistence on the order and harmony of the natural world makes what seems a conventional appeal to the argument from design. The hand of the artificer God is evident in the 'contrivance', 'apt disposition' and 'use' of the various parts of the universe. Philonous seems in particular to be invoking the cosmology of Bentley's Boyle lectures. Bentley too had dwelt on the alternation of night and day and on the progress of the seasons as tokens of God's goodness. More famously, he had celebrated the power of the heavens to 'excite and elevate our minds to his adoration and praise'. Philonous seems also to be echoing Bentley's account of the limitations of Newtonian gravity: that 'circular Revolutions in concentric orbs about the Sun or other central Body could no-wise be attain'd without the power of the Divine Arm'.[7] And in noting the 'negligent profusion' of the stars, Philonous touches on Bentley's argument that God must also over-ride gravity between the solar systems, lest they pull together in one great burning mass. Yet how could Philonous propound a cosmology so obviously materialist? Was not Bentley's purpose to redeem matter, to transform it from the 'Atheist's God' into the raw material of the world machine, a machine moved by divine gravity?

Philonous seems, however, to transcend Bentley's cosmology in the latter half of his speech. At the verges of sense and imagination, we can no longer comprehend God's art, but witness instead the 'energy of an all-perfect mind displayed in endless forms'. These ruminations complement a novel aesthetic strain in the passage.[8] There is a mysterious

---

[7] *A Confutation of Atheism from the Origin and Frame of the World* (London: H. Mortlock, 1692), Part II (being the seventh of Bentley's Boyle lectures), p. 35.

[8] In its heightened rhetoric, the passage resembles the rhapsody in Shaftesbury's *The Moralists*: ' – See! with what trembling Steps poor Mankind tread the narrow Brink of the deep

'something' in nature that 'transports the soul', fills it with 'pleasing horror', and shows us the 'glorious beyond expression and beyond thought'. In these sublime experiences we apprehend intuitively, perhaps even immediately, the energy of the world, the God in whom, to cite Berkeley's favourite text, 'we live, move, and have our being'. Philonous asks how a world could be counted unreal in which God so evidently expresses, not just his art, but his very being. The challenging questions with which the reader and Hylas are confronted at the end of this speech cut deep. If we account the 'beauty of the creation a false imaginary glare', is this not tantamount to the atheist's rejection of God?

Philonous' final-questions put us on the spot, asking us to make sense of this extraordinary turn of argument with its many contradictions. Once again Hylas expresses our feelings of confusion and resentment:

HYLAS. Other men may think as they please: but for your part you have nothing to reproach me with. My comfort is, you are as much a *sceptic* as I am.
PHILONOUS. There, Hylas, I must beg leave to differ from you.
HYLAS. What! have you all along agreed to the premises, and do you now deny the conclusion, and leave me to maintain those paradoxes by myself which you led me into? This surely is not fair. (II.211)

Having brought us to scepticism, Philonous now abandons us. Having destroyed Hylas' confidence in his senses, he further torments him by mocking him, it seems, for his scepticism. But another turn is at hand for the *Three Dialogues*. After this aporetic nadir, elenchus serves only a secondary role in the conversation. Having used it to purge Hylas of his preconceptions about the world, Philonous can now drop his sceptical guise and reveal his own theses. The remainder of the Second Dialogue falls into two parts. In the first, he adumbrates immaterialism as a positive doctrine. Reviving the theological note sounded in his description of the heavens, Philonous offers his striking and original 'continuity argument' for the existence of God: that if things *'really exist, they are necessarily perceived by an infinite mind'*.[9] Philonous goes on to describe God as one who not only 'perceives' our ideas, but 'exhibits' them to us, 'affecting' our minds (II.214). The seeds of this radical theory were sown in Philonous' rhapsody on nature, which suggested that we directly apprehend the energy of the Author of nature – that there is, as it were, a meeting of

Precipices!' (*Characteristicks*, Vol. II, pp. 389–91). Likewise his imagery Berkeley echoes Addison's *Spectator* 420, published the previous summer, in which Addison tells *'How the Authors of the New Philosophy please the Imagination'*. Several of Berkeley's essays in *The Guardian* explore themes from Addison's *Spectator* on the imagination.

9 Luce has pointed out that this is an important change; in the *Principles*, Berkeley was more concerned to account God the 'cause' of our percepts than 'the *upholder* of sensory things when they are not being perceived by us' (II.152). This new emphasis has implications for the rhetoric of immaterialism as it concedes to our strong presumption that even when no one is perceiving the book in the study it is somehow still 'there'.

minds as we look about us. Moreover Philonous' demonstration of his mind's power to recreate and transcend the sensible lays the ground for this system in which the divine mind thinks our world into existence. The apparent contradictions and confusions of Philonous' rhapsody thus begin to resolve themselves as Philonous reveals, for the first time, what *he* believes.

But even more important in preparing for this exposition was the descent to scepticism effected by the elenchus of the First Dialogue, which asked us to doubt that there was anything 'out there'. The perplexing yet rigorously logical process made us curious to see how the puzzle would resolve itself. Philonous' reconstruction of the world, and particularly the continuity argument's readmission of a permanent natural order, make us very conscious of precisely what it was that Philonous doubted in the First Dialogue: not the reality of the world, but only the existence of an insensible matter. Berkeley chose the elenchus to dramatize for the reader that despite appearances he is no sceptic. But the elenchus's doubting questions are essential to Berkeley's rhetoric in another way. The reception of the *Principles* had made it clear that the world was not prepared to entertain criticisms of its notion of matter. So the opening of the *Three Dialogues* addresses itself to the primary rhetorical task of bringing Berkeley's philosophical problems to life, challenging us to confront the doubts and difficulties that lie beneath the commonplace assumptions we hold about the world. With the elenchus of the First Dialogue Berkeley impresses upon us that whatever seems sceptical in his own philosophy is, in fact, the legacy of the materialists. He thus devotes time, in a way he did not in the *Principles*, to making it painfully evident to the reader that there can be no complacency about the epistemology of modern materialism.

In the remainder of the Second Dialogue Hylas shows a reluctance to relinquish his cherished *matter*. He wonders if it might not have some intermediate role in the divine expression of nature. The elenchus begins again as Philonous attacks a diminishing list of possible accounts of matter put forward by Hylas, with the result that matter is finally proved impossible. The Third Dialogue moves from this second aporetic state to present a second positive account of immaterialism as a realist, theocentric philosophy. In this dialogue elenchus is abandoned save for three brief and unsuccessful attempts by Hylas, and is replaced by catechetical exposition in the form of extended explanations and defences of immaterialism. In his Preface, Berkeley admits the importance of this formal movement from doubt, to exposition, and finally to defence:

It remains, that I desire the reader to withhold his censure of these Dialogues, till he has read them through. Otherwise, he may lay them aside in a mistake of

their design, or on account of difficulties or objections which he would find
answered in the sequel. A treatise of this nature would require to be once read
over coherently, in order to comprehend its design, the proofs, solution of difficulties, and the connexion and disposition of its parts. If it be thought to deserve
a second reading; this, I imagine, will make the entire scheme very plain . . .

(II.169)

Berkeley is obviously very conscious of the extent to which the meaning
and impact of his work is a function of its 'scheme' or 'design'. He is
worried that a negligent reader might lay the *Three Dialogues* aside in
the middle, and with good reason, because the conclusions of the First
Dialogue are strikingly different from those of the Third. Yet, at the same
time, Berkeley does not reveal in the Preface exactly what the scheme of
his work will be. Dialogue's strength lies in the uncertainty of its form, in
its potential revolutions in tone and argument and its ability to approxi-
mate to something like dramatic narrative. The impact of the *Three Dialogues* depends both on our commitment to the whole progress of the
work, and on our inability to project its outcome.

Only in the very conclusion of the *Three Dialogues* can Hylas finally
renounce his anxious scruples and adopt Philonous's assured tone:

I have been a long time distrusting my senses; methought I saw things by a dim
light, and through false glasses. Now the glasses are removed, and a new light
breaks in upon my understanding. I am clearly convinced that I see things in
their native forms; and am no longer in pain about their unknown natures or
absolute existence.   (II.262)

The imagery is apt. Hylas has won not only perspicuous knowledge, but
literal clarity of vision. The world he now sees has a new integrity as he
recognizes that his own philosophical materialism was sceptical, denying
the sufficiency of our sense-data. But Hylas' imagery, which echoes Paul's
'For now we see through a glass, darkly; but then face to face' (I Cor.
13.12), reveals how this has been for him a spiritual discovery as well.
Philonous has revealed the presence of God in the world. In the closing
exchanges of the work, Hylas finds himself straddling two stools, believing both the philosopher and the common man. Philonous attempts to
explain:

I do not pretend to be a setter-up of *new notions*. My endeavours tend only to
unite and place in a clearer light that truth, which was before shared between the
vulgar and the philosophers: the former being of opinion, that *those things they
immediately perceive are the real things*; and the latter, that *the things immediately
perceived, are ideas which exist only in the mind*. Which two notions put together, do
in effect constitute the substance of what I advance.   (II.262)

Hylas agrees:

You set out upon the same principles that Academics, Cartesians, and the like sects, usually do; and for a long time it looked as if you were advancing their philosophical *scepticism*; but in the end your conclusions are directly opposite to theirs. (II.262)

In this final vision of the harmony between common sense and philosophy, Berkeley asks us to appreciate the form his work has taken and so insists again on the strictly limited role doubt plays in his thought.

Philonous' extraordinary tactic of forcing an opponent into an unsavoury position and then turning about and mocking him for it has some striking Platonic precedents. In the late dialogue *Cratylus*, Socrates begins by arguing that words are not arbitrary, but express the natures of the things they name. Cratylus, who had favoured this view, gloats over these findings until, in the middle of the dialogue, Socrates turns on him and proceeds to doubt everything that has just been said. The logic of language, it now seems to Socrates, might well be flawed by the ignorance of the original word-makers. The comedy of this device lies both in the questioner's glaring self-contradiction and even more in the plight of the poor answerer. Hylas is confuted at the very moment he confesses resolute *aporia*. But whereas the *Cratylus* changes from an absurd confidence in the logic of language to a more sensible scepticism, the *Three Dialogues* does just the opposite. Philonous' perplexing rhapsody on nature is the pivot on which the *Three Dialogues* turns from scepticism to confidence.[10] Thus Berkeley uses the concerns, doubts and curiosity generated by the sceptical elenchus to make his immaterialism more prized by the reader. By first depriving us of confident knowledge, he makes us hungrier for the truths he then readily supplies. The comic moment of Philonous's abandonment of Hylas is thus the herald of a larger comedy in the *Three Dialogues*. Its movement from doubt to confidence is accompanied by a thematic transition from purely epistemological to spiritual concerns. All Berkeley's major writings share something of the fully-developed comic narrative of the *Three Dialogues*, from the *New Theory of Vision*'s sudden revelation of sight as God's language, to *Siris*'s steady ascent from tar-water to the Trinity. Looking back to the Preface of the *Three Dialogues*, it becomes clear that Berkeley is entirely conscious of the emotional impact achieved by his comic forms:

this return to the simple dictates of Nature, after having wandered through the wild mazes of philosophy, is not unpleasant. It is like coming home from a long voyage: a man reflects with pleasure on the many difficulties and perplexities he has passed through, sets his heart at ease, and enjoys himself with more satisfaction for the future. (II.168)

[10] Jonathan Rée finds a comparable comic pattern of doubt followed by confidence in Descartes's *Meditations*; see 'Descartes' Comedy', *Philosophy and Literature*, 8 (1984), 151–66.

The trials and doubts of the elenchus ultimately conspire to make the safe haven of immaterialism so much the more sure and precious to us.

The *Three Dialogues* is, then, a narrative of a learning process, as Albert William Levi puts it, a 'convincing spectacle of actual ideological change'.[11] More specifically, it is a drama of learning through doubt, which concentrates on the changing phases of Hylas' mind as he moves from his initial perplexity to become himself a sceptic trapped in his own speculations. Richard H. Popkin describes Hylas as 'the picture of a man who has arrived at "la crise pyrrhonienne" ',[12] but Berkeley shows us more than Hylas' angry, all consuming scepticism. Hylas is one who can admit the reasonableness of an argument, and yet still have difficulty treating it as a truth:

To deal frankly with you, Philonous, your arguments seem in themselves unanswerable, but they have not so great an effect on me as to produce that entire conviction, that hearty acquiescence which attends demonstration.   (II.223)

Even near the end of the Third Dialogue, when Hylas has exhausted all the possible objections which might have justified his dissent, he still admits that reason is not enough: 'Nothing now remains to be overcome, but a sort of unaccountable backwardness that I find in my self toward your notions' (II.256). Philonous tells Hylas, when he doggedly maintains the existence of matter against reason, 'you are loth to part with your old prejudice' (II.221). Hylas' scruples and questions, which fill the Third Dialogue, show a mind struggling to reconstruct his knowledge to incorporate Philonous' new truths and exclude matter. In this the plot of the *Three Dialogues* has an exemplary function. In Hylas, Berkeley portrays the difficulties we as readers have in attaining a 'hearty acquiescence' regarding immaterialism, objectifying the very learning process upon which we are embarked. By displaying for us the struggle between Hylas' reason and his prejudices, Berkeley places us in a better state to analyse our own reluctance to admit Philonous' proofs.

In his concluding speech, Philonous appreciates the dialogue's comic movement from isolation and competition to a reconciliation:

You see, Hylas, the water of yonder fountain, how it is forced upwards, in a round column, to a certain height; at which it breaks and falls back into the basin from whence it rose: its ascent as well as descent, proceeding from the same uniform law or principle of *gravitation*. Just so, the same principles which at first view lead to *scepticism*, pursued to a certain point, bring men back to common sense.

(II.262–3)

Both Elizabeth Merrill and Donald Davie are, in different ways, critical of these closing words. For Merrill 'they are undramatic, and they are

[11] 'Philosophy as Literature', p. 9.
[12] 'Berkeley and Pyrrhonism', p. 232.

academic in tone, connected with the life of the student rather than that of the world outside the college walls'. Davie uses this final speech to support his argument that Berkeley was wary of metaphor, and consistently used language that preserved a strong distinction between spirit and idea: 'the tone indicates that it is fanciful, no more'.[13] True, Berkeley does not give us a detailed literal description of the fountain, but this is not necessarily 'undramatic'. I have attempted to show that what is dramatic in the *Three Dialogues*, its characters and plot, arises from the play of ideas. Is it not appropriate to Philonous' character that he should end with a conceit, turning like Socrates from the elenchus to the analogy, to that particularly dense and suggestive mode of expression in which a multiplicity of meanings can co-exist? Philonous has throughout shown himself a master of subtle word-play, as witty as he is eloquent. His rhapsody in the Second Dialogue is revealed as a masterpiece of implicit argument, full of irony and playful self-consciousness as it foreshadows the central tenets of immaterialism. To see the fountain as merely fanciful, a cautious concession to art, the intellectual business of the dialogue done, does not do justice to its complex allusiveness. In this delightful and evocative piece of word-play, Philonous encapsulates and reflects upon the themes and the plot of the *Three Dialogues*.

First, Philonous stresses the symmetry of the fountain's movement, evoking the theme of the harmony and beauty of nature he took to such heights in his rhapsody on the universe. But again he pushes beyond the commonplace cosmological argument to touch on immaterialism's new proof for the existence of God. The fountain is, of course, a traditional symbol for the grace of God. The *Three Dialogues* has revived this symbol by proving that the world as we know it does emanate constantly from the divine mind. Moreover Philonous transforms the fountain into an emblem of the *Three Dialogues* itself; the movement of the water, he tells us, embodies the movement of the dialogue from scepticism to common sense. In particular, he stresses the actual uniformity of this apparently contradictory movement, reminding us that, despite appearances, he pursued 'the same principles' throughout the dispute.

In the same self-conscious vein, when he identifies '*gravitation*' as the single principle at work in the fountain Philonous makes a joke about the linguistic progress of the conversation. *Gravity* is a word that has been refashioned in the course of the debate. It ostensibly assumes the existence of matter, and Philonous at first rejected *gravity* along with the other abstract primary qualities put forward by Hylas. But later, the law of gravity seems to be a principle informing Philonous' Bentleian celebration of the harmony of the heavens: 'So fixed, so immutable are the laws

---

[13] Merrill, *Dialogue*, p. 97; Davie, 'Berkeley and Philosophic Words', *Studies*, 44 (1955), 322.

by which the unseen Author of Nature actuates the universe' (II.210). This confusion is resolved in the Third Dialogue, however, when Philonous reinterprets Newton to free gravity from the encumbrance of an active material substance:

> That there is magnitude and solidity, or resistance, perceived by sense, I readily grant; as likewise that gravity may be proportional to those qualities, I will not dispute. But that either these qualities as perceived by us, or the powers producing them do exist in the *material substratum*; this is what I deny.   (II.242)

By applying this purified meaning of *gravity* to the college fountain, Philonous makes a playful reflection on how the dialogue, itself a model of a linguistic community, has managed to forge a language in which immaterialism can live. Hylas, having been throughout the dispute the victim of Philonous' irony, is for the first time able to share the humour. He is now in a position to appreciate exactly what '*gravitation*' means, a knowledge won through the logical trials and contentions of the elenchus.

PART III

Alciphron

9

Argument into satire

Alciphron: or, the Minute Philosopher (1732), Berkeley's second philosophical dialogue, followed the *Three Dialogues* by nearly twenty years, years in which Berkeley was preoccupied with the struggle for preferment and the promotion of his Bermuda project. *Alciphron* itself was written during an unexpected lull in Berkeley's affairs as he waited in vain on Rhode Island for Walpole to release the funds for his college. Despite the fact that *Alciphron* and the *Three Dialogues* share a genre, they are in both form and purpose very different works. The *Three Dialogues*, like the *Principles*, was a model of concise exposition. It worked its single metaphysical theme into a tight comic shape. Its coherence reflected the simplicity and unity of the immaterialist system it propounded. But *Alciphron* is a much longer work, and its subject matter of much broader scope. In the course of its seven dialogues it examines a variety of ethical views and touches on most of the key points of Christianity. The reason for this breadth is clear from Berkeley's title-page, which claims the book contains 'an APOLOGY for the Christian Religion *against those who are called* Free-thinkers'. *Alciphron* is an apology. The fact that Berkeley is able to work some of his personal metaphysical notions into the debate – his rejection of abstract ideas, for example, and his psychological theory of perception – shows, more than anything else, the extent to which his religious and metaphysical tenets are integrated in his own mind. Berkeley is not here expounding his own novel metaphysical system, but vindicating a great body of orthodox thought in ethics and religion. The subject matter of *Alciphron* is determined by his opponents, the 'free-thinkers'. The First Dialogue provides a general account of the tenets of free-thinkers, while the Second and Third refute the particular ethical systems propounded by Mandeville and Shaftesbury. The challenge raised by both these thinkers to Christian notions of reward and punishment in the afterlife lead Berkeley naturally to religious apology. In the four remaining dialogues he defends the existence of God and the truth of Christianity, responding throughout to the myriad direct reflections on orthodox Christianity made by the prominent free-thinkers Toland, Tindal and Collins. Berkeley leaves no criticism of the Church or of faith without its logical rejoinder.[1]

This change of stance from exposition to apology demanded changes in the way Berkeley handled the dialogue form. One of the features that most strikingly distinguishes *Alciphron* from the *Three Dialogues* is that it is narrated. Berkeley adopts the convention of pretending that the dialogue is a transcript of an actual conversation, recorded by one who was present. Dion has little to say in the course of the discussion, but remains 'impartial' and 'attentive' throughout so that he might 'take notes of all that passeth during this memorable event' (III.108 and 141). Unlike the *Three Dialogues*, *Alciphron* does not immerse us immediately in dialogue, but begins as a letter from Dion to his friend, Theages, in which we learn the circumstances of the conversation, and even something of Dion himself. He alludes to a matter of personal concern, telling Theages of the miscarriage 'of the affair which brought me into this remote corner of the country' (III.31). Dion then explains that he has recorded the ensuing debate for his friend because he found it entertaining and instructive, providing him 'some amends for a great loss of time, pains, and expense' (III.31). This is Berkeley's signature to *Alciphron*, a thinly veiled reference to his own public disappointment in America, and a way of offering his book to the public, many of whom had supported his project generously, as some recompense for their pains.

Dion's stoic reflections raise issues and images which help set the scene for the dialogue. He remarks on the contrasts between his new-found 'liberty and leisure in this distant retreat' and 'that great whirlpool of business, faction, and pleasure, which is called *the world*'. Dion's urban pursuits, his 'life of action' which depended on 'the counsels, passions, and views of other men', brought him only 'trouble and disquiet'. He is happy now to find the time to reflect on what has passed, and to attend to the important spiritual issues which are raised in the debate. These candid personal reflections create a context into which Berkeley introduces the four main interlocutors of the debate. For these, it turns out, fall on either side of the distinction Dion makes between the contemplative rural life and the distracting bustle of the world. Dion first gives us a portrait of his friend

---

[1] *The Fable of the Bees* was almost universally condemned as vicious, but the *Characteristicks* was, at least on the surface, a moral book. In the *Theory of Vision Vindicated and Explained* Berkeley finds himself obliged to defend his inclusion of Shaftesbury amongst the free-thinkers as one who would undermine the most powerful incentives to virtue (I.252). At the same time Shaftesbury *did* patronize Toland, and the *Characteristicks* is strident in its attacks on the clergy and does insinuate doubts about revelation. Mandeville, whose own work is highly critical of Shaftesbury's ethics, approved none the less of 'the many admirable Things he has said against Priestcraft, and on the Side of Liberty and Human Happiness'; see *A Letter to Dion, Occasion'd by his Book call'd* Alciphron, or the Minute Philosopher (London: J. Roberts, 1732), p. 48.

Euphranor, who 'unites in his own person the philosopher and the farmer'. Euphranor balances study with agricultural labour, 'his health and strength of body enabling him the better to bear fatigue of mind' (III.32). Dion then relates how Euphranor's friend, Crito, first described the two free-thinkers who will participate in the dispute:

Alciphron is above forty, and no stranger either to men or books. I knew him first at the Temple, which, upon an estate's falling to him, he quitted, to travel through the polite parts of Europe. Since his return he hath lived in the amusements of the town, which, being grown stale and tasteless to his palate, have flung him into a sort of splenetic indolence.   (III.32)

We also learn that Alciphron's protégé Lysicles is at an earlier stage of a similar career, having fallen in 'with men of pleasure and free-thinkers'.

Through this epistolary introduction, Berkeley creates the impression that his dialogue is true to life. The ensuing debate is not only presented as some sort of compensation for Dion's disappointment, but seems to grow out of his experience, embodying in its characters the contrasts he had recently discovered between business and reflection, and between urban and rural life. Berkeley also intends that we read the dialogue as an extension of individual lives. We learn something of the station, habits and history of each interlocutor. These hints not only establish the characters in our minds, but command our interest in how each speaker will flesh out his portrait. Berkeley promises us a contest of originals, pitting a philosopher-farmer against modern, philosophical libertines.

As the debate proceeds, Dion's narrative voice sustains this focus on character. He often notes, for example, the tone of Alciphron's speeches, which are delivered 'with an air of pity' (III.35) or 'an air of triumph' (III.45). In these touches we come to see Alciphron as vain and self-inflated. Likewise Dion registers the free-thinkers' responses to their opponents' speeches: sometimes they listen with 'uneasiness' (III.54), or even 'staring full' in disbelief (III.222); sometimes they smugly display 'great composure of mind and countenance' (III.116). At one point, while hearing Euphranor's defence of theism, Lysicles looks 'like one that wished in his heart there was no God' (III.59). This ongoing, third-person commentary encourages us to examine the free-thinkers' speeches as expressions of character and be alive to their tone. Likewise, as we learn which notions are most precious to them, Berkeley encourages us to question their motives. Upon finishing a diatribe against 'statecraft and priestcraft', Alciphron, we are told, 'having uttered it with no small emotion, stopped to draw breath and recover himself' (III.36–7). This reflection subtly underlines the irony of an avowed enemy of 'superstition and enthusiasm' so much in the grip of his own passions.

While, in the *Three Dialogues*, Hylas' full emotional response to Philonous' sceptical line of argument was essential to the comedy of the work, there was nothing like the constant critical attention to character that prevails in *Alciphron*. This difference is due, in part, to a change of subject. The *Three Dialogues* was a study in epistemology, and Berkeley there used dialogue to challenge our metaphysical preconceptions and dramatize sensory experiments which illustrated his argument. *Alciphron*'s argument is primarily ethical, and it was not only conventional in Berkeley's day to illustrate ethical and religious discourse with 'characters' and *exempla*, but dialogue itself was praised for its power to complement ethical argument by representing moral characters in action. Shaftesbury had recognized the implicit ethical discourse displayed in Plato's dialogues, which, as they taught morals, 'exhibited 'em *alive*, and set the Countenances and Complexions of Men plainly in view'. He hoped that his own *Moralists* would achieve this same 'Moral Painting, by way of *Dialogue*'.[2] While Berkeley rejects Shaftesbury's ethical theory, he takes very seriously Shaftesbury's challenge to bring philosophy out of the academy and into the world by imitating modern characters and conversation.

This development of character in *Alciphron* is also appropriate given Berkeley's own moral theory, which, unlike Shaftesbury's, is extremely pragmatic. At the end of the First Dialogue, Euphranor lays the groundwork for a utilitarian ethic when he asks, 'is not the general good of mankind to be regarded as a rule or measure of moral truths, of all such truths as direct or influence the moral actions of men?' (III.60).[3] In the following dialogue Berkeley argues that Shaftesbury's aesthetic and introspective ethical theory suffers from vagueness and abstraction from human situations. While obviously well-intentioned, the *Characteristicks*' high-minded promotion of a natural impulse to virtue is in danger of underestimating the destructive powers of self-love. In Berkeley's more conservative view, the common man needs practical restraints to keep him from vice and immediate incentives to virtue. In the Third Dialogue Berkeley argues that Mandeville misleads us by perversely tracing improbable consequences from vicious acts. Both Shaftesbury and Mandeville are condemned for failing to provide a just representation of human behaviour. In contrast *Alciphron*'s ethical debate concentrates on practical evidence, mooting questions such as 'Is the man of pleasure happy?' or 'Do we need incentives to virtue?', questions which can only

---

[2] *Characteristicks*, Vol. I, p. 194 and Vol. II, p. 188. I cite the second edition of 1714 which incorporates Shaftesbury's final revisions. The editions of 1723 and 1727 are generally faithful to this text, with the exception of their omission of 'A Letter Concerning Design'.

[3] Paul J. Olscamp, in *The Moral Philosophy of George Berkeley* (The Hague: M. Nijhoff, 1970), pp. 78–9 and 230, shows that in *Passive Obedience* Berkeley asserts the primacy of divine law in ethical decisions, but that the law itself reveals God's desire that we should strive for the general good.

be answered with evidence of the behaviour of individuals in determinate situations.

Perhaps more surprisingly, Berkeley's views on religion have a similarly practical tendency, a tendency which was first revealed in his *Advice to the Tories who have taken Oaths* (1715). The *Advice* makes a direct appeal to all Jacobite Tories, warning them of the consequences for the Church should they break their oaths to George I. The argument from utility is the foundation of Berkeley's case: 'Two things there are which influence men with a regard for religion – a sense of its truth, and a sense of its usefulness' (VI.53). Tory perjury on a large scale would give the Whigs proof that the Established Church had no good influence on Tory hearts. While both here and in *Alciphron* Berkeley insists that the authority of the Church does not rest on the utility argument alone, he is none the less very conscious of its appeal: 'That which, in the eye of reason, gives any Church or religion the advantage above others is the influence it hath upon the lives of its professors' (VI.56). Evidence of a church's benign influence may 'cause even infidels to pay an outward respect to that whereon they apprehend the common welfare to depend' (VI.53). Ethics and religion are thus mutually dependent in Berkeley's eyes on particular evidence of moral action. In *Alciphron*, where Berkeley confronts modern infidelity, he naturally relies heavily on utilitarian arguments. The Fifth Dialogue in particular is devoted to a proof of 'the usefulness of the Christian religion' (III.218) against Alciphron's claims for the superior morality of the Greeks and Romans. In making his case Crito takes an extended 'survey of the prevailing notions and manners of the country where we live' (III.185). And Berkeley warns us throughout *Alciphron* that as free-thinking begins to supplant Christianity, 'Englishmen are not the same men they were' (III.139). With so much of the debate in *Alciphron* devoted to determining the moral character of the modern Englishman, it is appropriate that Berkeley should develop the characters of his disputants. They become in the course of the debate exemplary of the utility of both Christianity and modern free-thought.

In its concentration on the motives and behaviour of modern free-thinkers, *Alciphron* develops a tone and a purpose quite different from those of the *Three Dialogues*. Hylas was a sufficiently ordinary and sympathetic character to become a surrogate for our difficulties with immaterialism. In contrast, *Alciphron*'s critical concentration on the more fully realized and less attractive characters of the free-thinkers is primarily satiric. Like Plato's *Protagoras* and *Gorgias*, *Alciphron* is not simply a debate on ethical issues, but a polemic against a recognized group of philosophical opponents. Like the sophists in Plato's Athens, the free-thinkers had made themselves heard in Berkeley's England, rising to particular prominence with the publication in 1713 of Collins's *Discourse of Free Thinking*, which provoked responses from Swift, Bentley and Steele. In his parody, *Mr. C—ns's Discourse*, Swift complained of the freedom and vigour with which the modern free-thinker aired his heterodox views: '*Free Thinking* signifies nothing, without *Free Speaking* and *Free Writing*'.[4] If free-thought had lost some of its novelty by the time Berkeley wrote *Alciphron*, its proponents had lost none of their energy. Both Collins's *Discourse Concerning Ridicule and Irony* and the second volume of Mandeville's *Fable* were first published in 1729, and in 1730 Tindal's exhaustive *Christianity as Old as Creation* appeared. Berkeley's satiric purpose in *Alciphron* is the exposure of this social phenomenon; Lysicles and Alciphron are not just reflections of the moral and religious ideas they propound, but renderings of a recognizable social type. In the Advertisement to *Alciphron* Berkeley claims that his design is 'to consider the free-thinker in the various lights of atheist, libertine, enthusiast, scorner, critic, metaphysician, fatalist and sceptic', but warns that not 'every one of these characters agrees with every individual free-thinker, no more being implied than that each part agrees with some or other of the sect' (III.23). Alciphron and Lysicles arc not proposed, then, as lampoons of Shaftesbury and Mandeville, but as more universal figures designed to capture the many particular traits which characterize free-thinkers.

It is Crito who keeps the satire in sharp focus with his direct reflections on free-thinkers as a sect. He tells us that while some members are 'old sharpers in business . . . most free-thinkers are proselytes of the drinking club' (III.95–6). Appropriately, then, both Berkeley's free-thinkers are men of 'the world'. Crito also identifies two main psychological types amongst the free-thinkers:

> That sect, you must know, contains two sorts of philosophers, the wet and the dry. Those I have been describing are of the former kind. They differ rather in practice than in theory, as an older, graver, or duller man, from one that is younger, and more capable or fond of pleasure. The dry philosopher passeth his time but dryly. He has the honour of pimping for the vices of more sprightly men, who in return offer some small incense to his vanity. Upon this encouragement, and to make his own mind easy when it is past being pleased, he employs himself in justifying those excesses he cannot partake in.   (III.92)

This account is a key to the characters of Alciphron and Lysicles. The younger Lysicles, a self-confessed 'man of pleasure' (III.165), is obviously the embodiment of the 'wet' free-thinker. Crito has just anatomized this character, the modern English rake, in some detail. His life is comprised of 'momentary pleasures' separated by 'long and cruel intervals of spleen'

---

[4] *The Prose Works of Jonathan Swift*, ed. Herbert Davis, 16 vols (Oxford: Blackwell, 1939–74), Vol. IV, p. 36. This particular sentiment is echoed by Lysicles (III.100). In an appendix to his edition of *Alciphron* (III.336–7), Jessop suggests that Swift's satires on free-thought were influential for Berkeley.

(III.91). He is torn between his brute appetites and a remorse rendered ineffectual by 'habitual sloth and indolence' (III.92). This description is borne out by Lysicles' own confession that he is devoted to cards as 'a most admirable anodyne to divert or prevent thought, which might otherwise prey upon the mind' (III.91). Throughout *Alciphron* Lysicles shows himself true to Crito's account in both the tenor and the matter of his argument. He is irascible and rude, and his interest in intellectual matters proves limited. Dion notes that by the end of the dialogue 'Lysicles seemed heartily tired of this conversation' (III.323). He contributes much less to the debate than Alciphron, save in the Second Dialogue, where he expounds Mandeville's 'private vices, publick benefits' theory. Crito's characterization of 'wet' free-thinkers in this same dialogue helps explain the reason for Lysicles' attraction to Mandeville's maxim, as well as his later espousal of absolute atheism – an addiction to the fulfilment of his appetites. Lysicles is a philosopher only so far as he may use reason to undermine those laws, human and divine, which threaten to rob him of his pleasure.

Alciphron, a 'dry' philosopher, is a more complex figure. Having surfeited in his youth, he is now employed 'in justifying those excesses he cannot partake in'. In the Third Dialogue Crito offers us a further insight into the 'dry' free-thinker in a lampoon of Shaftesbury under the name 'Cratylus'. Cratylus' 'crazy constitution', we are told, inhibited his 'capacity for sensual vices', but he did, instead, 'under the pretence of making men heroically virtuous, endeavour to destroy the means of making them reasonably and humanly so' (III.132). Crito proposes that the 'dry' free-thinker is not motivated by appetite, but panders to immoral youths in return for some 'small incense to his vanity'.[5] This charge of vanity is implicit in the lampoon of Shaftesbury; Cratylus has 'a conceited mind, which will ever be its own object, and contemplate mankind in its own mirror' (III.132). Alciphron's arguments reveal this ruling passion at work. His espousal of Shaftesbury's high moral aesthetics reflects a desire to be seen as a man of refined sensibilities. And in his conversation he imitates the effusive style of the *Characteristicks* with its posturing, egotism,

---

[5] Berkeley may have taken a hint for his portrait of the 'dry' free-thinker from *Tatler* 135, ed. George H. Aitken (London: Duckworth, 1898–9), Vol. III, pp. 116–17, where Steele laughs at the prospect of the 'chaste infidel' who has 'neither passions nor appetites to gratify, no heats of blood nor vigour of constitution that can turn his systems of infidelity to advantage'. So too 'The Disabled *Debauchee*' promises

> Thus *States-man*-like, I'll sawcily impose,
> And safe from Action valiantly advise,
> Shelter'd in impotence, urge you to blows,
> And being good for nothing else, be wise.   (ll.45–8)

See *The Poems of John Wilmot, Earl of Rochester*, ed. Keith Walker (Oxford: Blackwell, 1984), p. 99.

and self-conscious gentility. While the attack on Shaftesbury's character
seems hardly fair, Berkeley's moral purpose is clear. He wants to diminish
Shaftesbury's public influence, preventing those who would use Shaftesbury's language to justify their own immorality.

Berkeley's exposition of the vices that motivate free-thinkers depends,
to a great degree, on the direct satiric portraits provided by Crito. But
these are substantiated and elaborated more subtly in the tone of the free-
thinkers' own speeches. Berkeley's satiric method taken as a whole is
characterized by lightness and reserve. Crito, in fact, has a double role in
Alciphron. Like Plato's Crito, he is a man with a working knowledge of the
world, but as his experience enables him to castigate the free-thinkers, it
also permits him to mimic them, and he soon proves a skilled parodist.
In the First Dialogue, having been told the general principles of the free-
thinkers, Euphranor asks 'who are these profound and learned men'
(III.47), and the ensuing debate attends to the characters that make up
the sect and the methods they employ. Alciphron and Lysicles readily
provide the particulars, beginning with the approved method of free-
thinking education. According to Alciphron they reject 'Academical
study' with its emphases on thought and reading: 'Proper ideas or
materials are only to be got by frequenting good company' (III.48).
Lysicles agrees, wagering that one educated in this 'modern way, shall
make a better figure, and be more considered in any drawing-room or
assembly of polite people, than one . . . who hath lain by a long time at
school and college'. At this point Crito joins in, in apparent agreement,
and completes the picture. When Euphranor asks where all this polite
learning takes place, Crito replies:

Where our grave ancestors would never have looked for it – in a drawing-room,
a coffee-house, a chocolate-house, at the tavern, or groom-porter's. In these and
the like fashionable places of resort, it is the custom for polite persons to speak
freely on all subjects, religious, moral, or political; so that a young gentleman who
frequents them is in the way of hearing many instructive lectures, seasoned with
wit and raillery, and uttered with spirit. Three or four sentences from a man of
quality, spoke with a good air, make more impression and convey more knowledge than a dozen dissertations in a dry academical way.   (III.48)

Of course we are already aware that Crito holds the free-thinkers and
their ways in contempt. Here, however, Crito restrains his indignation,
and adopts the tone, the diction and the attitudes of his opponents. He
picks up Alciphron's and Lysicles' concern that education should, above
all, prepare the student for polite conversation, and mimics their scorn
for traditional methods. But his apparent approbation only thinly dis-
guises his criticisms, and we are alerted by his comically descending list of
deistical meeting-places – from the drawing-room to the groom-porter's –
of his ironic intent. Crito's comments point out the dangers of coffee-

house learning: that the free-thinkers discourse freely 'on all subjects, religious, moral, or political', and do so in the presence of the young. His closing hyperbole asks us to consider if this new way of education can be anything but superficial.

Crito employs parody on several occasions in the first half of *Alciphron*, particularly to comment on the free-thinkers' ethical theories. In the Second Dialogue Crito takes Lysicles' account of Mandeville's ethics *ad absurdum*, and burlesques the Shaftesburian notion of a natural love of the beauty of virtue in the Third. At the end of Alciphron's long exposition of this ethical theory, Crito deftly picks up the train of thought:

> The love therefore that you bear to moral beauty, and your passion for abstracted truth, will not suffer you to think with patience of those fraudulent impositions upon mankind, Providence, the Immortality of the Soul, and a future Retribution of rewards and punishments; which, under the notion of promoting, do, it seems, destroy all true virtue, and at the same time contradict and disparage your noble theories, manifestly tending to the perturbation and disquiet of men's minds, and filling them with fruitless hopes and vain terrors.   (III.118)

There is nothing in this speech that was not in Alciphron's, which was itself a remarkably fair synopsis of the main moral argument of the *Characteristicks*. All that Crito does here is place certain of Alciphron's attitudes in relief to show the essential flaws in his thinking. The irony of the piece emerges only from the illogicality of the argument, a fallaciousness which is hinted at in Crito's 'it seems' and 'manifestly'. Of course a love of virtue and a notion of divine retribution are not mutually exclusive. Nor is Alciphron right in assuming that thoughts of the afterlife must fill men's minds with 'disquiet and perturbation'.

Crito's mimicry rivals, in its sophistication, Swift's burlesque *Mr C—ns's Discourse*. But within the dialogue form Berkeley has chosen, parody takes on new functions. The success of Swift's ironic abstract depends on the reader's ability to remember the particulars of Collins's argument, and to recognize how its features are being only slightly distorted to create a monstrosity of atheist thought. But *Alciphron*'s representation of several distinct voices means that Berkeley's ironic *exposés* may be juxtaposed with the 'straight' exposition of the views of his opponents. This useful proximity leaves Berkeley free, as we have seen, to make quite precise and yet very subtle ironic reflections on the free-thinkers' logic, while apparently giving them a fair hearing and their own voice in the text. The free-thinkers seem to condemn themselves. As *Alciphron* progresses, Crito's ironic renditions of the free-thinkers' speeches encourages a similarly critical attitude in the reader. Irony's implicit condemnation places the burden of the satire on the reader, who must elicit the second and subversive strain of meaning from the text. It is just this double reading

that Berkeley wants us to apply to all the articulations of the free-thinkers.
Crito warns us that their specious claims must be scrutinized for implicit
fallacies and deceits, for unrevealed consequences, and for motives other
than the search for truth.

In tandem with Crito's parody, Euphranor employs his own distinctive
analytic method. He uses the elenchus to wrest a great variety of valuable
concessions from the free-thinkers: that reason should be considered
'natural' to men (III.57); that sensual pleasure is not a primary good
(III.89); that beauty is an object of the mind and not the eye (III.123–4);
that we do, in a sense, 'see' God (III.145–6); and that obscurity is not
necessarily a defect in Scripture (III.233–4).[6] As in the *Three Dialogues*,
the elenctic exchanges are often comic in their effect. Here, for example,
Euphranor dissects Alciphron's claims that

> for men of rank and politeness, we have the finest and wittiest *railleurs* in the
> world, whose ridicule is the sure test of truth.
>
> EUPHRANOR. Tell me, Alciphron, are those ingenious *railleurs* men of knowledge?
> ALCIPHRON. Very knowing.
> EUPHRANOR. Do they know, for instance, the Copernican system, or the circu-
> lation of the blood?
> ALCIPHRON. One would think you judged of our sect by your country neighbours:
> there is nobody in town but knows all those points.
> EUPHRANOR. You believe, then, antipodes, mountains in the moon, and the
> motion of the earth?
> ALCIPHRON. We do.
> EUPHRANOR. Suppose, five or six centuries ago, a man had maintained these
> notions among the *beaux esprits* of an English Court; how do you think they would
> have been received?
> ALCIPHRON. With great ridicule.
> EUPHRANOR. And now it would be ridiculous to ridicule them?
> ALCIPHRON. It would.
> EUPHRANOR. But truth was the same then as now?
> ALCIPHRON. It was.
> EUPHRANOR. It should seem, therefore, that ridicule is no such sovereign touch-
> stone and test of truth as you gentlemen imagine.   (III.137)

While Euphranor's method seems radically different from Crito's, its
effect it surprisingly similar – an ironic rereading of the free-thinkers'
words. As with Crito's parodies, the end is a comic self-negation in which
the voice of free-thought is made to contradict itself. Here Alciphron is

---

[6] In the early 1720s, when Berkeley was an active senior fellow at Trinity, he was once
again responsible for moderating the students' elenctic disputes. Sometime later Berkeley
himself played the interlocutor in disputations at Court with Sherlock, Clarke and Hoadly.
In her additions to the life of Berkeley in the *Biographia Britannica*, Anne Berkeley remem-
bers that 'It was from a hope of advancing the interest of his College, that Dr. Berkeley
submitted to the drudgery (for such he esteemed it) of bearing a part in the fruitless
weekly debates.'

brought to the point where he must admit the direct opposite of his initial proposition. And the elenchus, like the parody Crito practises, is equally demanding of the reader. As I have argued earlier, the elenchus's indirect, puzzling movement from question to question encourages our involvement. We are inevitably drawn in as we wonder what Euphranor's teasing questions about the Copernican system and the mountains on the moon can have to do with the validity of ridicule in the pursuit of truth. But where, in the *Three Dialogues*, elenchus served the purpose of undermining our preconceptions about the nature of the sensible world, in *Alciphron* the sceptical method is turned against the sceptics.

Like all satire, *Alciphron* is designed to encourage and direct our feelings of contempt and resentment. In all his ethical writings Berkeley admits the role of emotions in moral action, not just the 'public spirit' described in the *Essay towards preventing the Ruin of Great Britain* (1721), but the hope for heavenly rewards and the fear of divine retribution that he emphasizes in *Alciphron*.[7] In Berkeley's day satire was often celebrated for providing a similar emotive constraint on the vicious man, playing upon his fears of rejection. But satire also appeals widely to public spirit, stirring our anger against those who threaten the *status quo*. Berkeley seems to have felt such a resentment very personally; at the time that he was writing *Alciphron*, he told Percival that 'free thinking seems to me the principal root or source not only of opposition to our College but of most other evils in this age' (VIII.212). Yet, despite Crito's caustic characterizations of free-thinkers in *Alciphron*, in its two prominent discursive modes, parody and elenchus, Berkeley's ridicule is effected through the subtler medium of irony. Both ironic techniques involve the reader, asking him to interpret and reflect so that he may himself judge and condemn. Likewise, Berkeley develops the dialogue as a form in which the free-thinkers may appear to condemn themselves.

Berkeley's reliance on irony in preference to explicit and direct condemnation ultimately makes for sophisticated and entertaining satire. But it also seems to reflect some reservations about satire in relation to philosophical writing. In his early notebooks he made these two strict memoranda about the tone he should adopt in the *Principles*:

Mem: upon all ocasions to use the Utmost Modesty. to Confute the Mathematicians wth the utmost civility & respect. not to stile them Nihilarians etc:

N.B. to rein in y^r Satirical Nature.   (PC 633–4)

Despite these plans to be firm with himself, Berkeley's 'Satirical Nature'

---

[7] David E. Leary, in 'Berkeley's Social Theory: Context and Development', *JHI*, 38 (1977), 635–49, argues for a dichotomy in Berkeley's ethical writing between 'social appetite' and 'private passions'.

showed through in the *Principles'* ironic *exposé* of Locke's theory of abstraction. And when he came to write the *Guardian* papers against free-thinkers he gave his satiric talents full rein. *Guardian* 39 is a vigorous Swiftian satiric fantasy in which Berkeley voyages through the mind of Anthony Collins to discover an intellectual anarchy, a mob rule of vanity, passion and imagination. In No. 55, however, where he first formulates his criticisms of Shaftesbury, Berkeley adopts an approach suitable to the more substantial thought of the *Characteristicks*. He begins this paper with a repudiation of the method he had applied so devastatingly to Collins a few weeks before:

It is usual with polemical writers to object ill designs to their adversaries. This turns their argument into satyr, which, instead of shewing an error in the under-standing, tends only to expose the morals of those they write against. I shall not act after this manner with respect to the Free-thinkers.   (VII.198)

Berkeley here maintains that satire's attention to the motives of the indivi-dual or group satirized distracts from the central business of confutation. Berkeley's commitment to a rational defence of orthodox religion was, in his own mind, at odds with his satiric method. As *Guardian* 55 proceeds, he insists that he is taking the Shaftesburians at their word, assuming that they are 'well-meaning souls' and that once they have been shown the errors of their theory, they will abandon it. Indeed, Berkeley's frequent insistence throughout the paper that the free-thinkers must be 'innocent creatures', 'destitute of passion', and 'a set of refined spirits' becomes an ironic subcurrent, spurring us to speculate as to whether these characters might not, after all, be pursuing 'ill designs'.

This tension between the conflicting demands of satire and reasonable refutation is a feature of *Alciphron*, determining the form and tone of the work and becoming itself a subject for debate. Part of Berkeley's problem as an Anglican satirist was that his opponents considered that they had appropriated ridicule as the proper voice of dissent. In the *Characteristicks* Shaftesbury had frequently claimed that 'nothing is ridiculous except what is deform'd': because we have an aesthetic sense of virtue, all that is vicious naturally seems to be deformed and ridiculous.[8] This notion that satire is a test of moral truth is explored by Collins in his *Discourse concern-ing Ridicule*, which argues that 'Decency and Propriety will stand the Test of Ridicule, and triumph over all the false Pretences to Wit.' In the course of his book Collins paints satire as the only tool which can prise the shackles of religious bigotry from the mind. He claims, moreover, that irony in religious debate arose from the 'want of Liberty to speak plainly', citing Shaftesbury's maxim, ' 'Tis the persecuting Spirit has rais'd the

---

[8] *Characteristicks*, Vol. I, p. 128.

bantering one.'[9] Collins also claims that most religious tenets and rituals are inherently ridiculous in their violation of reason. The *Discourse concerning Ridicule* employs his favourite device of citing the texts of orthodox churchmen to show, in this case, that high-church satire is misdirected and falls flat. For Collins, Tory humour is not a test of truth, but the means of religious persecution.

In *Alciphron* Berkeley's free-thinkers make appropriately loud claims for wit and raillery as their favourite mode of inquiry, often resorting to wit to evade serious and sustained argument. In the Seventh Dialogue, Alciphron's various concessions on revelation unnerve Lysicles, who suggests that 'it would be more prudent to abide by the way of wit and humour than thus to try religion by the dry test of reason and logic' (III.296). As we have seen, Euphranor employs the elenchus to demonstrate to Alciphron that wit has often been misdirected and is no absolute test of truth. But Berkeley is also willing to analyse the satiric method of the free-thinkers on its own terms. In the *Characteristicks* Shaftesbury had placed great weight on the distinction between the 'railer' and the *'railleur'* – between the blunt, malicious invective of the Tories and the good-humoured, rallying banter of his own writing. Berkeley was not impressed. He goes to some lengths in *Alciphron* to show that the *Characteristicks'* portrait of the clergy is a kind of *'caricatura'* (III.196), a conscious perversion of nature for comic effect which violates Shaftesbury's own aesthetic principles. And Berkeley exposes the maliciousness which informs Shaftesbury's allegedly rational satire when he quotes the various epithets used against churchmen and teachers in the *Characteristicks*: 'the black tribe, magicians, formalists, pedants, [and] bearded boys' (III.198). This critique of free-thinking wit becomes most acute when Alciphron reads out Shaftesbury's gibe at squabbles amongst churchmen:

ALCIPHRON. To use the words of the most ingenious Characterizer of our times: – 'A ring is made, and readers gather in abundance. Every one takes party and encourages his own side. "This shall be my champion! – This man for my money! – Well hit, on our side! – Again, a good stroke! – There he was even with him! – Have at him the next bout! – Excellent sport!" '

CRITO. Methinks I trace the man of quality and breeding in this delicate satire, which so politely ridicules those arguments, answers, defences, and replications which the press groans under.   (III.197)

Beside Crito's dry irony, Shaftesbury's bear garden jest seems low and clumsy, the very sort of coarse wit he so loudly eschewed.

In *Alciphron's* dialogue form Berkeley finds a way of preserving what he saw as the conflicting demands of polemical writing: the need on one

---

[9] *A Discourse concerning Ridicule and Irony in Writing* (London: J. Brotherton, 1729), pp. 21 and 24.

hand to stir public resentment against a genuine threat to society, and on the other to refute reasonably and candidly a body of false doctrine. First, and most significantly, in the characters of Alciphron and Lysicles Berkeley grants his opponents apparently autonomous voices in which to express their views. This is more than merely an easy gesture so that he may claim intellectual candour. *Alciphron* presents us with a critical forum and a high level of intellectual exchange, such that Swift, Gay and Bolingbroke all complained that the book was 'too speculative'.[10] Alciphron may, ultimately, be proved wrong, but he is far from stupid. As Berkeley satirizes the motives and methods of the free-thinkers, he also permits them to expound, very much in their own terms, their objections to orthodox Christianity and morality. *Alciphron* is as thorough a representation as a refutation of modern free-thought, a fact that Berkeley recognized when he decided against sending copies to friends in America. He told Johnson that he feared 'it might do mischief to have it known in that part of the world what pernicious opinions are boldly espoused here at home' (VIII.214).[11]

Dialogue's distinct voices and its pretence to be the record of an actual conversation also permit Berkeley to distance himself somewhat from the negative *ethos* of the satirist. Satire's anger and complete condemnation imply a conviction and a judgmental attitude that run counter to both Christian humility and the spirit of philosophical inquiry.[12] But Crito is not Berkeley, and Crito's knowing condemnation of the free-thinkers is balanced by Euphranor's rural innocence. While both characters devote much of their time to logical refutation, the intellectual rigour of Euphranor's elenctic questioning establishes the integrity of Berkeley's case. *Alciphron* develops, even more than did the *Three Dialogues*, the Socratic paradox of the teacher willing to play the student. Euphranor entreats Alciphron and Lysicles 'to bear with my defects' (III.70), 'to rid me of some scruples about the tendency of your opinions' (III.108), 'to consider me as a patient, whose cure you have generously undertaken' (III.236). This humility, despite the gentle irony of its appeal to the free-thinkers' vanity, shows us a mind truly open and receptive. Euphranor is

[10] *The Correspondence of Alexander Pope*, ed. George Sherburn, 5 vols (Oxford: Clarendon Press, 1956), Vol. III, pp. 286 and 289; *The Correspondence of Jonathan Swift*, ed. Harold Williams, 5 vols (Oxford: Clarendon Press, 1965), Vol. IV, p. 45.

[11] And this despite Berkeley's being 'creditably informed that great numbers of all sorts of blasphemous books published in London are sent to Philadelphia, New York, and other places, where they produce a plentiful crop of atheists and infidels' (VIII.212). Collins, in *A Discourse of Free-Thinking* (London: n.p., 1713), p. 91, had teased the Tory apologists that they actually encouraged the spread of atheism by introducing atheistical characters in their '*Treatises in Dialogue*'.

[12] Edward A. and Lillian D. Bloom comment on the contradiction between Christian humility and satire, in *Satire's Pervasive Voice* (London: Cornell University Press, 1979), p. 198.

tireless in his appeals to reason and his efforts to bring truth to light. Like the voice of the opening of *Guardian* 55, he assumes that the free-thinkers' motives are pure. In Euphranor's character, Berkeley provides an exemplary moral strain of humility to balance Crito's satiric sallies.

Dialogue also frees Berkeley from the moral ambiguity that characterizes much prose satire. It avoids satire's unstable ironic *persona*, the voice which must be the object of its own irony. In his *Fable of the Bees*, Mandeville struggles to create a critical perspective within the voice of his callous projector, and must finally turn to incipient dialogue to distance himself from the most extreme expressions of his calculus of vice. He invokes a 'good humour'd Antagonist' to make the devastating proposal that gin is actually good for the nation.[13] Much of the difficulty of the satiric voice lies in the fact that it must rely on established moral attitudes which may be only obliquely evoked by the text. Much of the prose satire of writers like Swift and Mandeville disconcerts us because its irony lacks a clear centre. While this disconcerting moral vagueness is often a positive feature, challenging us to probe our own moral standards and, perhaps, to recognize some of our own culpability, it can lead to a dangerous confusion over important issues. Berkeley displays the dangers of satire's reliance on implied standards in the character of Lysicles, someone who has read the *Fable* as straight moral theory. When Lysicles voices Mandeville's own vindication of the *Fable* – that he is simply being 'plain and frank', cutting beneath the hypocrisy of society to expose vice – Crito remains unimpressed: 'I do verily think that in this country of ours, reason, religion, law are all together little enough to subdue the outward to the inward man' (III.131–2). It is not enough to expose the failings of society; one must establish rules and remedies. Berkeley follows his own advice in *Alciphron*, where Crito and Euphranor, as they destroy the false learning of the free-thinkers, establish true principles in its place. In dialogue Berkeley can write polemics which represent the practical evidence of modern moral and religious behaviour, and yet move on to reinforce, through reasonable discourse, essential ethical and religious principles.

There is, none the less, a way in which satire's attention to 'ill designs' does not necessarily detract from the argument of *Alciphron*, where proof lies to such a great extent with the moral character of the modern Englishman. At the beginning of the Fifth Dialogue, when the debate shifts from the truth of theism to the social benefits of Christianity, Berkeley employs his third-person narrator to reassert a focus on character. Here Dion relates a comic but not insignificant incident:

---

[13] *The Fable of the Bees*, 2nd ed. (London: E. Parker, 1723), p. 92. F. B. Kaye's edition reproduces the text of 1732.

we had hardly seated ourselves and looked about us when we saw a fox run by the foot of our mount into an adjacent thicket. A few minutes after, we heard a confused noise of the opening of hounds, the winding of horns, and the roaring of country squires. While our attention was suspended by this event, a servant came running, out of breath, and told Crito that his neighbour Ctesippus, a squire of note, was fallen from his horse, attempting to leap over a hedge, and brought into the hall, where he lay for dead. Upon which we all rose, and walked hastily to the house, where we found Ctesippus just come to himself, in the midst of half-a-dozen sun-burnt squires, in frocks, and short wigs, and jockey-boots.

(III.174–5)

Ctesippus escaped with only a broken rib, and the hunters stayed to dine with Crito and his company, after which 'They passed the afternoon in a loud rustic mirth, [and] gave proof of their religion and loyalty by the healths they drank.' The next day, the four disputants return to their discussion, but not without some reflections on this interlude. The rural Tory boobies, drawn by Berkeley in a few broad comic strokes, seem in every way the antithesis of the free-thinkers and, not unexpectedly, Lysicles cannot forbear expressing his 'contempt for the rough manners and conversation of fox-hunters'.[14] 'How much more elegant', he exclaims, 'are the diversions of the town!' Euphranor has rather different thoughts:

There seems . . . to be some resemblance between fox-hunters and free-thinkers; the former exerting their animal faculties in pursuit of game, as you gentlemen employ your intellectuals in the pursuit of truth. The kind of amusement is the same, although the object be different.   (III.175)

Euphranor's point is that the free-thinkers' method of ethical and religious inquiry resembles the hunters' noisy, headlong charge. He also subtly implies that the free-thinkers, like the hunters, aim at the destruction of their quarry. In this particular instance, the hunters had blundered, and the fox escaped.

---

[14] Addison's essays in *The Freeholder* had fixed this caricature of the Tory squire: 'For the Honour of His Majesty, and the Safety of His Government, we cannot but observe, that those who have appeared the greatest Enemies to both, are of that Rank of Men, who are commonly distinguished by the Title of *Fox-Hunters*'; see *The Freeholder*, ed. James Leheny (Oxford: Clarendon Press, 1979), p. 130. In the course of *The Freeholder* Addison's popular fox-hunter mellows into an amiable 'humorist' in the mould of Sir Roger de Coverley. When the fox-hunter learns that, contrary to country rumours, London is not a hive of republicanism and dissent, he becomes 'a Convert to the present Establishment, and a good Subject to King *George*' (p. 241). *Alciphron*'s comic confrontation between town and country had featured in many earlier satires on free-thought. In Steele's *Spectator* 234 (Vol. II, p. 412) a Devonshireman judges that the fashionable free-thinker just come from London is 'little better than a Heathen'. In *The Drummer*, Lady Truman resolves to entertain the free-thinker Tinsel because 'an *infidel* is such a Novelty in the Country'; see *The Miscellaneous Works of Joseph Addison*, ed. A. C. Guthkelch, 2 vols (London: G. Bell, 1914), Vol. I, p. 438.

When Lysicles replies that he would rather 'be compared to any brute upon earth than a rational brute', Crito suggests that the free-thinkers are more like the hounds than the hunters:

For, said he, you shall often see among the dogs a loud babbler, with a bad nose, lead the unskilful part of the pack, who join all in his cry without following any scent of their own, any more than a herd of free-thinkers follow their own reason.
(III.175)

Here is Berkeley at his most derogatory, and yet this ludicrous analogy between the ways of free-thinkers and the chaos of the chase proves far from insignificant. In the following pages one of the keynotes of Crito's argument is that in England the moral incentives of Christianity have, against all odds, managed to 'soften the rugged manners of northern boors into gentleness and humanity' (III.184–5). Climate and a backward genius in the race have conspired against the civilization of this island, and 'what but religion', Crito asks, 'could kindle and preserve a spirit towards learning in such a northern rough people?' (III.201). These arguments draw upon the opening of the Fifth Dialogue with its satiric description of the fox-hunters, characters of the coarsest grain in their drunken and violent amusements, and yet eager to proclaim 'their religion and loyalty by the healths they drank'.

The hunters' conformity to the Church and loyalty to the Crown contrast with the subversive attitudes of the free-thinkers. As the Fifth Dialogue progresses, Lysicles' behaviour and comments show that the free-thinkers are just as much in need of moral constraints. He confesses at one point that he does not necessarily disapprove of the modern habit of duelling (III.187), and then innocently reveals why he has nothing against universities: 'I had the spending three hundred pounds a year in one of them, and think it was the cheerfulest time of my life. As for their books and style, I had not leisure to mind them' (III.197). The *beaux esprits*, it seems, are just as devoted to rough 'diversions' as their country cousins. In Berkeley's eyes the worst of these recreations is, perhaps, their baiting of the clergy. Throughout the Fifth Dialogue, Alciphron and Lysicles display the ugly malice they bear 'the black tribe', whom they censure in the most demeaning fashion. Crito is finally moved to classify the free-thinker as a sort of cowardly 'tame bully', who vents his spleen where his insults are least likely to be taken up (III.187).[15] In all, the Fifth Dialogue dramatizes the ways in which the free-thinkers share the violence and coarseness of the fox-hunters, but none of the moral constraints of

---

[15] So Swift had argued in *The Abolishing of Christianity in England*, observing that the great advantage of the clergy is that it permits the wits 'to exercise and improve their Talents, and divert their Spleen from falling on each other, or on themselves; especially when all this may be done without the least imaginable *Danger to their Persons*' (*Works*, Vol. II, p. 36).

Christianity which might render them tractable members of society. The opening encounter with the local squires becomes a point of departure for an analysis of the English temperament, and here at least, Berkeley seems able to transform 'satyr' into argument.

10

Conversations with ingenious men

When he arrived in London for the first time in January 1713, Berkeley was immediately befriended by Steele, and he soon found himself regularly in the company of Addison, Pope, Arbuthnot and Swift. These friendships naturally revolved around the coffee-houses and it was in making the rounds of such establishments that Berkeley first encountered the modern free-thinker in person. The town was full of talk of Collins's recently published *Discourse of Free Thinking*, and Berkeley's first letter to Percival from London, dated 26 January, condemns it as 'a very bold and pernicious book' (VIII.58). But free-thinking was then as thriving in conversation as it was in print. In the Advertisement to *Alciphron*, Berkeley adamantly defends his claim that some free-thinkers are atheists and asserts: 'This the author knows to be true, and is well assured that one of the most noted writers against Christianity in our times declared he had found out a demonstration against the being of a God' (III.23). The grounds for this claim are explained in Samuel Johnson's autobiography. Berkeley once described to Johnson how he had sought out the deists in London, and had 'been several times in their clubs in quality of a learner and so perfectly knew their manner . . . On one of these occasions . . . he heard Collens [sic] declare that he had found a demonstration against the being of a God'.[1]

Certain circumstances cast doubt on the accuracy of this anecdote, not least the fact that it would have been difficult for Berkeley to have met Collins during his first stay in London. Collins left London for the Continent shortly after the publication of the *Discourse*, perhaps as early as 2 January, and did not return until the autumn, about the time when Berkeley himself left for Sicily.[2] Collins's notoriety stemmed, however,

---

[1] See Herbert and Carol Schneider, *Samuel Johnson, President of King's College: His Career and Writings* (New York: Columbia University Press, 1929), Vol. I, p. 26. See also Thomas Chandler, *The Life of Samuel Johnson, D.D.* (New York: T. and J. Swords, 1805), p. 59. David Berman discusses this anecdote in arguing that Collins was, in fact, an atheist; see 'Anthony Collins and the Question of Atheism in the Early Part of the Eighteenth Century', *Proceedings of the Royal Irish Academy*, 75 (1975), section C, 88–9.

[2] James O'Higgins, *Anthony Collins: The Man and His Works* (The Hague: M. Nijhoff, 1970), p. 79.

not just from his authorship of the *Discourse*, but from his prominent role in an atheistical club that met at the Grecian Coffee-House.[3] Johnson claims that it was at the meeting of such a club that Berkeley heard of Collins's atheism, and Berkeley was certainly aware that Collins frequented the Grecian, a point he alludes to in his lampoon of Collins in *Guardian* 39 for 25 April. It seems possible, then, that even if he did not hear Collins's atheistical conversation at first hand, he had it related to him by Collins's fellow deists at the Grecian. Indeed, Berkeley's first contribution to the *Guardian*, the letter from 'Misatheus' in No. 9 for 21 March, seems to allude to just such an encounter:

I happened to be present at a publick conversation of some of the defenders of this *Discourse of Free-Thinking* and others that differed from them; where I had the diversion of hearing the same men in one breath perswade us to freedom of thought, and in the next offer to demonstrate that we had no freedom in anything.   (VII.176)

And when defending *Alciphron* in the *Theory of Vision Vindicated and Explained* (1732), Berkeley again speaks unequivocally of a personal knowledge of the clubs and conversation of the free-thinkers:

But to return, if I see it [atheism] in their writings, if they own it in their conversation, if their ideas imply it, if their ends are not answered but by supposing it, if their leading author hath pretended to demonstrate atheism, but thought fit to conceal his demonstration from the public; if this was known in their clubs, and yet that author was nevertheless followed, and represented to the world as a believer of natural religion; if these are so (and I know them to be so), surely what the favourers of their schemes would palliate, it is the duty of others to display and refute.   (I.254–5)

Here Berkeley reveals that his early personal encounters with free-thinking in its boldest and most dangerous declarations became the impetus for *Alciphron*, where he is at last able to fulfil his moral obligation to 'display and refute'. Of course one detail in Johnson's story rings very true, that Berkeley entered the club 'in quality of a learner', the attitude adopted by Euphranor to draw the free-thinkers into an open expression of their views.

Berkeley drew two clear lessons from his own early dialogues with the atheists, lessons which he applied in composing *Alciphron*. First, he learned that the free-thinkers were willing to go much farther in their clubs than in their published writings. Berkeley came to see that the deism cautiously insinuated in the pages of Collins's *Discourse* was but a pale

---

[3] O'Higgins, *Collins*, p. 12. Shortly after the publication of the *Discourse*, one George Paul of Oxford, who had frequented the Grecian and conversed with Collins there, felt obliged to write a public declaration of his own orthodoxy. See *An Account of a Discourse at the Grecian Coffee-House, on February the 11th 1712/13* (London: H. Clemens, 1713).

reflection of his true beliefs and intended only as a gentle introduction to atheism. For this reason *Alciphron* is clearly directed, not just at the books, but at the conversation of atheists. Lysicles and Alciphron are not meant as caricatures of Mandeville and Shaftesbury, but men of fashion who, enamoured of the notions and argumentative style of those writers, have made them part of their conversation. While Alciphron is a particularly enthusiastic disciple of Shaftesbury – 'I am never without something of that noble writer about me' (III.198) – he also cites Hobbes (III.47), and propounds generally atheistical views that are not treated in the *Characteristicks*. In the Advertisement for the second edition, Berkeley felt obliged to clarify this point, warning us that 'the author hath not confined himself to writing against books alone', and that as for the characters of Alciphron and Lysicles, 'a gentleman in private conversation may be supposed to speak plainer than others write, to improve on their hints, and draw conclusions from their principles' (III.23).

The second and not unrelated lesson Berkeley took to heart was that the club was, for a variety of reasons, a much more powerful and efficient organ than the press for the dissemination of infidelity. Berkeley is at some pains to make this clear to the reader of *Alciphron*. In passages cited earlier from the First Dialogue, Alciphron and Lysicles advocate a free, witty, coffee-house conversation as a cure for the 'pedantry of a college education' (III.48). In this milieu, learning has 'grown an amusement', hence 'the great number of minute philosophers' (III.49). Alciphron claims that the advantages of this modern education lie in its informality; polite conversation's rapid transition from subject to subject 'keeps the mind awake and active, exercising its faculties, and calling forth all its strength and spirit' (III.50). This glowing account of 'polite' learning and concomitant depreciation of the universities was something of a commonplace in Berkeley's day, but Berkeley has reservations. Euphranor worries at the lack of method in such an education: 'I always thought that some order was necessary to attain any useful degree of knowledge; that haste and confusion begat a conceited ignorance' (III.48). And Berkeley expresses other doubts in the course of the dialogue. In conversation superficial minds often absorb ideas on nothing more than the reputation of the speaker. This is dramatized in the Fourth Dialogue, where Berkeley casts Lysicles as one who overheard Collins's claims to a proof against the existence of God.[4] Lysicles expounds what Berkeley presumably once

---

[4] This atheistical argument is an elaboration of one made in *Free-thinking*, p. 50. Johnson testifies that the argument Berkeley overheard was one Collins 'soon after published, in a pretended demonstration that all is fate, and necessity, which among other things is here briefly but excellently confuted'; see Schneider, *Johnson*, Vol. I, p. 26. But *Alciphron* does not confute Collins's fatalist arguments. Johnson may be thinking of Collins's point in the Introduction to *A Philosophical Inquiry concerning Human Liberty* that we can have no 'idea' of God, an argument which Alciphron expounds at length in the beginning of the

heard himself in the Grecian Coffee-House – that if God's attributes are, as Peter Browne had argued, quite unlike human attributes, then we can have no real knowledge of God as a mind or first cause. Lysicles concludes this argument for atheism with an apology:

You wonder perhaps to hear a man of pleasure, who diverts himself as I do, philosophize at this rate. But you should consider that much is to be got by conversing with ingenious men, which is a short way to knowledge, that saves a man the drudgery of reading and thinking.   (III.165)

Conversation has replaced not only reading, but critical reflection as well.

Crito points out in the Fifth Dialogue that the 'curiosity' which inspired the ancients' 'learned conversations . . . is among our people of fashion treated like affectation, and as such banished from polite assemblies' (III.201). The social constraints on fashionable conversation actually inhibit free and inquiring thought. Crito argues that 'there are many who, believing in their hearts the truth of religion, are yet afraid or ashamed to own it, lest they should forfeit their reputation with those who have the good luck to pass for great wits and men of genius' (III.53). Alciphron is one such thinker who, particularly chary of his reputation, is prone to conform to the views of the club against his own judgment. At the opening of the Fourth Dialogue Dion discovers him pacing alone in the garden, and Alciphron then admits that it is much easier to deny the existence of God 'When half-a-dozen ingenious men are got together over a glass of wine' than in his solitary walks, where he finds himself 'haunted by a sort of panic' (III.143–4). Yet when he later confesses these doubts to Lysicles, he is sharply upbraided for abandoning the cause, and Dion notes how Lysicles's scolding 'touched Alciphron to the quick, who replied nothing but showed confusion in his looks' (III.209). In this exchange Berkeley dramatizes the chief danger of modern education: that the ethos of the club, with its insistence on loyalty and conformity, involves an emotional extortion that stifles both dissent and candour.

Alciphron's dialogue form is, then, more than just a medium which facilitates philosophical satire. It is the genre in which Berkeley can best display the true character of the free-thinker. To portray free-thinkers in conversation is to reveal them at their most open and most dangerous, to confront them in the medium they have chosen to disseminate their true opinions. But Berkeley also makes it clear that the example of free-thinking conversation he gives us in *Alciphron* is not entirely typical. Dion observes in the Sixth Dialogue

that the foregoing week our conferences had been carried on for a longer time and with less interruption than I had ever known, or well could be, in town, where

Seventh Dialogue. This argument is clearly related to Lysicles's attack on God's attributes in the Fourth Dialogue; both are designed to turn *God* into a meaningless word.

men's hours are so broken by visits, business, and amusements, that whoever is content to form his notions from conversation only must needs have them very shattered and imperfect.   (III.219)

While *Alciphron* displays some of the superficial banter that characterizes conversation in town, it manages, through Crito and Euphranor, a more concerted and penetrating discourse. As *Alciphron* thrives on the contrast between the views of Christian and atheist characters, it also attends with considerable care to their very different methods of conversation. As in the *Three Dialogues*, the style of dialogue is itself a central issue, and *Alciphron* comes to exemplify the modes of true and false discourse.

Richetti, in his discussion of *Alciphron*, shows how 'Berkeley's polemic is as much against improper language and its deluding satisfactions as it is against the generalizing doctrines of Deism and materialism.'[5] Richetti follows this theme in a careful study of the strain of horticultural imagery which runs through the work. Alciphron and Lysicles employ inflated images of 'weeding' and 'stubbing' when they talk of the need to clear the mind of prejudices. For Richetti, the free-thinkers display a 'self-satisfied extravagance and utter confidence in language', while 'Berkeley and his surrogates refuse to soar.'[6] The free-thinker's indulgence in metaphor is but one of many specific abuses of language that Berkeley identifies in *Alciphron*. The radical nature of free-thought and its need for a covert expression of its tenets demanded that its proponents twist the language of religious discourse. As early as 1697, Peter Browne was complaining that Toland and his fellows 'have agreed to speak of plain things in a peculiar dialect of their own'.[7] And Swift's technique in *Mr C—ns's Discourse* is to make Collins's covert argument explicit, to render his insinuations against the Church in plain, bold English. As Swift's officious Whig editor makes clear, 'this Writer, when he speaks of *Priests*, desires chiefly to be understood to mean the *English* Clergy, yet he includes all *Priests* whatsoever, except the antient and modern *Heathens*, the *Turks*, *Quakers*, and *Socinians*'.[8] It is just this Swiftian decoding that Crito takes upon himself when he provides this bald summary of the free-thinkers' principles at the end of the Second Dialogue:

that there is no God or providence: that man is as the beasts that perish: that his happiness as theirs consists in obeying animal instincts, appetites, and passions: that all stings of conscience and sense of guilt are prejudices and errors of education: that religion is a State trick: that vice is beneficial to the public: that the soul of man is corporeal . . .   (III.107)

---

[5] *Philosophical Writing*, p. 165.
[6] *Philosophical Writing*, pp. 165 and 172.
[7] *A Letter in Answer to a Book entitled* Christianity Not Mysterious (Dublin: J. North, 1697), p. 3.
[8] *Works*, Vol. IV, p. 28.

Stripped of their specious presentation, the free-thinkers' tenets have little to recommend them.

Like Swift, Berkeley renders the language of free-thought in the vernacular and so teaches us to recognize its deceptiveness. Even when filling his notebooks in 1707 and 1708 Berkeley was aware that much polemical diction achieves its effect through ambiguity:

> We read in History there was a time when fears & jealousies, Privileges of Parliament, Malignant Party & such like expressions of too unlimited & doubtfull a meaning were words of much sway. Also the Words Church, Whig, Tory etc. contribute very much to faction & Dispute.   (*PC* 608)

In *Alciphron* the free-thinkers use abstract catchwords like 'prejudice' and 'liberty' to make their case more appealing, but the dialogue's critical forum is one in which the vocabulary of atheism can be isolated and examined. Of all their terms, the title 'free-thinker' is particularly suspect. In *Spectator* 234 Steele wished 'that they who value themselves upon that conceited Title, were a little better instructed what it ought to stand for'. Likewise Ambrose Philips claimed that in calling his journal *The Free-Thinker*, he hoped 'to rescue the Word from Infamy . . . by taking it out of the Hands of Libertines'.[9] In the First Dialogue of *Alciphron* Euphranor expresses confusion at the name because it is 'too general and indefinite, inasmuch as it comprehends all those who think for themselves' (III.46). Alciphron's doubts about the immortality of the soul make Euphranor invoke Cicero's *De senectute*, wherein the elder Cato names the Epicureans 'minute philosophers'. Cicero 'understood the force of language', and Euphranor politely suggests that this name might more fittingly and precisely denominate men of Alciphron's persuasion.[10] Crito agrees; the modern deists, like the Epicureans, are 'minute' in that they 'diminish all the most valuable things, the thoughts, views, and hopes of men' (III.46). By making their coded meanings explicit, and questioning their claims to certain powerful words, Berkeley robs atheistical conversation of much of its effectiveness. He comes ultimately to portray their specious vocabulary as nothing more than a philosophical version of the euphemistic cant of high life. Lysicles readily admits that the free-thinking beaux speak a special 'dialect' that they 'may enjoy their vices without incurring disagreeable appellations' (III.69). From this point on Crito takes it upon himself to translate Lysicles' self-indulgent talk of 'love, and wine, and play' into the vulgar and the specific – 'cheat, whore, betray, get drunk' (III.84).

[9] *The Spectator*, Vol. II, p. 142; *The Free-Thinker* (London: n.p., 1722–3), Vol. I, p. 5.
[10] Again Berkeley seems to be indebted to Steele, who in *Tatler* 135 (Vol. III, p. 116) applied Cicero's epithet to the modern free-thinkers.

In its scrutiny of the free-thinkers' dialect, *Alciphron* reasserts the integrity of public usage over the esoteric meanings of the club. But Berkeley also counters more open attacks on language, showing us how the free-thinkers have consistently striven to rob us of a language of faith. In the Fourth Dialogue, for example, Lysicles follows Collins in trying to turn 'God' into nothing more than an empty sound. Lysicles delights in the prospect of proving the divine attributes unintelligible, 'For how are things reconciled with the divine attributes when these attributes themselves are in every intelligible sense denied, and, consequently, the very notion of God taken away, and nothing left but the name without any meaning annexed to it?' (III.164). In the same manner Alciphron consistently denies the meaningfulness of spirit words on the Lockian grounds that they conjure up no 'idea'. In the Sixth Dialogue, he engages, like Shaftesbury, in a derisory punning on 'inspiration':[11]

The word *inspiration* sounds indeed big, but let us, if you please, take an original view of the thing signified by it. To *inspire* is a word borrowed from the Latin, and, strictly taken, means no more than to breathe or blow in; nothing, therefore, can be inspired but what can be blown or breathed; and nothing can be so but wind or vapour, which indeed may fill or puff up men with fanatical and hypochondriacal ravings. This sort of inspiration I very readily admit.   (III.237)

Euphranor responds by taking a word Alciphron accepts and uses without question – 'discourse' – and reducing it in just the same way to its original Latin meaning – 'to run about' – thus exposing Alciphron's word-play as facile and impertinent. Clearly, in modern English 'inspiration' does not mean 'puffed up with wind', but, as Euphranor explains, is now used 'to denote an action of God, in an extraordinary manner, influencing, exciting, and enlightening the mind of a prophet or apostle' (III.238). Throughout *Alciphron*, Berkeley exposes an atheist plot to establish new meanings while enervating the language of Christianity, a project consistent with their larger efforts to weaken the bonds of society.

Another potentially dangerous feature of free-thinking rhetoric is the *exemplum*. Berkeley is specifically concerned with the free-thinkers' reliance on the sort of anecdote which Mandeville had employed in his *Fable*. The second, enlarged edition of the *Fable* enjoyed great notoriety, and the book made three further editions before the end of the decade. In Lysicles Berkeley gives us a character who has not simply absorbed the *Fable*'s idiosyncratic moral theory, but has made Mandeville's rhetoric his own as well. In the Second Dialogue, Lysicles follows the *Fable* in leavening moral argument with appealing narratives of individual characters:

---

[11] *Characteristicks*, Vol. I, p. 45. Swift elaborates the pun in his account of the learned Aeolists; see *Works*, Vol. I, p. 95.

Suppose a fool of quality becomes the dupe of a man of mean birth and circumstance who has more wit? In this case what harm doth the public sustain? Poverty is relieved, ingenuity is rewarded, the money stays at home, and has a lively circulation, the ingenious sharper being enabled to set up an equipage and spend handsomely, which cannot be done without employing a world of people. But you will perhaps object that a man reduced by play may be put upon desperate courses, hurtful to the public. Suppose the worst, and that he turns highwayman; such men have a short life and a merry. While he lives, he spends, and for one that he robs makes twenty the better for his expense; and, when his time is come, a poor family may be relieved by fifty or a hundred pounds set upon his head.

(III.67–68)[12]

These narrative details, these touches of life, make Mandeville's *Fable* and Lysicles' conversation readily digestible. While they distract us from considering his ethical system objectively, they give it a disconcerting plausibility.

Berkeley's response to Mandeville is directed in the first place, not at his ideas, but at his powerful and persuasive rhetoric. Crito, playing once again the expositor of free-thought, matches Lysicles' *exempla* with two tales drawn from his own experience:

I can illustrate this doctrine of Lysicles by examples that will make you perceive its force. Cleophon, a minute philosopher, took strict care of his son's education, and entered him betimes in the principles of his sect. Callicles (that was his son's name), being a youth of parts, made notable progress; insomuch that before he became of age he killed his old covetous father with vexation, and ruined the estate he left behind him, or, in other words, made a present of it to the public, spreading the dunghill collected by his ancestors over the face of the nation, and making out of one overgrown estate several pretty fortunes for ingenious men, who live by the vices of the great.   (III.70)

Crito then tells of one Telesilla, who 'was instructed by her husband in the tenets of the minute philosophy, which he wisely thought would prevent her giving anything in charity'. But Telesilla foiled these frugal plans, as free-thought soon encouraged her to deep play and extravagant dress, not to mention promiscuity. In both *exempla* Crito works, typically, by parody and irony. On the surface he maintains the 'private vices, publick benefits' theme, but he deftly turns it on the heads of its promulgators. Crito bluntly eschews the 'long train of consequences, relations, and dependences' (III.68) which is a feature of Lysicles' involuted anecdotes. The proliferation of vice and the squandering of wealth are now cast as the direct consequences of modern free-thinking.

But Crito's parody transforms his opponent's moral tales in another

---

[12] In this passage Berkeley reproduces in part Mandeville's *exemplum* of the highwayman and the thief-catchers; see *Fable*, pp. 84–6. F.B. Kaye describes the *Fable*'s vogue in the mid-century, in 'The Influence of Bernard Mandeville', *Studies in Philology*, 19 (1922), 86–90.

way. Mandeville and Lysicles had traced the stories of isolated individuals and the ultimate benefits of their self-indulgence to society at large. Whatever ill consequences attend on vice, Lysicles argues, 'are inconvenient only to private persons' (III.99). Crito, by contrast, tells us of members of families.[13] Cleophon is a patricide. Telesilla ruins her husband. This simple change of subject gives these tales a strikingly personal dimension and affective impact. Crito speaks in the same callous, almost academic tone that characterized the *persona* of the *Fable*, but his tales are plots of tragedies. The pain and pathos of the vicious life are made suddenly immediate. By invoking the powerful and universal bonds of the family, Berkeley endows Mandeville's otherwise ambiguous irony with a firm moral centre. Crito proceeds to make this new style of *exemplum* – his antidote to the rhetoric of Mandeville's *persona* – a feature of his own discourse for the rest of the dialogue. He provides us, in all, with a dozen such stories, all of which represent the ugly extremes of vice. We hear of Charmedes the suicide and of Cleon, who was tutored in Collins's atheistical club, and after a riot of self-indulgence 'died before thirty . . . childless and rotten' (III.98). In each case Crito exposes the chaos brought to families by free-thought, pointing us to the fallacy of Mandeville's purely economic calculations of public good.

Alciphron is, then, a thorough critique of the style of free-thinking debate, exposing its abuses of language and its deceptive rhetoric. But Berkeley goes beyond style to examine the logic that lies beneath free-thinking discourse, a scrutiny inspired by free-thought itself, which claimed to be the very voice of reason. On the opening page of the *Discourse of Free-Thinking* Collins proffers this definition:

> By *Free-Thinking* then I mean, *The Use of the Understanding, in endeavouring to find out the Meaning of any Proposition whatsoever, in considering the nature of the Evidence for or against it, and in judging of it according to the seeming Force or Weakness of the Evidence.*[14]

Free-thought, as its name suggests, is nothing less than philosophical inquiry, and Collins implies that the religious scepticism of the *Discourse* is a natural product of reasonable reflection. Creating a false dichotomy between reason and religion, Collins casts all Christians as the '*Unthinking*' and accuses priests of '*discouraging Examination* into the Truths of Religion'.[15] Collins's claims to reason are echoed by Alciphron in the First Dialogue. He boasts that the 'Herculean labour' of the modern deist is

---

[13] Olscamp, in *Moral Philosophy*, p. 181, touches on this in his summary of Berkeley's disagreement with Mandeville, which was 'not philosophical but factual . . . that society is composed of family units, which are individually not helped by vice, and thus there is no reason to think that society as a whole would be helped'.

[14] *Free-Thinking*, p. 5.

[15] *Free-Thinking*, p. 97.

none other 'but the subduing prejudices and acquiring true knowledge'
(III.33). But in the course of the debate it becomes clear that the free-
thinkers work with a very limited logic. In the Fourth Dialogue Alciphron
eliminates those kinds of arguments he believes have no bearing on the
debate concerning the existence of God:

> First, then, let me tell you I am not to be persuaded by metaphysical arguments;
> such, for instance, as are drawn from the idea of an all-perfect being . . . Secondly,
> I am not to be persuaded by the authority either of past or present ages, of
> mankind in general, or of particular wise men . . . Thirdly, all proofs drawn from
> utility or convenience are foreign to the purpose.   (III.142)

In the following dialogues Berkeley shows the importance of each of
these three arguments to religious inquiry; metaphysical arguments from
the nature of spirit, the authority of Scripture and the utility of Christianity are given special prominence by Crito and Euphranor. Collins had
claimed that he and his fellows were 'able to comprehend in their minds
the whole compass of human Life',[16] a claim Berkeley had first disputed
in *Guardian* 70. There he likened the deist to a fly on a pillar in St Paul's,
conscious only of the minor imperfections in the surface of the stone and
incapable of appreciating the grandeur of the building. In the same way,
the deists magnify a few minor flaws 'without comprehending the scope
and design of Christianity' (VII.207). In *Alciphron* Berkeley repeats this
charge against the 'minute philosophers', who are 'over-positive in judging, and over-hasty in concluding' (III.172).[17] Crito argues that his
opponents should be more circumspect, proceeding in their inquiries
'more modestly and warily' (III.242).

As Berkeley balances negative with positive characters, and false tenets
with true principles, so, in the discourse of Euphranor and Crito, he
strives to illuminate valid philosophical inquiry against the narrow logic
of the free-thinkers. Crito's own cautious and thorough defences of
Christianity are described as 'a more comprehensive view of the connection, order, and progress of the divine dispensations' (III.282). But, as in
the *Three Dialogues*, it is the elenchus that substantiates the integrity of
Berkeley's argument, here providing a model of logical discourse against
the club banter of his opponents. Berkeley draws our attention to the
logical qualities of Euphranor's interrogative method in the conclusion.
Euphranor is cut short by Alciphron: 'It is now time to set out on our
journey: there is, therefore, no room for a long string of question and
answer' (III.313). This forces Euphranor to make an extended refutation

---

[16] *Free-Thinking*, p. 121.
[17] Gregory Hollingshead, in 'Bishop Berkeley and the Gloomy Clerk: Pope's Final Satire
on Deism', *Durham University Journal*, 75 (1982–3), 19–27, traces some details of Berkeley's
characterization of free-thinkers in Book IV of *The Dunciad*. Pope's gloomy clerk is
'Prompt to impose, and fond to dogmatize'.

of Alciphron's theories, a method which he dislikes as 'more dogmatical' than his customary 'joint and leisurely examination of the truth' (III.317). Indeed, the qualities that have distinguished the elenchus throughout *Alciphron* are its careful attention to detail and to the meanings of words and its insistence on the agreement of questioner and answerer. Euphranor asks Alciphron at the end of one elenctic bout:

> Throughout this whole inquiry, have we not considered every step with care, and made not the least advance without clear evidence? You and I examined and assented singly to each foregoing proposition: what shall we do then with the conclusion?   (III.147)

Beside the guarded and aggressive speeches of Alciphron and Lysicles, Euphranor's elenchus seems an extremely candid and constructive method. And, as in the *Three Dialogues*, elenchus's rules are clearly shown to be the rules of logic. The same fundamental fallacies that Philonous revealed in Hylas' materialism are at work in the main objections that the free-thinkers level against Christians. Crito summarizes these for us:

> I know no sort of sophism that is not employed by minute philosophers against religion. They are guilty of *petitio principii*, in taking for granted that we believe contradictions; of *non causa pro causa*, in affirming that uncharitable feuds and discords are the effects of Christianity; of *ignoratio elenchi*, in expecting demonstration where we pretend only to faith.   (III.319)

Here, in the concluding pages of *Alciphron*, while challenging the free-thinkers' claims to be the sole champions of reason, Berkeley asserts the rationality of his religion.

Despite the primacy of satire in *Alciphron*, with its focus on the flawed morals and methods of Alciphron and Lysicles, Berkeley does portray something of the learning process that gave the *Three Dialogues* its dramatic shape. Of the two free-thinkers, Lysicles is the most obviously unregenerate. He has no faith in philosophical dialogue and holds his principles inviolate to question or rational scrutiny. When pressed to admit an error, he retorts: 'My notions sit easy. I shall not engage in pedantic disputes about them. They who do not like them may leave them' (III.247). But as it becomes clear that Lysicles is incapable of doubt and thus an enemy to true dialogue, Berkeley turns our attentions to Alciphron. The latter half of *Alciphron* unfolds along lines of his choosing. Alciphron's own difficulties with 'the received notions of a God and Providence' instigate the shift from moral to religious debate at the end of the Third Dialogue (III.140). Likewise the Fifth Dialogue is in response to his ignorance of the utility of Christianity (III.173) and the Sixth to his belief that he holds 'unanswerable objections' to Christian revelation (III.218). Alciphron's state of belief becomes a main point of interest, and he proves more tractable in argument and more susceptible to reason than Lysicles. As the dialogue progresses, Berkeley even foreshadows his eventual conversion to Christianity. If less candid than Hylas, Alciphron does display some of Hylas' struggle with prejudice. At several points Alciphron admits that there is at least 'some foundation' in his opponents' arguments, and he does stop to meditate on what has been said. In summing up the various concessions Alciphron has made, Dion remarks that he hopes to see the Christians and the free-thinkers 'come to an entire agreement in the end' (III.220). These hopes are encouraged by Alciphron himself, who makes this challenge to Euphranor and Crito: 'if you, gentlemen, can but solve the difficulties which I shall propose to-morrow morning, I promise to go to church next Sunday' (III.219).

But having encouraged us with these hints to expect Alciphron's conversion from atheism, Berkeley proceeds to frustrate our predictions and his own apparent design. In sharp contrast to the comic climax of the *Three Dialogues*, *Alciphron* ends with a disturbing dissolution of community and a failure of dialogue. While in one sense the dialogue is complete in that Euphranor now admits he has learned all of free-thinking he cares to know, the free-thinkers seem to have learned nothing. They simply break off the debate because they must return to London, back to the intellectual and moral vacuum of the club. The ultimate failure of *Alciphron* to reach some sort of agreement is a result of the free-thinkers' scepticism; Alciphron's parting revelation is that the ultimate conclusion of free-thinking is that everything is supposition (III.321). Despite their pretences, the free-thinkers in fact deny the efficacy of human reason. Truth is relative, and its pursuit in conversation nothing more than a game to fight off the fierce boredom that marks the days of a man of pleasure.

This unresolved ending is true to *Alciphron*'s satiric purposes. The free-thinkers' simple abandonment of the debate completes their portraits as evasive and narrow-minded men, more concerned with the pleasures of the town than with truth, or even their own spiritual welfare. But the disconcertingly open-ended nature of *Alciphron* also enhances the impact of Berkeley's satire on the reader, for Alciphron, unlike Hylas, is not the embodiment of our own thoughts and doubts. However much we may find new confidence from the proofs offered by Crito and Euphranor, they are proofs of truths we already hold. In portraying Alciphron's attempts to grasp the truth, Berkeley provides us with an image of someone who must be brought over to our faith. Berkeley presents us with the possibility of this conversion, but leaves the task incomplete. The dissatisfaction that inevitably attends *Alciphron*'s ending becomes a motivation, a challenge to the reader to 'display and refute', to persevere with the dialogue's moral task. Likewise the satiric emotions that Berkeley's language has engendered in the course of the dialogue – indignation at the free-thinkers and even fear of the threat they pose to our world – are not satisfied by the conclusion to *Alciphron*. Alciphron and Lysicles do not suffer, but remain blithely unrepentant and unconcerned. Berkeley offers us little of the gratifying humiliation in which Pope immerses his dunces. Instead, our anger is, in the closing pages of *Alciphron*, given a specific object and purpose.

Alciphron, like all satire, is not directed solely at those members of society it satirizes, but is written for the community as a whole, a community composed not of free-thinkers, but of condoning and complacent Christians. Berkeley's arguments are fit for those who may have flirted with atheistical notions, but they are of primary value to those who have succumbed to the pressures of the club, who failed to engage the free-thinker in open debate or raise their voice in defence of their faith. For this latter reader *Alciphron* is designed as a handbook for Christian apology. It provides a thorough list of reasonable replies to all the objections that the deists have raised against morality and faith. But it also, in its dialogue form, immerses us in apologetic debate itself. The purpose of Berkeley's attention to style is the education of the reader in appropriate methods of discourse. Berkeley has taught us how to unravel the deceptive rhetoric of the coffee-house philosophers, how to decode their specious diction and recognize the flaws in their appealing analogies, *exempla* and rhapsodies. And all the while Berkeley has illuminated, in the discourse of both Crito and Euphranor, a style that is both logically valid and rhetorically effective. He has taught us how to draw the deists out with questions, to press for definitions, and even how to name the fallacies of their most fundamental arguments.

To the end of Berkeley's *Guardian* 39 – the comic voyage through Collins's mind – Steele added a postscript which offers advice to 'whoever undertakes the reformation of a modern Free-thinker'.[18] His hints towards a 'proper cure' are at once comic and practical. Steele counsels the reader that 'it will be necessary to bring him [the infidel] into good company, and now and then carry him to church' (VII.190). Berkeley shows this same attention to the practical means of reforming freethinkers at the end of *Alciphron*. After the free-thinkers have departed, Dion, Crito and Euphranor reflect on what has passed, and come to treat of the method of achieving what *Alciphron* itself has failed to do. When Dion remarks that 'whatever may be said for reason, it is plain the sceptics and infidels of this age are not to be cured by it', Crito replies: 'in order to cure a distemper, you should consider what produced it'. He goes on to explain that while it is true that free-thinkers are seldom motivated by reason,

<hr>

[18] See E. J. Furlong, 'How much of Steele's *Guardian* No. 39 Did Berkeley Write?', *Hermathena*, 89 (1957), 76–88.

It may, nevertheless, be worth while to argue against such men, and expose their fallacies, if not for their own sake, yet for the sake of others; as it may lessen their credit, and prevent the growth of their sect, by removing a prejudice in their favour, which sometimes inclines others as well as themselves to think they have made a monopoly of human reason.   (III.326)

Here Berkeley provides a justification of *Alciphron* as an attempt not just to reform free-thinkers, but also to challenge their authority and limit their influence in the community as a whole.

Having thus asserted the importance of confronting deists in public, Crito proceeds to lay down in plain terms our immediate responsibilities if we are to prove *true* free-thinkers. With a sensible economy, Berkeley asks us to keep only three things in mind when we engage with minute philosophers. First, following the example set in *Alciphron*, 'he that would convince an infidel who can be brought to reason ought in the first place clearly to convince him of the being of a God' (III.327). Crito explains that this is the most fundamental point of disagreement, but he also notes that it is 'capable of clear proof', and proceeds to warn us of the dangers of imbruing ourselves in defences of divine mysteries. Berkeley is fearful lest we should, like Peter Browne, give a handle to deists with our more ingenious justifications of the ways of God. Crito's second rule is a simple but invaluable rhetorical commonplace:

But, on all occasions, we ought to distinguish the serious, modest, ingenuous man of sense, who hath scruples about religion, and behaves like a prudent man in doubt, from the minute philosophers, those profane and conceited men, who must needs proselyte others to their own doubts. When one of this stamp presents himself, we should consider what species he is of: whether a first or a second-hand philosopher, a libertine, scorner, or sceptic, each character requiring a peculiar treatment. Some men are too ignorant to be humble, without which there can be no docility.   (III.327–8)

Notice how Berkeley has adopted the first person plural, including the reader in his plans, making us, with Crito, spokesmen for Christianity. Of course, having read *Alciphron*, we are now in a position to make these judgments about the characters of our opponents as Crito advises. *Alciphron* has been an introduction to the different 'stamps' and 'species' of free-thinker – Lysicles the ignorant libertine and Alciphron the second-hand philosopher and sceptic. We have learned, moreover, how each character responds to its 'peculiar treatment'.

With Crito's third and final methodological hint, Berkeley gives us a final judgment on the efficacy of satire for shaming, if not confuting, the most recalcitrant free-thinkers:

But though a man must in some degree have thought, and considered, to be capable of being convinced, yet it is possible the most ignorant may be laughed out of his opinions. I knew a woman of sense reduce two minute philosophers, who had long been a nuisance to the neighbourhood, by taking her cue from their predominant affectations. The one set up for being the most incredulous man upon earth, the other for the most unbounded freedom. She observed to the first, that he who had credulity sufficient to trust the most valuable things, his life and fortune, to his apothecary and lawyer, ridiculously affected the character of incredulous by refusing to trust his soul, a thing in his own account but a mere trifle, to his parish priest. The other, being what you call a beau, she made sensible how absolute a slave he was in point of dress, to him the most important thing in the world, while he was earnestly contending for a liberty of thinking, with which he never troubled his head . . .   (III.328)

Crito relates these direct, personal rebuffs, not just as models of effective ridicule, but also as pithy *exempla* for the reader's own use. Memorable and easily interjected in conversation, these anecdotes point to the paradoxes in the lives of modern free-thinkers, revealing how they make themselves, by their own professions, ridiculous. Crito ends his counsel with a warning that the task *Alciphron* sets us is no easy one. We must be prepared, above all, for the assertive and self-assured manner of our opponents, 'there being something in the air and manner of these second-hand philosophers very apt to disconcert a man of gravity and argument' (III.328).

   This theme of the difficulty of debating with free-thinkers is the note on which *Alciphron*, itself a failed dialogue, ends. The last exchange between Euphranor and Crito brings into sharp relief Berkeley's own doubts about the ultimate efficacy of polite conversation as a method for learning. Collins had joked that the Tory divines, Swift included, should be shipped abroad to propagate the Gospel, leaving England in peace.[19] Berkeley turns the joke back on him, as Euphranor, in his last speech, proposes that there should be

erected in the midst of this free country a Dianoetic Academy, or seminary for free-thinkers, provided with retired chambers, and galleries, and shady walks and groves, where, after seven years spent in silence and meditation, a man might commence a genuine free-thinker, and from that time forward have licence to think what he pleased, and a badge to distinguish him from counterfeits.
                                                                                (III.328)

It is not just that the free-thinkers should be made to think, but that they must first be silent and solitary, denied the superficial banter of the club on which they have relied. Crito agrees with Euphranor and proceeds to reassert the value of a traditional education, based on the reading of Plato and Aristotle, against the new methods of the club and the groom-porter's:

What can be expected where those who have the most influence have the least

---

[19] *Free-Thinking*, p. 43. The badging of free-thinkers is an appropriately Swiftian proposal.

sense, and those who are sure to be followed set the worst example? where youth so uneducated are yet so forward? where modesty is esteemed pusillanimity, and a deference to years, knowledge, religion, laws, want of sense and spirit?

(III.329)

This critique of modern polite education is itself incomplete: 'While Crito was saying this, company came in, which put an end to our conversation' (III.329). This last line of *Alciphron* seems at first trivial, but even here Berkeley enforces his theme that learning and polite discourse do not agree. The constraints of company render inquiry by way of conversation superficial, disjointed, and uncandid. As much as *Alciphron* is a guide to apologetic debate, and as much as it challenges us to prove ourselves men and women 'of gravity and argument' who will publicly engage Christianity's detractors, Berkeley warns us that conversation is seldom the way to truth. Much reading and more meditation are the methods of the true and inquiring free-thinker.

PART IV

Siris

11

The rude essay

In January 1734, three years after his return from America, Berkeley was consecrated Bishop of Cloyne. In the 1720s, Berkeley had devoted little time to his Deanery at Derry; the business of promoting the Bermuda project demanded his presence in London. At Cloyne, however, he proved himself an assiduous servant of the Church of Ireland. There he spent most of his twenty remaining years, visiting Dublin only once and not returning to England until shortly before his death. As Bishop he committed his energies to improving conditions in his impoverished see. He set up a spinning school in Cloyne, and introduced the cultivation of hemp and flax. When epidemics raged through Ireland in the early 1740s he tended the sick himself, discovering, in the process, the curative properties of tar-water.[1] But despite these consuming pastoral duties and his isolation from lettered society, these were not years of literary stagnation for Berkeley. He continued to write extensively on Irish affairs, often on themes inspired by his own experiences in Cloyne. These late works show no diminishment of Berkeley's literary powers, nor even of the inventiveness of his earlier writings. The same impulse that had led him to explore that most demanding of philosophical genres, the dialogue, inspired several radical experiments in form and style in his last years.

The most striking of these formal experiments is unquestionably *The Querist, containing several Queries, proposed to the Consideration of the Public.* This work first appeared serially, in three parts, between 1735 and 1737, and consisted wholly of a list of 895 rhetorical questions. Many of Berkeley's writings had made extensive use of questions. *The Analyst* (1734), for example, ends with a list of sixty-seven queries in parody of the conclusion of Newton's *Opticks.* An extended work composed of nothing but questions is, however, quite unprecedented. The *Querist*'s original format provides Berkeley with an open forum for proposing a variety of particular projects for a national recovery. He also finds opportunity to attack

---

[1] See Marjorie Nicolson and G. S. Rousseau, 'Bishop Berkeley and Tar-Water', in *The Augustan Milieu* (Oxford: Clarendon Press, 1970), pp. 102–37, in which they describe Berkeley's discovery of tar-water and the public response to his publication of the cure.

the vices of the gentry and the indolence of the Catholic poor. These ideas and proposals are not, however, presented in a coherent fashion; there is no immediately apparent method to Berkeley's relentless questioning:

> 113   Whether, if drunkenness be a necessary evil, men may not as well drink the growth of their own country?
> 114   Whether a nation within itself might not have real wealth, sufficient to give its inhabitants power and distinction, without the help of gold and silver?
> 115   Whether, if the arts of sculpture and painting were encouraged among us, we might not furnish our houses in a much nobler manner with our own manufactures?   (VI.114)

Each of these three questions opens a different issue that will be raised again by the *Querist*: alcoholism, the advantages of paper money, and the encouragement of the arts. Although these questions are all related to a general theme of economic self-sufficiency, Berkeley does not make this connection explicit. There is no reference between one question and the next, and Berkeley provides none of the connectives that we expect of continuous discourse. Only through repetition does he instil in us any sense of a continuity of thought or a priority of concerns. Even at those places where he does devote a sequence of queries to one issue, the uniform brevity of the units of discourse, and, indeed, their interrogative form, preclude anything like sustained exposition. Each question is explicitly incomplete, waiting on the reader's answer. In this vein Berkeley frequently includes proverbs or aphorisms: '84   How long it will be before my countrymen find out that it is worth while to spend a penny in order to get a groat?' (VI.112).[2] Such proverbs neatly encapsulate a situation, but the reader is obliged to bridge the gap between the proverb and the specific economic condition of Ireland to which it applies. Whatever larger message we derive from the *Querist* depends on our own willingness to respond to its open and demanding text.

Some of these stylistic concerns and strategies emerge in Berkeley's last major philosophical work, *Siris*. Appearing first in 1744, it was the most immediately influential of all Berkeley's books, with five editions in Dublin and London within the year. At the same time it is one of Berkeley's most perplexing works, and is most frequently ignored by modern Berkeley scholars. Some of the many difficulties it presents are evident even on the title-page:

---

[2] Berkeley's late *Maxims concerning Patriotism* (1750) shares many rhetorical features with the *Querist*, being a list of thirty-nine provocative aphorisms.

SIRIS:

A CHAIN OF

Philosophical Reflections

AND

INQUIRIES

Concerning the VIRTUES of

TAR WATER,

And divers other *Subjects* connected together
and arising one from another.

On one hand, this title suggests that the ensuing book will be an integrated, well-connected piece, a chain of arguments. Translated from the Greek *siris* itself means a small cord or chain. On the other hand, Berkeley implies that the connections in *Siris* might not be strictly logical. He is offering not proof, but rather 'reflections and inquiries'. And though they are said to arise one from another, the subjects the book will ultimately investigate are 'divers', implying, perhaps, a miscellany. The brief prefatory paragraph which begins the text does not resolve these confusions or elucidate Berkeley's proposed method. There he refers only obliquely to the fact that the book will fall into two parts:

What entertainment soever the reasoning or notional part may afford the mind, I will venture to say the other part seemeth so surely calculated to do good to the body that both must be gainers . . . And, as effects are linked with their causes, my thoughts on this low but useful theme led to farther inquiries, and those on to others, remote perhaps and speculative, but, I hope, not altogether useless or unentertaining.   (V.31)

This introduction prolongs the teasing mystification of Berkeley's project, alluding once more to those other, notional subjects and again refusing to tell us what they might be. This ambiguity is uncharacteristic of Berkeley's earlier philosophical works; the *Principles* and the *Three Dialogues* openly advertised those other subjects – God and religion – which he would handle as a consequence of his analyses of human sensation. Moreover the younger Berkeley was willing to make great claims for the integrity

of his method. Recall that the *Three Dialogues* opens with a promise 'plainly
to demonstrate the Reality and Perfection of Humane Knowledge, the
Incorporeal Nature of the Soul, and the Immediate Providence of a
DEITY'. Berkeley's tone in presenting *Siris* is altogether different. He
seems instead rather dubious about the outcome of his inquiries, telling
us he hopes, but is not certain, that they might at least provide the reader
with some entertainment. And he seems less than willing to take full
responsibility for the book, depicting himself as almost passive in the
writing process; he merely followed his thoughts as they 'led on' from
tar-water to more and more remote speculations.

Whatever else it may prove, Berkeley assures us that *Siris* does have
some specific and useful medical information to dispense. And *Siris*
begins very satisfactorily in the particular, with a receipt for the preparation of tar-water. This is followed by an account of the diseases which
it has cured, supported by an impressive number of medical case histories.
But as we read on the discussion becomes gradually more and more
abstract as Berkeley turns to consider the best sources of tar, and then
tar's chemical properties. The text gives us little sense of a structure; like
the *Querist*, *Siris* is open. Unlike the *Principles*, it does not adopt the format
of the classical oration with its distinct divisions into parts according to
style of argument. Nor is there any sense of argumentative continuity as
we pass from paragraph to paragraph. Berkeley's chain proves to be not
that of the syllogism, but rather the chain of being itself. *Siris* makes its
way, not from premise to conclusion, but from subject to subject. Medicine leads Berkeley to botany, botany to chemistry, chemistry to metaphysics, and *Siris* finally comes to rest on the nature of God. As Horace
Walpole quipped in a letter to Horace Mann, 'The book contains every
subject from tar-water to the Trinity.'[3] Its plot is a cautious induction
which moves from effect to cause so gradually that the transitions themselves are imperceptible.

Within this movement Berkeley is free to return to previous themes,
particularly to tar-water, so that the sensible and the rational merge in
this speculative ascent. Only once we are well engaged in Berkeley's more
speculative reflections on the nature and role of the *anima mundi* does he
stop to reflect on the nature of his work, justifying its method, albeit
rather apologetically, to the reader:

though, perhaps, it may not be relished by some modern readers, yet the treating
in physical books concerning metaphysical and divine matters can be justified by
great authorities among the ancients: not to mention that he who professedly

---

[3] *The Yale Edition of Horace Walpole's Correspondence*, ed. W.S. Lewis *et al.* (London: Oxford
University Press, 1937–83), Vol. XVIII, p. 452. Pope reported to Hugh Bethel, 'I have
had the Bishop's book as a present, and have read it with a good deal of pleasure'; see
Correspondence, Vol. IV, 514.

delivers the elements of a science is more obliged to method and system, and tied down to more rigorous laws, than a mere essay-writer. It may, therefore, be pardoned if this rude essay doth, by insensible transitions, draw the reader into remote inquiries and speculations, that were not thought of either by him or by the author at first setting out.   (V.138)

Here Berkeley hints at a rhetorical purpose for *Siris*'s apparent formlessness. In its fluid movement it can lead the modern reader only interested in the latest cure to consider divine subjects without his being aware of the transition.

There is, however, an interesting turn to this apology about the method of *Siris*. For Berkeley pretends that he, as much as the reader, is subject to the rhetoric of *Siris*, that he too is surprised by its speculative turn. The 'remote inquiries . . . were not thought of . . . by the author at first setting out'. *Siris* is a 'rude essay'. The distinction Berkeley makes here between methodical and free exposition was an important one in his day. Addison elaborated this same distinction when reflecting on his own work in *Spectator* No. 476:

Among my Daily-Papers, which I bestow on the Publick, there are some which are written with Regularity and Method, and others that run out into the Wildness of those Compositions, which go by the Name of *Essays*. As for the first, I have the whole Scheme of the Discourse in my Mind, before I set Pen to Paper. In the other kind of Writing, it is sufficient that I have several Thoughts on a Subject, without troubling my self to range them in such order, that they may seem to grow out of one another, and be disposed under the proper Heads. *Seneca* and *Montaigne* are Patterns for Writing in this last Kind, as *Tully* and *Aristotle* excel in the other.[4]

Johnson touches on these same notions of informality and spontaneity when he defines *essay* as 'A loose sally of the mind; an irregular undigested piece; not a regular and orderly composition.'[5] In introducing his own *Essay*, Locke goes to some lengths to recount the haphazard genesis of the work, how it was 'written by incoherent parcels; and, after long intervals of neglect, resum'd again, as my Humour or Occasions permitted'. This way of writing 'by catches', in which Locke followed his humour rather than any preordained structure, provides him with an excuse for the unevenness of the *Essay*, which he admits is sometimes too dense and

[4] *The Spectator*, Vol. IV, p. 185–6.
[5] *A Dictionary of the English Language* (London: J. and P. Knapton *et al.*, 1755). In *Rambler* 184 Johnson notes that 'the writer of essays, escapes many embarrassments to which a large work would have exposed him; he seldom harasses his reason with long trains of consequence . . . or burthens his memory with great accumulations of preparatory knowledge'; see *Works*, Vol. V, p. 201. Johnson defends the hasty resolutions and inconclusiveness of essays, arguing that, in the unpredictable world in which we live, a random reflection is just as likely to end profitably as a methodical treatise.

at others prolix and repetitious. He affects a relaxed attitude to his text, claiming to be 'too lazie, or too busie to make it shorter'.[6]

Berkeley consistently refers to *Siris* as an 'essay' – an important point in that he shows considerable care and precision when referring to the forms his works take. He calls the *Principles* a '*Treatise*' in recognition of its formal and thorough treatment of its chosen theme. Unlike *Siris*, it is a work which 'delivers the elements of a science', working deductively to establish the principles of human knowledge. But Berkeley has also called two of his earlier works 'essays'.[7] The *Essay towards a New Theory of Vision* is, as its title suggests, far from a thorough or definitive overview of the science in question. Instead it attends to our particular experiences of perceiving the depth, magnitude and situation of objects. Berkeley suggests that in each case the quality is not immediately sensed, but inferred from our past experiences. The radical doctrine that underlies these investigations, that the objects of sight and touch are hetero-geneous, is defended but not elaborated: 'I do not design to trouble my self much with drawing corollaries from the doctrine I have hitherto laid

---

[6] *Essay* (Epistle to the Reader), pp. 7–8. Rosalie Colie's 'The Essayist in his *Essay*', in *John Locke: Problems and Perspectives*, ed. John W. Yolton (Cambridge: Cambridge University Press, 1969), pp. 234–61, explores Locke's adoption and rhetorical exploitation of the genre, particularly its informality, intimacy and stylistic liberty. She goes on to argue convincingly that Locke saw his book as elastic, adding chapters at will, and that the chapters in themselves can stand as short essays. Colie does not address, however, the ways in which the *Essay* denies Locke's account of its genesis. It is, after all, a very long book which treats its admittedly imposing subject with some thoroughness. One does not need the marginal summaries added to the second and subsequent editions to recognize the logical progression that often underlies Locke's apparently casual exposition. Berel Lang has vigorously promoted the study of philosophical genres, proposing an initial division of all philosophical texts according to point of view: expository, performative and reflexive. It would seem that the eighteenth-century essay is a genre in Lang's perfor-mative mode, in which 'the process of the philosophical discourse unfolds not as an image or reflection of a state of affairs, but as a construction or performance of both the state of affairs and the philosopher himself'; see 'Space, Time, and Philosophical Style', in *Philosophical Style: An Anthology about the Writing and Reading of Philosophy*, ed. Berel Lang (Chicago: Nelson-Hall, 1980), p. 156.

[7] Berkeley refers to his essays in *The Guardian* as 'papers' rather than 'essays' (VII.181, 213 and 219). In them Berkeley displays an incredible range of styles, from the Swiftian satiric fantasies of the pineal gland traveller (Nos. 35 and 39) to the tightly-focused and well-organized papers on ethical and religious topics (Nos. 55, 77 and 83). In some papers, how-ever, Berkeley does exhibit the freedom, intimacy and casualness of the essayist. In No. 62, for example, he begins with a specific personal encounter which leads him into a chance reflection; the sight of young scholars at Westminster School permits him to expound his views on education. No. 70 also begins anecdotally with an account of how a fly on a pillar of St Paul's permitted him an apt 'occasional reflection' on the narrow views of free-thinkers. The intimacy and openness of these witty turns of thought can also be found in *Guardian* 89, on immortality. Here, however, the mood is appropriately pious as Berkeley candidly con-fesses the comfort he derives from reflections on the afterlife.

down' (I.232). And Berkeley concludes, not with a coherent summary of a new theory, but with the argument that the prevalent geometrical model of perception is inadequate. Of course the *New Theory of Vision* is an essay not just because it is a partial and explorative treatment, but because it was for Berkeley a tentative introduction to immaterialism. It is a cautious first step in which Berkeley shows us how visual ideas, and particularly visual depth, are mind-dependent. Berkeley's second effort in this genre is *An Essay towards preventing the Ruin of Great Britain* (1721), a work which in both subject and style looks forward to the *Querist*. Taking the bursting of the South Sea Bubble as its cue, this essay combines a variety of observations on the state of England with many proposals of 'effectual methods for restoring and promoting religion, industry, frugality, and public spirit' (VI.69). Much more than the *New Theory of Vision*, it shows throughout the essay's characteristic spontaneity and lack of order and priority. One subject simply 'calls to mind another' (VI.83). In a few pages Berkeley can jump from suggestions for the better management of poor taxes, to the need for public encouragements to propagation, and then on to lament the poor quality of the black used by English dyers. Berkeley's mood ranges, with his topics, from stern to witty. This rapid and random movement makes for a lively if irregular piece, but Berkeley has no pretensions about the work. He shows the essayist's customary humility. None of his remedies are offered as fool-proof, but proposed as just some 'general hints' which the author had simply 'thrown together' (VI.84).

In *The Ruin of Great Britain* Berkeley has learned to take advantage of informality to make a striking appeal. It is as entertaining as it is impressive with its varied themes, provocative proposals, and subtle modulation of tone. Here Berkeley joins Locke, Addison and Johnson in recognizing that the essay is, as its name suggests, a trial or an attempt at truth. It is heuristic rather than demonstrative, attempting to discover through language new truths, rather than set down something the author already knows. When, in *Siris*, Berkeley calls himself a 'mere essay-writer', he asks us to accept that at the beginning of the book he had no clear notion of how it would unfold. He also warns us that to look for a predetermined message is to mistake its genre. He does not demonstrate or establish elements or principles, but presents us instead with a history of a prolonged pondering, a drama of discovery in the spontaneous excursion of a mind. Where Berkeley's dialogues strove to exemplify legitimate debate, in *Siris* he provides us with a model of meditation, a lively first-hand account of philosophical inquiry.

Berkeley's apparently intentional abandonment of any predetermined order is as evident in the style as in the form of *Siris*. He was experimenting in his letters of the period with the curt prose of Seneca and

Montaigne,[8] an interest which is reflected in the style of *Siris*:

> Turpentine is on all hands allowed to have great medicinal virtues. Tar and its infusion contain those virtues. Tar-water is extremely pectoral and restorative; and, if I may judge from what experience I have had, it possesseth the most valuable qualities ascribed to the several balsams of Peru, of Tolu, of Capivi, and even to the balm of Gilead, such is its virtue in asthmas and pleurisies, in obstructions and ulcerous erosions of the inward parts. Tar in substance mixed with honey I have found an excellent medicine for coughs. Balsams, as hath been already observed, are apt to offend the stomach, but tar-water may be taken without offending the stomach, for the strengthening whereof it is the best medicine I have ever tried.   (V.38)

This random collection of notes about tar-water's virtues is the antithesis of the *Principles'* smooth, logical flow. In *Siris* Berkeley favours very short sentences, and these take the barest subject-copula or subject-verb-object form. But even the longer periods exhibit little subordination or syntactic projection; the third sentence here, for example, is accumulative, dedicated like the rest of the paragraph to cataloguing facts. Berkeley also enforces an unnatural parataxis, banishing connectives between his periods. Each sentence begins the discourse anew with its own subject, emphasizing the independence of each observation.

This paratactic prose is appropriate to Berkeley's 'rude essay'. It is an exploratory and unfinished style in which the ideas preserve their individual integrity and freshness, as if they were simply scribbled down as they arose in the writer's mind. Montaigne had established that the way of essay was the way of self-exploration: 'Je ne vise icy qu' à découvrir moi-mesmes.' Likewise Locke tells us that his *Essay* was written 'for my own Information, and the satisfaction of a few Friends'.[9]

---

[8] Berkeley adopts the curt style for a series of three public letters on military tactics for the *Dublin Journal* appearing between December 1745 and February 1746. With rebellion threatening, Berkeley had mustered and equipped a troop of horse at Cloyne. The trials of this task no doubt led him to these reflections on the advantages of an established and well-trained national militia: '*Pro aris et focis* hath been always esteemed the strongest motive to fighting. Foreigners want this motive, and therefore should not be depended on. Its own Militia and soldiers raised at home, are the natural Defence of a country. Great evils have ensued from calling in foreigners; History is full of such examples . . .' (VIII.280–1). Here the clipped style creates a valuable commonsense *ethos*. Berkeley obviously wants to suggest an author of military experience in these letters, a man not of the pen but of the battlefield. Montaigne had, after all, described his style as 'soldatesque'; see *Les Essais*, ed. Pierre Coste (London: J. Tonson and J. Watts, 1724), Vol. I, p. 167. See also the letter of 26 March 1742 to Percival's son, in which Berkeley speaks in favour of sumptuary laws in an antithetical and aphoristic style (VIII.262). Berkeley seems to allude to his late experiments in Senecan prose in a formal and self-effacing letter to Orrery of July 11, 1747: 'Your Lordsps lott is fallen in a pleasant land. For my part, I admire the *belles lettres* without possessing them (A truth I need not mention), my studies having been of the dry and crabbed kind, which give a certain gouty stiffness to the style'; see David Berman, 'Berkeley's Letter to Lord Orrery', *Berkeley Newsletter*, 3 (1979), 12–13.

[9] Montaigne, *Essais*, Vol. I, p. 139; Locke, *Essay* (Epistle to the Reader), p. 7.

Of course *Siris* never indulges in autobiography to the extent of Montaigne's *Essais*. It sustains none the less some of the intimacy of the essay's confessional rather than didactic mode, of the unguarded revelation of the author's thoughts. Richetti captures this quality of *Siris* which he describes as 'a release of Berkeley's implicit lyricism'.[10] Just as the larger form of *Siris* reflects a free excursion in thought, so the small movements of Berkeley's language depict for us an unconstrained mental searching. This drama of exploration can be found at even the most mundane moments:

Tar was by the ancients esteemed good against poisons, ulcers, the bites of venomous creatures; also for phthisical, scrofulous, paralytic, and asthmatic persons. But the method of rendering it an inoffensive medicine and agreeable to the stomach by extracting its virtues in cold water, was unknown to them. The leaves and tender tops of pine and fir are in our times used for diet-drinks, and allowed to be antiscorbutic and diuretic. But the most elaborate juice, salt, and spirit of those evergreens are to be found in tar, whose virtues extend not to animals alone, but also to vegetables. Mr. Evelyn, in his treatise on 'Forest Trees', observes with wonder that the stems of trees, smeared over with tar, are preserved thereby from being hurt by the envenomed teeth of goats and other injuries, while every other thing of an unctuous nature is highly prejudicial to them.   (V.34)

Here again Berkeley presents us with a list of facts. But in the antitheses established between the first and second, and third and fourth sentences, he also reveals some rudimentary attempt to work with this raw material. Within each pair, the fact given in the first sentence is qualified in the second, as Berkeley tests it against his growing suspicion that tar-water is a panacea. The 'But' which begins the second sentence in each case is too strong an antithesis, the initial over-reaction of a mind shifting between a general hypothesis and the particular facts that lie before it. It is this tentativeness and responsiveness that characterize the mind depicted in *Siris*. This passage does not end with an appropriate conclusion or summary, such as 'There is good evidence in both ancient and modern medical practice of the healing powers in tar.' Instead, in the middle of the fourth sentence, the thinker unexpectedly recalls something he read in Evelyn's *Sylva* and the discussion shoots off on a tangent. Suddenly we are no longer concerned with curing human illness, but with protecting trees from goats. What we are left with, in the end, is no more than a series of hints, with examples of several initial gestures towards a larger meaning as the author gathers together all the evidence he can find relating to tar and tar-water.

This probing, wayward discourse generates a cautious *ethos* as it depicts an almost nervously receptive mind hesitant to impose its own hypothesis

[10] *Philosophical Writing*, p. 177.

on the evidence it has gathered. Clearly, this is the *ethos* Berkeley wants to create in *Siris*. In his prefatory paragraph he adopts an apologetic tone, deferring to the reader's judgment as to whether or not his book will prove useful. He also protests his reticence to play author: 'charity obligeth me to say what I know' (V.58). These are not merely conventional gestures, but consistent with Berkeley's attitude throughout the work. In the *Principles* Berkeley made a conscious effort to 'speak positively' so that the reader would take his arguments seriously.[11] He achieved this confident tone largely through the regular inclusion of assertive phrases such as 'I dare be confident' or 'it is evident on all hands'. The *persona* of *Siris* makes quite different claims about his findings: 'If I am not greatly mistaken' (V.52); 'One would be tempted to suspect' (V.61); 'perhaps there may be something analogous to this' (V.45); and 'It should seem that' (V.45). 'Seem', 'suspect', and 'suppose' are the operative verbs in *Siris*, often worked into such evasive qualifications as 'thus much at least it seems not absurd to suppose' (V.61), a typical gesture in which Berkeley consciously restrains his speculative urges.

Only when recounting first-hand observations does the voice of *Siris* gain a degree of certainty. Berkeley *does* frequently remind us that his claims for tar-water are confirmed by experience. He relates how he administered the medicine to his family and neighbours (V.55), and even reveals that he treated his own nervous colic successfully: 'I owe my life to it' (V.72). And it is at these moments, when recounting actual medical histories, that Berkeley freely employs the first person in *Siris*:

> I never knew anything so good for the stomach as tar-water: it cures indigestion and gives a good appetite. It is an excellent medicine in an asthma . . . As it is both healing and diuretic it is very good for the gravel. I believe it to be of great use in a dropsy, having known it cure a very bad anasarca in a person whose thirst, though very extraordinary, was in a short time removed by the drinking of tar-water. (V.33)

Notice the off-hand manner with which Berkeley mentions the substantiating case history, and also how easily he handles the medical jargon. While displaying the author's practical competence, this language is not meant to intimidate the reader. Recent studies in eighteenth-century medicine show that the reading public had a sophisticated command of

---

[11] Revising the *Principles* for the second edition of 1734, Berkeley carefully struck most of these phrases from the text, an indication, perhaps, of a dissatisfaction with the didactic method of the *Principles* and a first gesture towards the *ethos* he would create in *Siris*. Something of this change of rhetorical outlook is also evident in the philosophical correspondence with Johnson of 1729, where Berkeley still defends immaterialism, but with a new note of deference: 'I had no inclination to trouble the world with large volumes. What I have done was rather with a view of giving hints to thinking men, who have leisure and curiosity to go to the bottom of things, and pursue them in their own minds' (II.281).

medical terminology. In particular, Roy Porter's study of medical articles in *The Gentleman's Magazine* shows not only the extent of lay participation in medical debate, but also that the eighteenth-century practitioner did not treat his knowledge as esoteric: 'medical knowledge was presented in the magazine, not *ex cathedra*, but openly and experimentally, so readers could see and do for themselves'.[12] It is appropriate too, that the confident tone disappears in *Siris*, along with the first person, as the discussion moves from case histories on to more 'notional' subjects. W.F. Bynum, in his study of medical writings in the century, finds that 'Not uncommonly, Enlightenment doctors drew fairly hard lines between fact and speculation; they were prepared to abandon any particular speculation but considered facts were sacred.'[13] In portraying himself as a man more comfortable with fact than with speculation, Berkeley would have impressed his readers as a sound medical adviser.

Berkeley clearly wants us to regard *Siris* at first as a 'physical book', one making 'philosophical' inquiries into tar-water. The cautious tone and hesitant, exploratory style is as appropriate to the inductive text of a modern natural philosopher as to the modern medical treatise. Bacon had described 'anticipation of mind' as the greatest stumbling-block to the advancement of natural philosophy. He had advocated, therefore, a disjointed, aphoristic style of the sort adopted by Berkeley, with 'short and scattered sentences, not linked together by an artificial method', and in which the author 'did not pretend or profess to embrace the entire art'.[14] Bacon's strictures set both the tone and the form of much scientific writing in the seventeenth century. Glanvill tells the Royal Society in his Dedicatory Epistle that his *Scepsis Scientifica*, 'which with a *timerous* and *unassur'd countenance* adventures into your *presence*, can pride itself on no higher title, then that of an *Essay*, or imperfect offer at a Subject'.[15] And just as Bacon confessed his ignorance of the scheme of nature, so Browne in his *Pseudodoxia Epidemica* protests: 'We are not Magisteriall in opinions, nor have we Dictator-like obtruded our conceptions; but in the humility of Enquiries or disquisitions, have only proposed them unto more ocular discerners.'[16] Perhaps the most famous gesture of scientific self-effacement comes in Newton's *Opticks*, a book to which Berkeley frequently refers in *Siris*. In the middle of the third book, Newton leaves off his transcripts of experiments, explaining that his investigation of the

[12] 'Laymen, Doctors and Medical Knowledge in the Eighteenth Century: The Evidence of the *Gentleman's Magazine*', in *Patients and Practitioners*, ed. Roy Porter (Cambridge: Cambridge University Press, 1985), p. 297.
[13] 'Health, Disease and Medical Care', in *The Ferment of Knowledge*, ed. G. S. Rousseau and Roy Porter (Cambridge: Cambridge University Press, 1980), p. 225.
[14] *Works*, Vol. IV, pp. 42 and 85.
[15] *Scepsis*, sig. C3ᵛ.
[16] *Pseudodoxia Epidemica*, 3rd ed. (London: N. Ekins, 1658), sig. A4ʳ.

bending of light rays was interrupted: 'And since I have not finish'd this part of my Design, I shall conclude, with proposing only some Queries in order to a farther search to be made by others.'[17] In the explicit incompleteness of these works, each scientific author insists that his comprehension of the subject is only partial. Berkeley himself makes this conventional gesture of deference to future 'ocular observers' in *Siris* when he offers tar-water as a cure for gout:

And I leave it to trial, whether tar-water be not that medicine, as I myself am persuaded it is, by all the experiments I could make. But in all trials I would recommend discretion; for instance, a man with the gout in his stomach ought not to drink cold tar-water. This Essay leaves room for future experiment in every part of it, not pretending to be a complete treatise.   (V.58)

Here Berkeley, like Glanvill, suggests that the essay as an explicitly incomplete form is the appropriate genre for the modern 'physical book'.

When Berkeley has left the empirical realms of medicine and botany, turning to chemical theory to consider the nature of tar's volatile acids, he interjects this cautionary note before resuming the discussion:

I am very sensible that on such subjects arguments fall short of evidence, and that mine fall short even of what they might have been if I enjoyed better health, or those opportunities of a learned commerce from which I am cut off in this remote corner. I shall nevertheless go on as I have begun, and proceed, by reason, by conjecture, and by authority, to cast the best light I can on the obscure paths that lie in my way.   (V.73–4)

Here Berkeley underlines the distinction between the evidence he could marshal in his own medical histories, and this theoretical discussion which lives in the realm of probability, dependent not on sensory evidence but on 'reason, conjecture, and authority'. But this section also affirms that the text itself is truly an essay, without a predetermined outcome. For the writer of *Siris* the text is a journey of discovery and the paths which lie in his way are 'obscure'. In such reflections Berkeley undermines his own authority, placing himself at parity with the reader. Both reader and author are confronting the same information for the first time, engaged in the same learning process, fellow-travellers on the same obscure path.

The treatise, especially an aggressive treatise like the *Principles*, concentrates on attaining the reader's assent to certain arguments. In the *Principles* Berkeley employs *prolepsis*, objections and the first and second persons to establish and maintain the distinct identities of writer and reader. The text becomes a debate in which the reader is cast as critic and the writer as defendant of immaterialism. *Siris* creates a much less competitive and public forum. Berkeley never uses the second person, and, as I have suggested earlier, once the initial medical discussion is

[17] *Opticks*, 2nd ed. (London: W. and J. Innys, 1717), p. 313.

superceded by more speculative topics, he abandons the first person as well.[18] In fact, in *Siris* Berkeley often begins sentences with anticipatory subjects, whereas in the *Principles* he opted for the more direct first person. Among the most frequent are 'It must be owned' (V.94, 110, 111, 122 and 163) for 'I admit', and 'It should seem' (V.76, 99 and 100) for 'I believe'. This suppression of the first person is, of course, appropriate to the tentative *ethos* of the piece, but it also inevitably diminishes the reader's consciousness of the author as a distinct character in the text. The effect is quite different from the critical atmosphere that predominates in the *Principles*. Instead of 'I' and 'you' polemics we are drawn into the intimacy of candid self-revelation. Rather than confronting and judging specific arguments, in reading *Siris*'s history of a free meditation we too become meditators, its tentative tone encouraging a sympathetic rather than a critical reading. *Siris*'s subtler method is just as effective as the *Principles*' rhetoric at ensuring that we remain participants rather than observers as we read.

Addison, in his discussion of the styles of discourse in *Spectator* No. 476, touches on the respective impacts of the treatise and the essay. He believes that the methodical text is the best mode for communicating ideas, because the reader 'comprehends every thing easily' and leaves the discourse with a clear, orderly impression of the main arguments and their relations: 'When I read a Methodical Discourse, I am in a regular Plantation, and can place my self in its several Centers, so as to take a view of all the Lines and Walks that are struck from them.' When Addison encounters an essay, however, he experiences a very different kind of pleasure: 'I fancy myself in a Wood that abounds with a great many noble Objects, rising among one another in the greatest Confusion and Disorder . . . You may ramble . . . a whole Day together, and every Moment discover something or other that is new to you.'[19] Like Berkeley's image of the text as an obscure path, Addison's wild wood captures the surprise and suspense that we feel as essay-readers, never quite sure what will loom into view. Notice too that in the course of this analogy Addison depicts the essay-reader as constantly in motion, 'rambling' about in the text. By contrast, the reader of treatises is static, taking an overview of the whole work from the several vantage points offered him by the structure of the piece. Addison shows that in an essay the onus is on the reader

---

[18] I have found only twelve instances where Berkeley uses the first-person pronoun in the latter eighty-nine pages of *Siris*: in four of these cases he is recording phenomena or cures he has witnessed himself (V.80, 104, 105 and 106); three others are evasive qualifying phrases such as 'if I mistake not' and 'if I may say so' (V.93, 118 and 119); and in three more he is referring the reader to an authority which he either does not transcribe or will not translate (V.98, 152 and 163). In the two remaining instances he says 'I believe' (V.111 and 154).

[19] *The Spectator*, Vol. IV, p. 186.

to discover what there is of beauty and value in the language before him. Locke makes the same point when he likens the pleasures he takes in writing the *Essay* to those of 'Hawking and Hunting, wherein the very pursuit makes a great part of the pleasure':

This, Reader, is the Entertainment of those, who let loose their own Thoughts, and follow them in writing; which thou oughtest not to envy them, since they afford thee an Opportunity of the like Diversion, if thou wilt make use of thy own Thoughts in reading.[20]

Locke regularly encourages us to use his *Essay* as a spur to our own thought, frequently insisting that we test his statements against our own experience. The essay, since it represents a process of inquiry antecedent to knowledge, is pointedly unfinished, 'undigested' as Johnson would have it. Berkeley's own *Essay towards a New Theory of Vision* is very conscious of this propaedeutic function. Indeed, both Berkeley's earlier essays look '*towards*' their subjects in their titles, emphasizing that the essay is a journey towards an ideal which, at the end of the text, is still to be attained. Likewise *Siris* presents us with an implicit challenge to complete the task at hand, to join the author in surveying his scattered facts and few loose conjectures, and to help him to determine their significance. It is we who must give the random and often hidden meanings of the essay some form. *Siris* demands of us throughout that sort of intuitive reading which any meditator must ultimately apply to his own free reflections.

The reader's full participation is further encouraged by the broken, paratactic prose that Berkeley practises in *Siris*. Its lack of closure demands that we compare and connect the discrete items strewn before us. In Berkeley's day rhetoricians like Ward rejected too terse a prose style as tending to obscurity, but Blair had some guarded praise for the response elicited by curt prose: 'The direct effect of short sentences, is to render the Style brisk and lively . . . By the quick successive impulses which they make on the mind, they keep it awake.'[21] The greatest fault of Senecan prose, its lack of solidity and logical progression, is, from a different viewpoint, its chief strength. It nettles the reader out of a complacent reading. It piques the curiosity without ultimately providing the satisfaction of logic's closure, and so stimulates reflection. The *Querist*'s disjointed discourse was clearly designed to involve the reader in this way. There, Berkeley's queries demanded participation, raising complex problems which admitted no easy solution, or disconcerting us by intimating the imminent collapse of Irish society. As Ellen Douglas Leyburn has shown, there is a strong satiric vein in the *Querist*.[22] The excesses of the

[20] *Essay* (Epistle to the Reader), pp. 6–7.
[21] *Lectures*, Vol. I, p. 375.
[22] 'Bishop Berkeley: The Querist', *Proceedings of the Royal Irish Academy*, 44 (1937–8), section C, 77. Donald Davie, in 'Irony and Conciseness in Berkeley and Swift', *The Dublin*

Irish gentry, who are Berkeley's readers, are made the object of ridicule. Berkeley thus insists that the reader accept his or her own culpability for the sorry state of Ireland. The last query reads: 'Whose fault is it if poor Ireland still continues poor?' (VI.154). Berkeley's purpose in the *Querist*'s threats and ridicule is the reformation of the habits and attitudes of his countrymen. He wants to spur them into action and to encourage them to implement any of the particular projects and reforms he has in mind. But he first uses the provocative and evasive form of the book to get his readers thinking:

315 Whether one, whose end is to make his countrymen think, may not gain his end, even though they should not think as he doth?
316 Whether he, who only asks, asserts? and whether any man can fairly confute the querist?   (VI.161)

The unconventional rhetoric of the *Querist* has, I have suggested, much in common with the form and style of *Siris*. It would seem, too, that in both texts Berkeley's primary goal is the same – the mental exertion of the reader. Berkeley's conviction in the importance of meditation emerges to qualify the somewhat sceptical mood of *Siris*'s conclusion. Having warned that the earthbound thinker must often be content with mere glimpses of knowledge, Berkeley finishes by insisting that we should not despair, but apply ourselves all the more vigorously:

It is Plato's remark, in his *Theaetetus*, that while we sit still we are never the wiser, but going into the river, and moving up and down, is the way to discover its depths and shallows. If we exercise and bestir ourselves, we may even here discover something.
368 The eye by long use comes to see even in the darkest cavern: and there is no subject so obscure but we may discern some glimpse of truth by long poring on it. Truth is the cry of all, but the game of few. Certainly, where it is the chief passion, it doth not give way to vulgar cares and views; nor is it contented with a little ardour in the early time of life, active perhaps to pursue, but not so fit to weigh and revise. He that would make a real progress in knowledge must dedicate his age as well as youth, the later growth as well as the first fruits, at the altar of Truth. Cujusvis est errare, nullius nisi insipientis in errore perseverare. CICERO
(V.164)

Noting the way in which Locke's *Essay* seems to run off its rails at the end of Book IV, Rosalie Colie remarks: 'open-endedness is, however, perfectly characteristic of books of essays . . . [which] do not characteristically wind up their coils neatly in a knot at the end, but let them trail, to be grasped by whoever comes after'.[23] Appropriately, then, *Siris* ends not with a conclusion or even a summary, but with a reflection on method. It

Magazine, 27 (1952), 20–9, argues that the query form, combined with Berkeley's conciseness and lack of irony, makes for trenchant satire.
[23] 'Essayist', p. 258.

is a text which has forced us to 'bestir ourselves' by refusing us clear
principles. As in the dark woods of Addison's essays, we have had to
ramble. We have had to move up and down 'to discover its depths and
shallows'.

There are two striking features of the language of this conclusion. The
first is the re-emergence of the first person, but now in the plural, an
affirmation that *Siris* has been a joint learning experience. And second,
Berkeley's paratactic prose turns sententious here, easily incorporating
the aphorisms which featured in the rhetoric of the *Querist*. Whether it is
Cicero's 'Cujusvis est errare' or his own memorable 'Truth is the cry
of all', Berkeley's maxims intensify the challenge to reflection that has
characterized the method of *Siris* throughout. Their pithiness asks for
elaboration, and their abstraction for some application, some specificity
that might tie them to their context. And, like those in the *Querist*, these
maxims disconcertingly solicit an application to our own lives. Clearly we
are the ones who have persevered in error, who have cried truth and yet
failed to pursue it. Like *Alciphron*, *Siris* does not end, but rather opens
outward, looking not at what has been accomplished, but at what is yet to
be done. Its final lines urge the reader 'to weigh and revise', to resume
the business of reflection and inquiry in which *Siris*'s open and demanding text has been an initiation.

12

The method of inductive analogy

We leave *Siris*'s disjointed text with little sense of the whole and no impression of any central tenet around which it was organized. No '*esse* is *percipi*' looms large in our memories. *Siris* presents such a variety of doctrines on so many subjects, and all in such a tentative fashion, that any clear perception of what the book was about is denied us. Instead *Siris* encourages us to participate in a mode of inquiry.[1] Its form and style ask us to join Berkeley in his reflections, and under his subtle direction we come to experience a technique of interpreting the natural world.

It is surprising to discover Berkeley investigating natural causes in *Siris*, let alone teaching a method of 'philosophical' inquiry. Much of his career was devoted to attacking modern natural philosophy on the grounds that it detracted from the more central and valuable sciences of theology, ethics and metaphysics. Berkeley's most thorough criticism of the method of contemporary science came in *De Motu*, a tract written in 1720 for a competition organized by the French Academy. There he warns physicists to be less dogmatic in attributing occult qualities to objects and more faithful to sensible evidence. Above all he insists they renounce their claims to identify causes in nature, a task which belongs to the metaphysician alone. He thus demotes the scientist to the position of nature's cataloguer, one permitted only to observe the regularities in natural phenomena and from these determine 'apparent', but not true causes and laws. In *De Motu* Berkeley's underlying philosophy of science is instrumentalist: scientific explanations are never perfect, but are only proposed as the best interpretations available. They are valued not because they are true, but because they are useful for predicting future natural occurrences. As W. N. Newton-Smith has pointed out, Berkeley's instrumentalism was a direct challenge to the bold claims of

---

[1] K. M. Wheeler describes Coleridge's *Biographia* as a text whose shifting discourse and startling metaphors are designed to lead the reader through a sequence of imaginative experiences to reach a higher self-consciousness. Wheeler notes that the *Biographia* and *Siris* share a method of serious irony and fragmentation; see *Sources, Processes and Methods in Coleridge's* Biographia Literaria (Cambridge: Cambridge University Press, 1980), p. 126.

contemporary physics. In a post-Newtonian world 'no viable theory of science can be built up using only observation vocabulary and eschewing any strong notion of causation'.[2]

There is ample evidence that this fundamental critique of contemporary natural philosophy was shaped as much by Berkeley's religious concerns as by his metaphysical principles. Berkeley's excursions into optics and physics were primarily rejections of the mathematical and mechanical trends of contemporary science, trends which extended the authority of the natural philosopher while deferring consideration of God's agency. Berkeley found science relegating God to a distant first cause in the administration of the world. In the *Principles* he draws attention to these tendencies, and casts the philosopher's material substance as 'the main pillar and support of *scepticism*' (II.81). These concerns find their most damning expression in the queries that end the *Analyst*:

> *Qu. 56* Whether the corpuscularian, experimental, and mathematical philosophy, so much cultivated in the last age, hath not too much engrossed men's attention; some part whereof it might have usefully employed?
>
> *Qu. 57* Whether from this and other concurring causes the minds of speculative men have not been borne downward, to the debasing and stupifying of the higher faculties? And whether we may not hence account for that prevailing narrowness and bigotry among many who pass for men of science, their incapacity for things moral, intellectual, or theological, their proneness to measure all truths by sense and experience of animal life?   (IV.101–2)

Mechanical philosophy was partially responsible, in Berkeley's eyes, for the narrow and sceptical character of much contemporary thought, for that 'minute philosophy' so thoroughly anatomized on the pages of *Alciphron*.

Despite the stridency of these attacks, Berkeley's views on natural philosophy cannot be simply dismissed as reactionary. He was by no means ignorant of contemporary scientific thought, and like many educated men and women of his day he too participated in the Baconian task of accumulating and recording observations of the natural world. As an undergraduate Berkeley was an officer of Trinity College's Philosophical Society, for which he prepared a paper recounting his explorations of the caves at Dunmore. Later, on his second Italian tour, he gathered data on the tarantula and went on to climb Vesuvius to study its exhalations. Berkeley's narrative of the latter adventure was promptly published by Arbuthnot in the *Philosophical Transactions*. Thomas Blackwell, who once planned to accompany Berkeley to America to be a fellow of the new college, later eulogized Berkeley as a master of the practical and mechanical as well as the liberal arts, recalling that Berkeley would 'sit for Hours

[2] 'Berkeley's Philosophy of Science', in *Essays on Berkeley*, ed. John Foster and Howard Robinson (Oxford: Clarendon Press, 1985), p. 154.

in Forges and Founderies to inspect their successive Operations'.[3] A second *Transaction* in 1747 on the petrifaction of wood and an article in the *Gentleman's Magazine* in 1750 on earthquakes show that Berkeley's interest in natural history was to continue until the very end of his life. While these papers display the caution demanded by the methods of modern science, they also reveal a mind well-versed in current scientific writing. This is borne out by the sale catalogue of Berkeley's library, in which the mechanical moderns make a substantial showing, again suggesting that Berkeley's interest in the study of nature was far from superficial.[4]

This tension between Berkeley's concern about the religious consequences of the practice of natural philosophy and his own fascination with the subject emerges in the *Principles*. Despite the metaphysical sanctions it imposes on the study of nature, the *Principles* works within these rules to advocate a constructive theory of scientific inquiry. While Berkeley warns against the dangers of scientific scepticism, he is at pains to point out that immaterialism does not necessarily 'destroy the whole corpuscular philosophy, and undermine those mechanical principles which have been applied with so much success' (II.62). In the latter pages of the *Principles* he elaborates a new method he envisions for the scientist, invoking the metaphor of language he has used to describe the nature of sense-data. Natural phenomena are 'marks or signs' from God about future occurrences; black clouds in the sky warn us that we will soon feel rain on our faces. In section 108 of the first edition of 1709, Berkeley suggests the implications of this view for the practice of natural philosophy:

The steady, consistent methods of Nature, may not unfitly be stiled the *language* of its *Author*, whereby He discovers His *attributes* to our view, and directs us how to act for the convenience and felicity of life. And to me, those men who frame general rules from the phenomena, and afterwards derive the phenomena from those rules, seem to be grammarians, and their art the grammar of Nature.

(II.88–9)

There is no doubt that Berkeley is being provocative here; 'grammarian'

---

[3] *Memoirs of the Court of Augustus*, Vol. II (Edinburgh: Hamilton *et al.*, 1755), p. 227.

[4] The Leigh-Southeby sale catalogue of Berkeley's library – British Museum S.–C.S. 28 (14) – is far from being a perfect record of Berkeley's collection. It includes, without distinguishing, the additions of George Jr and Monck Berkeley, but almost all the works dating from after Berkeley's death are either poetic or devotional. It is probable, then, that the philosophical and scientific items were Berkeley's own purchases. It is still only a partial record, since some of the works that Berkeley certainly owned, such as those he used at Cloyne when preparing *Siris*, do not appear. See R. I. Aaron, 'A Catalogue of Berkeley's Library', *Mind*, 41 (1932), 265–75. The catalogue does include: for optics, Barrow, Newton, Molyneux and Borelli; for botany, Grew, Ray, Bradley and Tournefort; for chemical physics, Glauber, Boyle, Power and Gilbert; and for medicine, Shaw, Robinson and Daniel LeClerc.

implies the sort of pedantic, book-bound scholarship rejected by the modern natural philosopher. Few scientists could be pleased with this demeaning comparison, but it does serve Berkeley's purposes well, neatly incorporating the controls he wants to set on scientific explanation. First, and most important, it denies the philosopher any talk of efficient causes, since each phenomenon in Berkeley's system is but the sign of a future phenomenon. Second, the 'rules' the scientist makes about these conventional relations will obviously be provisional. Berkeley praises Newton's *Principia* as 'The best grammar of the kind we are speaking of', only to attack it for making distinctions between the '*absolute* and *relative, true* and *apparent, mathematical* and *vulgar*' (II.89). Berkeley reminds us that grammatical rules, derived from linguistic practice, all have exceptions: 'as it is very possible to write improperly, through too strict an observance of general grammar-rules: so in arguing from general laws of Nature, it is not impossible we may stretch the analogy too far, and by that means run into mistakes' (II.89). In this the metaphor of a natural grammar usefully satisfies Berkeley's desire for natural laws that cannot be seen to impose any constraint on the divine will.

This linguistic analogy also supports Berkeley's conception of God's participation in natural events. Language is the best evidence we have of the operation of mind. If the scientist is encouraged to treat nature as a language, he will be less likely to ignore Berkeley's tenet that all phenomena are the productions of God's mind. The *Principles*' emphasis on the essential benevolence of nature, a nature created for the well-being of mankind, prepares us for this, Berkeley's final account of the true hermeneutics of the sensible world:

As in reading other books, a wise man will choose to fix his thoughts on the sense and apply it to use, rather than lay them out in grammatical remarks on the language; so in perusing the volume of Nature, methinks it is beneath the dignity of the mind to affect an exactness in reducing each particular phenomenon to general rules, or shewing how it follows from them. We should propose to our selves nobler views, namely to recreate and exalt the mind, with a prospect of the beauty, order, extent, and variety of natural things: hence, by proper inferences, to enlarge our notions of the grandeur, wisdom and beneficence of the Creator: and lastly, to make the several parts of Creation, so far as in us lies, subservient to the ends they were designed for, God's glory, and the sustentation and comfort of our selves and fellow-creatures.   (II.89)

Here, in section 109, science seems little more than pointless pedantry. Berkeley reveals that the true significance of the book of nature – its sense rather than its grammar – is its expression of God's character and will, those final causes so disparaged by the modern experimental philosophers.

If few scientists would be satisfied with the peripheral role offered them in sections 108 and 109 of the *Principles*, neither, ultimately, was Berkeley. For the second edition of 1734 he reworked section 108, eliminating the phrases in which he calls scientists 'grammarians, and their art the grammar of nature', and speaks instead of the scientist as one who finds 'analogy' amongst natural signs. This is still consistent with the linguistic metaphor of the discussion; in grammar 'analogies' are specifically those regularities of language which suggest grammatical rules. But 'analogy' has been used more expansively a few pages earlier in the *Principles* with regard to the scientist's task, and Berkeley's emendations help bring sections 108 and 109 in tune with this earlier account. In section 104 Berkeley had admitted the validity of 'attraction' as a rule of nature (II.86). To attain this rule the scientist compared phenomena, attentive to 'likeness', 'conformity' and 'a certain similitude of appearances'. Having observed 'the falling of a stone to the ground . . . the rising of the sea towards the moon . . . cohesion, crystallization, etc.', the scientist then formulated a rule of attraction between bodies. In section 105 Berkeley proceeds to tell us that natural philosophers differ from other men

in a greater largeness of comprehension, whereby analogies, harmonies, and agreements are discovered in the works of Nature, and the particular effects explained, that is, reduced to general rules, see *Sect.* 62, which rules grounded on the analogy, and uniformness observed in the production of natural effects, are most agreeable, and sought after by the mind.   (II.87)

While still not granting certainty to scientific explanations, Berkeley here seems to admit both their usefulness and the pleasure that attends them. Where the grammarian's rules seemed peripheral to a 'wise man's' reading of nature, here the analogist is seen to make a valid contribution to human knowledge. It appears also that the analogical method which Berkeley prescribes to philosophers involves the comparison of relations between phenomena, and that these phenomena themselves can be, as in the example of attraction, strikingly different in kind. Moving within 'a larger compass of Nature', the true philosopher applies the same process of interpretive comparison that, in the *New Theory of Vision*, Berkeley had argued was an integral part of all our sensory experiences. The constant 'predictions' we make at every moment of our waking lives, the philosopher can make 'at very great distances of time and place' (II.87).

In *Siris* Berkeley repeats, almost verbatim, the theory of scientific investigation first formulated in the *Principles* more than thirty years before:

There is a certain analogy, constancy, and uniformity in the phenomena or appearances of nature, which are a foundation for general rules: and these are a grammar for the understanding of nature, or that series of effects in the visible world whereby we are enabled to foresee what will come to pass in the natural course of things.   (V.120)

But *Siris* goes further than the *Principles* and illustrates precisely what Berkeley means by this analogy; as an essay, it is able to portray the mental processes involved in his method of exploring nature. Berkeley shows us analogical induction arising naturally from his own random observations. As we have seen, in the early pages of *Siris*, when discussing the curative properties of tar, he recalls a remark from Evelyn's *Sylva*: 'that stems of trees, smeared over with tar, are preserved thereby from being hurt by the envenomed teeth of goats' (V.34–5). This correspondence between the health of humans and that of plants is not pursued at this point, but left as a simple coincidence. The notion crops up again, however, a few pages later in the simile Berkeley chooses to describe trees rich in tar. Old fir trees, he remarks, 'like old men, being unable to perspire, and their secretory ducts obstructed, they are, as one may say, choked and stuffed with their own juice' (V.37). But chance figure of speech soon becomes mode of argument when Berkeley turns to plant physiology and seriously considers that 'wonderful similitude of analogy between the mechanism of plants and animals' (V.41–2):

Those who have examined the structure of trees and plants by microscopes have discovered an admirable variety of fine capillary tubes and vessels, fitted for several purposes, as the imbibing or attracting of proper nourishment, the distributing thereof through all parts of the vegetable, the discharge of superfluities, the secretion of particular juices. They are found to have ducts answering to the tracheae in animals, for the conveying of air; they have others answering to lacteals, arteries, and veins. They feed, digest, respire, perspire, and generate their kind, and are provided with organs nicely fitted for all those uses.   (V.41)

Notice the empirical detail with which Berkeley elaborates the analogy, taking time to mention each particular organ and function shared by plants and animals alike. In this passage he cites the work of Nehemiah Grew, whose discovery of capillaries in plants complemented, in botany, Harvey's famous discovery of the circulation of the blood. Berkeley proceeds to sketch for us the present status of Grew's analogy, remarking that some now deny the circulation of sap in plants. Most prominent among these dissenters was Stephen Hales, who had, albeit with considerable caution and respect, pointed out the fact that plants have nothing like a heart.[5] Hales had also described numerous experiments which cast the descent of sap in doubt and suggested instead that plants lose moisture through their leaves.

---

[5] *Statical Essays*, 2nd ed. (London: W. Innys *et al.*, 1731), Vol. I, p. 143. Hales was rector of Teddington and a friend of Pope.

Taking such objections into account, Berkeley shows the diffidence appropriate to an essayist:

I shall not take upon me to decide this controversy. Only I cannot help observing that the vulgar argument from analogy between plants and animals loseth much of its force, if it be considered that the supposed circulating of the sap, from the root or lacteals through the arteries, and thence returning, by inosculations, through the veins or bark-vessels to the root or lacteals again, is in no sort conformable or analogous to the circulation of the blood.   (V.43)

While this seems at first inconclusive, it soon becomes clear that Berkeley finds more food for thought in the circulation of sap. He proceeds to expand the analogy, suggesting that both plants and animals have lacteal glands, and even comparing bark to subcutaneous fat (V.44). Obviously in this open and exploratory frame of mind Berkeley is not willing to dismiss the analogy simply because it may fail in some particulars, and, moreover, seems to feel that in a doubtful case such as this we could do worse than let analogy guide our thoughts. Indeed, as his discussion returns to medical matters, Berkeley keeps this analogy in mind. Considering how his tar-water can work as a panacea, he wonders if scurvy, then a generic name for diseases which hindered the absorption of nourishment from the blood, might not 'contain the seeds and origin of almost all distempers' (V.62). Tar, as concentrated sap, is rich in the 'vegetable soul' of the tree, which, in the analogy, corresponds to the '*vis vitae*' of the blood. Berkeley comes to imply that by ingesting these volatile acids found in tar we may cure all scurvies, replenishing the cleansing and animating spirits in our own blood.

The plant/animal analogy suggests a further subject for reflection to the inquirer of *Siris*, namely the nature of this *vis vitae* that is shared by plants and animals. And this line of investigation proceeds under the guidance of a second and more far-reaching analogy, that of microcosm to macrocosm. Again Berkeley shows the analogy emerging naturally from the course of his meditation, rather than being a consciously chosen and imposed method:

The *calidum innatum*, the vital flame or animal spirit in man, is supposed the cause of all motions in the several parts of his body . . . In the same sense, may not fire be said to have force, to operate and agitate the whole system of the world, which is held together and informed by one presiding mind?   (V.83–4)

Berkeley's tentative proposal of this ancient conceit in the form of a question encourages us to weigh the analogy before he proceeds to enumerate the particular phenomena wherein the *calidum innatum* of the macrocosm manifests itself – in earthquakes and in the focus of a burning glass. Here again analogy lights the way for Berkeley's meditator. From the corresponding roles of life-giving aether in the human body and in the corporeal world, Berkeley is led naturally to see that the world, like man, must have some animating intelligence. As with the plant/animal analogy, Berkeley is careful to test his comparison with natural phenomena. And again Berkeley candidly explores the limitations of his analogy, admitting, for example, that God is not sentient in the way the human soul is sentient, for this implies passivity (V.82 and 134).[6] But again such contrary features, once recognized, are outweighed by the correlations and harmonies suggested to the mind by the natural world.

As he works through these two inductive analogies with the reader, Berkeley is self-conscious, drawing attention to his method and pointing out in each case its strengths and weaknesses. Moreover he cites authorities both ancient and modern to testify to the universality of this way of thought. Of these, the modern authorities show that inductive analogy was a recognized method of scientific inquiry in Berkeley's day. In the *Novum Organum* Bacon had listed it among the prerogative instances or sorts of natural evidence. 'Analogies' or 'Physical Resemblances', Bacon admitted, are not much use for his central task of determining the natural kinds of the world, but analogy does have a place in those more advanced studies which lead the experimenter to comprehend the unity and configuration of the whole.[7] As *Siris* makes plain, the plant/animal analogy was a central issue for botanical research in the early eighteenth century.[8] Even Newton's *Opticks*, with its concentration on hard empirical evidence, gave an explicit if limited role to analogy. In the second book, Newton advances his theory '*Of the permanent Colours of natural Bodies, and the Analogy between them and the Colours of thin transparent Plates*'. And although he does not permit himself to develop this analogy for the reader, Newton hints suggestively at a likeness between musical scales and the patterns adopted by dispersed light.[9] In the *Conduct of the Understanding* Locke recognized that analogy plays a central if often implicit role in 'happy and successful Experiments',[10] and in Book IV of the *Essay*, he shows how it is the means by which the natural philosopher can exceed the limits of sensory evidence. Our ideas of 'the manner of operation in most parts of the Works of Nature' are extrapolations from experience. From the heat of bodies rubbed together 'we have reason to think, that what we call Heat and Fire, consists in a violent agitation of the imperceptible minute parts of the burning matter'. Locke goes on to argue that the existence of angels may be proved analogically from our perception of 'the several

---

[6] Newton had expressed similar reservations about this analogy at the end of the *Opticks* (p. 379).

[7] *Works*, Vol. IV, pp. 164–7.

[8] See Philip C. Ritterbush, *Overtures to Biology* (London: Yale University Press, 1964), pp. 58–67.

[9] *Opticks*, pp. 219, 110–11 and 186.

[10] *Some Thoughts on the Conduct of the Understanding* (n.p., 1741), p. 96.

ranks of Beings' in nature and how by 'gentle steps Things ascend upwards in degrees of Perfection'.[11]

This notion that we may reason analogically from the natural to the spiritual order became a central theme in eighteenth-century popular theology. Scientists like George Cheyne and apologists like Joseph Butler explored the harmony between these two worlds.[12] Berkeley himself had a prominent part in this developing discussion. In *Alciphron* he defended the validity of analogy from the human soul to God against Peter Browne's *Procedure, Extent, and Limits of Human Understanding*. But he had explored this analogy as early as 1713, in *Guardian* 62, wherein he reasons from physical to spiritual 'appetites' in order to prove the immortality of the human soul:

Shall every other passion be rightly placed by nature, and shall that appetite of immortality, natural to all mankind, be alone misplaced, or designed to be frustrated . . . In a word, shall the corporeal world be all order and harmony, the intellectual discord and confusion? He who is bigot enough to believe these things must bid adieu to that natural rule of *reasoning from analogy*; must run counter to that maxim of common sense, *That men ought to form their judgments of things unexperienced from what they have experienced.*   (VII.181–2)

Again, in *Guardian* 126, Berkeley likens the forces at work in the cosmos to those impelling the human soul:

And as the attractive power in bodies is the most universal principle which produceth innumerable effects, and is a key to explain the various phenomena of nature; so the corresponding social appetite in human souls is the great spring and source of moral actions.   (VII.227)[13]

Berkeley goes on to argue in this paper that if love and charity are, like gravity, natural laws, the selfish man must then be viewed as 'a sort of monster or anomalous production'. The analogy also provides 'a signal proof of the divinity of the Christian religion', because Christ's message of love is in accord with the presiding forces of the created universe. Berkeley's argument here is striking in the way it exceeds the simple elaborations of the cosmological argument offered by authors like Bentley and William Derham. In the *Guardian* Berkeley's analogies

[11] *Essay* (IV.xvi.12), pp. 665–6.
[12] E. R. Wasserman offers an overview of the discussion in 'Nature Moralized: The Divine Analogy in the Eighteenth Century', *ELH*, 20 (1953), 39–76. In particular, he traces the Shaftesburian ethical/natural strain of analogical argument and suggests its implications for poetry in the period.
[13] This paper may well have inspired George Cheyne's account of a spiritual cosmos driven by love; see *Philosophical Principles of Religion*, 2nd ed. (London: G. Strahan, 1715), p. 49. G. Bowles's study, 'Physical, Human and Divine Attraction in the Life and Thought of George Cheyne', *Annals of Science*, 31 (1974), 474–88, follows the course of the analogy through Cheyne's career.

permit him to go beyond proofs of the being and nature of God, to determine final causes. Berkeley makes specific applications of our knowledge of nature for the establishment of principles at work in the moral realm.

This powerful analogy between the natural and the spiritual pervades Berkeley's work. While immaterialism insisted that spirit and idea are fundamentally different in kind, it did not deny that their distinct realms are in harmony. The sensible world is God's language, an expression of his character and will. Donald Davie has shown in a number of articles how this analogy also surfaces in *Siris*.[14] He has noted how Berkeley's medical discussion elaborates a correlation between the spiritual and the physical, as when, for example, Berkeley suggests that 'the worst prison is the body of an indolent epicure, whose blood is inflamed by fermented liquors (Sect. 66) and high sauces, or rendered putrid, sharp and corrosive by a stagnation of the animal juices through sloth and indolence' (V.66). Davie also shows this metaphoric ambiguity at work when Berkeley applies adjectives to tar-water which suggest human qualities. Tar-water is 'grateful' (V.72), 'kindly' (V.73), 'congenial and friendly' (V.105), 'benign and comfortable' (V.106). Davie notes how Berkeley's botanical discussion often relies on the terms 'spirit' and 'soul' to name the vital essences in plants, words which have specific scientific meanings but which also inevitably suggest their more common spiritual denotations. This sort of word-play disturbs Davie, because it seems to violate Berkeley's professed dualism in which spirit and idea are radically different.[15] But is this such a radical change for Berkeley, who did, despite disclaimers, use physical terms to describe spirit in the *Principles*? In *Siris* he goes so far as to admit the inevitability of this practice: 'all speech concerning the soul is altogether, or for the most part, metaphorical' (V.89). Davie is right in noticing a freer and more frequent appeal to such metaphors in *Siris*, and in so doing touches on the change of genre that *Siris* involved for Berkeley: 'the work is a chain of reflections. And one could argue that it has its own logic, the logic not of philosophy but of poetry.'[16] *Siris*'s open, exploratory and intimate form allows Berkeley an ambiguous diction that a treatise would not permit. In fact Berkeley's suggestive metaphors serve the larger rhetorical purpose of the essay. When he speaks of a 'vegetable soul' captured in tar-water he is encourag-

---

[14] Davie discusses *Siris*'s metaphoric diction in 'Berkeley's Style in *Siris*', *Cambridge Journal*, 4 (1950–1), 427–33; 'Berkeley and "Philosophic Words" ', *Studies*, 44 (1955), 319–24; and *The Language of Science and the Language of Literature, 1700–40* (London: Sheed and Ward, 1963), pp. 50–9.

[15] 'Berkeley's Style in *Siris*', p. 429.

[16] 'Berkeley's Style in *Siris*', p. 432.

ing the reader to look beyond the merely 'philosophical' meaning to the spiritual. Ambiguity is part of *Siris*'s denial of easy knowledge, of its explicit uncertainty and challenging openness. Berkeley's expansive language asks us to engage in the larger analogical reading of the world that is the business of *Siris*.

Reading *Siris*, it is easy to see why inductive analogy appealed to Berkeley, and why he felt moved to illustrate its method in an essay. Inductive analogy obeys the strictures immaterialism imposes on natural science, and yet still provides a heuristic mode of inquiry. First, in his far-reaching analogies Berkeley can preserve the integrity of the sensory object as complete and significant in itself. *Siris* does not elaborate a hypothetical supra-sensory corporeal reality in order to account for the world of sense. Second, Berkeley's analogies encourage a breadth of vision. Seeking similarities between disparate entities, Berkeley crosses the boundaries between natural kinds and between branches of learning. In contrast to the specialist tendency of conventional induction, analogy depicts the diversity and harmony of all nature. Bacon had advised that the scientist should, for the most part, concentrate on efficient mechanical causes, and Berkeley's violation of this rule caused much consternation amongst the natural philosophers who responded to *Siris*. Stephen Hales tactfully attempted to bring tar-water back down to earth in a series of experiments measuring the solubility of various tars.[17] The prominent physiologist Malcolm Flemyng criticized Berkeley for 'linking Heaven and Earth',[18] but the anonymous pamphlet *Anti-Siris* was most direct of all:

'Tis in Truth a Chain, but such a one as no Man ere saw wove together in Print before. 'Tis Law, Gospel, Physics, Metaphysics, every Thing but what it should be . . . he travels but a very little Way in his Work, when he forgets Tar, and overlooks Physicians, to fall foul on all the modern Philosophers, but particularly on his own Countryman, the great *Newton*.[19]

Berkeley's rejection of this modern attitude is of long standing. The very form of the *Principles*, with its transition from empirical to spiritual evidence, insisted on the unity of human knowledge and the inextricability of faith and reason, of the human and the divine. In *Siris*, as in *The Guardian*, Berkeley uses analogy to bring the study of the world to bear on the moral and the spiritual.

As Berkeley had made clear in the *De Motu*, the greatest error in modern mechanical philosophy was its violation of the metaphysical principle that spirit is the only cause. Despite his apparent attribution of secondary

[17] *An Account of Some Experiments and Observations on Tar-Water* (London: R. Manby and H.S. Cox, 1745).
[18] *A Proposal for the Improvement of the Practice of Medicine . . . [with] some Remarks on a Book entitled* Siris, 2nd ed. (Hull: G. Ferraby, 1748), p. 142.
[19] *Anti-Siris: or, English Wisdom Exemplifi'd* (London: M. Cooper, 1744), p. 32.

causes in *Siris*, Berkeley still holds to this principle and takes some care
to explain his double-talk:

We have no proof, either from experiment or reason, of any other agent or
efficient cause than mind or spirit. When, therefore, we speak of corporeal agents
or corporeal causes, this is to be understood in a different, subordinate, and
improper sense.   (V.83)

Berkeley goes on to say that he indulges in this 'gross and popular' talk
in order to be understood, and insists again that whatever seems to act in
the world is, in fact, only God's 'instrument'. But we soon learn that
'instrument' itself only crudely conveys Berkeley's meaning, for instruments are very different things for God from what they are for us: 'Without instrumental and second causes there could be no regular course of
nature. And without a regular course, nature could never be understood'
(V.84–5). The apparent physical causes in the world are instituted for
our sakes; they form the established grammar of the language God speaks
through our senses. God does not need these instruments; we do. But at
the same time, Berkeley shows us in *Siris* how God uses these arbitrary
and symbolic causes, not just to create an environment in which our
limited beings can function, but also to teach us about the true and only
Cause at work in nature. Analogy helps us to transcend apparent causes
to find God. As Berkeley works out before us his two natural analogies
of plant to animal and microcosm to macrocosm, he slowly discovers a
central sign, a recurrent and significant element which he identifies as
aether. Aether is that vital principle which manifests itself in the curative
and volatile spirit of tar, in the vital heat of the human body, and in the
solar energy which seems to nourish the whole world. This common
essence is characterized by 'purity, lightness, subtlety, and mobility'
(V.89). Though itself invisible, aether is no occult element, but clearly
known in nature through its qualities of heat and light.

However arcane and alchemical this sort of elemental explanation
might seem today, it was far from such to the eighteenth-century
reader. In the queries appended to the second English edition of the
Opticks, Newton wondered if a universal aetherial medium might be
the cause of the diffraction of light, or even, by virtue of an inherent
'elastic' or repulsive force, of gravity itself. Newton likewise saw that
aether could be the medium through which mind and matter interact.
A little later Boerhaave developed his complementary theory of a pure
elemental fire which, like Newton's aether, permeated all things, was
elastic, and was directly responsible for keeping the universe in motion.
Berkeley invokes and conflates Newton's aether and Boerhaave's fire
in *Siris*, and he was not alone in so doing. In his recent study of aether
theories in the early part of the century, P. M. Heimann argues that

'by the 1740's natural philosophers had developed dualistic theories in which *"elemental fire"* was considered to be an ethereal substance "endowed with active powers distinct from those of other matter" '.[20] The aether Berkeley discloses through analogy, was, both for himself and for his contemporaries, a recognized natural element suspected to be the prime efficient cause by which God animates the world.

In the latter pages of *Siris*, Berkeley explores the true meaning of the sensible language that God has instituted in nature. Berkeley reads, through analogy, 'the bright and lively signatures of a divine Mind, operating and displaying itself in light and fire throughout the world' (V.89). Aether is not God, nor truly active, but is a sign of the true cause; as the least corporeal of the elements, aether 'leads us naturally and necessarily to an incorporeal spirit or agent' (V.135). In remarking on the important place fire has in the imagery of all religions, including Christianity, Berkeley interprets the meaning of the highest link in the chain: 'The cleansing quality, the light and heat of fire, are natural symbols of purity, knowledge, and power' (V.93). The sensible world, if a dark mirror, is one in which we can glimpse the world of spirit.

Stephen Leo Carr, in an article entitled 'The Rhetoric of Argument in Berkeley's *Siris*', is disconcerted by Berkeley's distinction between true and apparent causes: 'Berkeley's disclaimer of this manner of speaking about physical causes points towards an ideal philosophic correctness, but he does not even try to enact such a standard.'[21] Carr interprets this contradiction, along with the tentative tone of *Siris*, as an expression of Berkeley's own dissatisfaction with his text. For Carr, 'This self-consciousness of *Siris*'s limitations suggests that its apparent method is really a rhetoric strategy.' That is, *Siris*'s medical, botanical, and chemical discussion is for Berkeley just a ploy for engrossing 'a stolid and worldly-minded audience', that he may, by the end of *Siris*, coax them into a 'purely logical philosophic inquiry'.[22] I disagree with Carr to the extent that, as I have argued, the method of inductive analogy seems both significant and viable for Berkeley. *Siris* depicts a speculative movement in which the empirical can reveal the spiritual. Why should Berkeley devote the bulk of *Siris* to a discussion that is, in his view, nothing more than bait for the reader? And why should the 'purely logical inquiry', purportedly Berkeley's goal in *Siris*, be just as tentative and inductive as the scientific discussion from which it grows?

There is, however, much that supports the general thrust of Carr's reading. Carr worries about the contradiction between Berkeley's own

[20] 'Ether and Imponderables', in *Conceptions of Ether*, ed. G. N. Cantor and M. J. S. Hodge (Cambridge: Cambridge University Press, 1981), p. 70.
[21] *University of Toronto Quarterly*, 51 (1981–2), 52.
[22] 'Rhetoric', pp. 54 and 58.

gradual method and the attitude of the Platonic thinkers cited at the end of *Siris*, who believe that the transition from the world of sense to the world of intellect demands a sharp rupture. Moreover, as Carr stresses, Berkeley does express concern about the worldly reader of *Siris*. But both these issues must be placed in the context of Berkeley's sense of his own task, and his larger view of the processes of learning:

> The perceptions of sense are gross; but even in the senses there is a difference. Though harmony and proportion are not objects of sense, yet the eye and the ear are organs which offer to the mind such materials by means whereof she may apprehend both the one and the other. By experiments of sense we become acquainted with the lower faculties of the soul; and from them, whether by a gradual (Sect. 275) evolution or ascent, we arrive at the highest. Sense supplies images to memory. These become subjects for fancy to work upon. Reason considers and judges of the imaginations. And these acts of reason become new objects to the understanding. In this scale, each lower faculty is a step that leads to one above it. And the uppermost naturally leads to the Deity, which is rather the object of intellectual knowledge than even of the discursive faculty, not to mention the sensitive. There runs a chain throughout the whole system of beings. In this chain one link drags another. The meanest things are connected with the highest. The calamity therefore is neither strange nor much to be complained of, if a low sensual reader shall, from mere love of the animal life, find himself drawn on, surprised and betrayed into some curiosity concerning the intellectual.
>
> (V.140)

Berkeley is conscious of the rhetorical impact of his work, that the reader may feel 'surprised and betrayed' at being 'drawn on' unsuspecting into a theological discussion. But this reflection also makes it clear that *Siris*'s early 'experiments of sense' are somehow different from the deceits of presentation that Berkeley practises in the *Principles*, where he intentionally concealed the theme of immaterialism until the reader's mind was engaged and prepared. For while Berkeley maintains in this section that the objects of sense and reason are distinct, he shows that they are not unconnected. Ruminations on nature do ultimately, indeed 'naturally', lead to God. The point, that Berkeley enforces with the gentlest irony, is that we should not feel 'betrayed' by *Siris*. The progress of the work, it turns out, is 'neither strange nor much to be complained of'.

In the section cited above, Berkeley provides a synopsis of the customary growth of the human mind from sense to reason, a progress which Locke had plotted out in large in Book II of his *Essay*. But here Berkeley emphasizes a correspondence between mind and world that Locke did not: parallel to the chain of being, Berkeley depicts a chain of human faculties. And he gives a significant role to 'fancy' or 'imagination' as the faculty which links sense and reason, transforming sensible objects into rational objects. *Siris*'s study in analogy is, of course, a study in the imagination's initial daring attempts to bring harmony to the world of sense. In this passage Berkeley shows that the form of *Siris* is a mirror of the natural processes of the acquisition of knowledge. Carr's response to the form of *Siris* misses the complex repercussions of Berkeley's chosen genre. The tentative tone that Carr reads as an admission of doubt is the appropriate voice of the essayist. The text is a natural history of the mind of the writer, an enactment of the birth of the intellect, of the slow but natural progress from sense to reason. Most important, our relation to the text is not that of victim, so much as that of participant. As this passage makes clear, the purpose of his text is not didactic but exploratory and, ultimately, hortatory. *Siris* does not, in its latter pages, lay down metaphysical principles, but throughout strives to challenge the reader's mind, to awaken 'some curiosity concerning the intellectual'.

The complex interaction of the intellectual and the sensible is a recurrent theme in *Siris*. In the passage above, as elsewhere, Berkeley depicts a balance in which the mind and the world each have a part to play in the attainment of knowledge: 'Though harmony and proportion are not objects of sense, yet the eye and ear are organs which offer to the mind such materials by means whereof she may apprehend both the one and the other.' While he recognizes this interdependence, Berkeley warns against being content with sense alone (V.124). He also notes that the world is aggregate in character, in contrast to the simplicity and unity of mind. On this point Berkeley cites Aristotle and Themistius, who believed that the mind 'maketh each thing to be one' and 'by virtue of her simplicity, conferreth simplicity upon compounded beings' (V.160). This central function of mind is the central task of *Siris*. Analogy, unlike limited induction, attempts to disclose the implicit unity of the universe, making the many one.[23]

Berkeley captures this difficult balance of the sensible and the intellectual in the title of *Siris*. '*Reflections and Inquiries*' epitomizes the wayward and tentative progress of a mind turning alternately inward upon itself and outward to the world around it. Likewise Berkeley points to the tension between an imposed order and an organic form in the work when he claims that his subjects are at once 'connected together' and 'arising One from Another'. This tension is crystallized in Berkeley's choice of '*Siris: A Chain*' as his presiding metaphor. Throughout the work he makes extensive use of the ancient conceit of the chain of being, and applies it to the work itself, which effectively climbs from the lowest to highest

---

[23] Lester S. King appreciates this feature of eighteenth-century medical theory, in *The Philosophy of Medicine: The Early Eighteenth Century* (Cambridge, Mass.: Harvard University Press, 1978), p. 256: 'Sound analogy penetrates, somehow, to the essence of things and takes as its point of departure certain properties that share in the essence. An observer tries to identify particular features that relate to the essence; these he follows with the eye of reason until he reaches the more central core, deeper and more essential.'

being. But all the while, Berkeley quietly nurtures a subversive strain of related images. He describes aether as a '*vinculum*' (V.97), a chemical 'fetter' which binds other elements together, but he also says that aether is often 'imprisoned, and detained in gross bodies' (V.100). Picking up on his earlier account of the epicure's body as a prison for a tortured soul, Berkeley goes on to invoke 'the ligaments that chain the soul down to the earth' (V.140). Then he recites the Platonists' descriptions of the mind as eager 'to disengage and emancipate herself from those prejudices and false opinions that so straitly beset and cling to her' (V.145). In these struggles towards the light of truth, however, 'she is soon drawn backward and depressed by the heaviness of the animal nature to which she is chained' (V.154). By the end of *Siris* the image of the title is fully laden. 'Chain' implies both the order and connection that mind can bring to the world, and the world's painful restraint on the innate aspirations of the mind. The image remains, none the less, an appropriate title for *Siris*, which seeks not to resolve, but simply to narrate the tension between world and mind. The essayist recounts his own slow and cautious labour to exceed the sensory. *Siris* dramatizes the difficulty and uncertainty, but also the ultimate possibility, of discovering God in nature.

13

The hoary maxims of the ancients

One of the most disconcerting features of *Siris*'s rhetoric is its frequent citation of the works of other philosophers. At first such authorities are few and scattered. In the course of his initial botanical discussion Berkeley only occasionally invokes the opinions of such experts as Theophrastus, Evelyn and Ray. These authorities do not seem inappropriate because, like Berkeley, they are men of science with first-hand experience of the subject. But as *Siris* moves towards metaphysics and theology, the authorities come thicker and faster until the discourse virtually proceeds in terms of the opinions and writings of other thinkers. *Siris* becomes like Burton's *Anatomy of Melancholy*, a cento or a patchwork of learned opinions. That Berkeley should adopt so cumbersome and antiquated a mode of exposition is disturbing. It moved G. J. Warnock to dismiss *Siris* as 'Gothic',[1] and even a sympathetic reader like Jessop longs for the 'clean, stripped, athletic pages of the *Principles*' (V.18). Berkeley's reliance on the argument from authority is stranger still in that it had been loudly and almost universally denounced in the seventeenth century as a feature of outmoded, scholastic learning. The most vociferous critics had been the apologists for the new natural philosophy. One of the first critics of *Siris*, the physician James Jurin, derides Berkeley for borrowing two-thirds of his material from other authors: 'the *Ipse dixit* of your Lordship will not, with men of Science, stand against Experience and well-founded Knowledge'.[2] While Bacon had argued that scholastic science was too speculative and dogmatic, Thomas Browne showed in his *Pseudodoxia Epidemica* that the little empirical evidence it had to work with was inaccurate.[3] But the *ipse dixit* was judged as dangerous for modern epistemology as for natural philosophy. In fact, two of the most thorough critics of the

---

[1] *Berkeley* (Oxford: Blackwell, 1952), p. 223.
[2] *A Letter to the Right Reverend the Bishop of Cloyne* (London: J. Robinson, 1744), p. 18.
[3] Browne remarks (p. 19) that 'of all men a Philosopher should be no swearer', and Glanvill (*Scepsis*, p. 106) agrees with Malebranche that the scholastics use their memories and not their judgments: ' 'Tis better to own a Judgment, though but a *curta supellex* of coherent notions; than a *memory*, like a Sepulchre, furnished with a load of broken and discarnate bones.'

argument from authority were the two thinkers most influential on Berkeley's early career – Locke and Malebranche.

In Book II of his *Recherche de la Vérité*, Malebranche made the objection, by that time something of a commonplace, that there is no good reason to suppose the ancients had a better purchase on truth than the moderns:

On ne considère pas qu'Aristote, Platon, Epicure étoient hommes commes nous, & de même espèce que nous: & de plus, qu'au tems où nous sommes, le monde est plus âgé de deux mille ans, qu'il a plus d'expérience, qu'il doit être plus éclairé.[4]

Both Locke and Malebranche took the sheer diversity of human opinion as further evidence against learned authority. In their eyes philosophical history was no better than political history – a long tale of discord, with no apparent progress and no tradition of truth. Locke returned to this theme several times in Book IV of the *Essay*, eventually satirizing those gullible thinkers who trust the writings of the ancients:

The Tenet has had the attestation of reverend Antiquity, it comes to me with the Pass-port of former Ages, and therefore I am secure in the Reception I give it: other Men have been, and are of the same Opinion, (for that is all is said,) and therefore it is reasonable for me to embrace it. A Man may more justifiably throw up Cross and Pile for his Opinions, than take them up by such Measures.[5]

In their respective discussions of learned authority, both Locke and Malebranche drew a strong distinction between meditation and reading. For Locke, learning is quite certainly a matter of personal experience and reflection, and he warns us that 'we may as rationally hope to see with other Mens Eyes, as to know by other Mens Understandings'.[6] Likewise his Baconian sense of the manifold abuses of language made him suspicious of book-learning. In his essay 'Of Study' Locke argues that reading can, at best, only provide the raw materials of the edifice of knowledge, an edifice which is planned and built by meditation alone.[7] Malebranche went farther, suggesting that our minds actually atrophy as we pore over the tomes of the ancients. The prime reason we rely on the ancients and devote ourselves to reading is 'la paresse naturelle des hommes, qui ne veulent pas se donner la peine de méditer'.[8] If we wish to read constructively, Malebranche advises that we first consult the book's table of contents and then carefully formulate our own thoughts on the topics to be handled. Only then will we be in a position to guard against the imposition of false learning. But as for uncritical and unprepared readers, 'plus ils ont de lecture, plus leur esprit devient foible &

---

[4] *Œuvres Complètes*, ed. André Robinet *et al.* (Paris: J. Vrin, 1958–70), Vol. I, p. 283.
[5] *Essay* (IV.xx.17), pp. 718–19.
[6] *Essay* (I.iv.23), p. 101.
[7] *Educational Writings*, p. 422.
[8] *Œuvres*, Vol. I, p. 281.

confus'.[9] For Malebranche, the scholastic mind is calcified through its own inactivity and confounded by a jumble of unassimilated opinions.

Having determined, then, that the argument from authority is most certainly invalid, Locke and Malebranche proceed to show that it was never employed as an argument in the first place. It is, they decide, a rhetorical strategy adopted by feeble-minded academics to make their writings seen impressive. According to Malebranche, the scholastics praise Plato and Aristotle in order to enhance their own *ethoi*, borrowing some of their glory while creating the impression of great learning. In his *Essay*, Locke reveals a more dangerous rhetorical strategy at work when he styles authority the '*Argumentum ad Verecundiam*' – the argument to shamefacedness.[10] Locke argues that authorities are employed in a philosophical text to cow the timid reader into an intellectual submission. The scholastic never encourages us to ponder whether or not Aristotle's dicta are true; he only dares us to disagree with the great thinker, and by implication, with his own book. In sum, then, Locke and Malebranche seem to agree that the citation of authorities is a means of discouraging reflective reading, a strategy for ensuring a bland and uncritical receptivity in the reader's mind.

Berkeley had many specific objections to the writings of Locke and Malebranche, but in this matter of authority he seems in agreement with his predecessors. His early books never use this form of argument, and in fact, in the Introduction to the *Principles*, he joined Locke and Malebranche in mocking the schoolman's submission on hearing the words '*Aristotle hath said it*':

And this effect may be so instantly produced in the minds of those who are accustomed to resign their judgment to the authority of that philosopher, as it is impossible any idea of his person, writings, or reputation should go before.

(II.38)

Here Berkeley seems to agree that the purpose of the scholastic's authorities is rhetorical rather than argumentative, inducing a deferential attitude without presenting a reasonable proof. And, like Locke and Malebranche, Berkeley holds that the schoolman is a perfect example of one who is content with words rather than ideas.

How can the author of these modern sentiments write at the end of his career a tome so apparently scholastic in its method as *Siris*? Clearly, if we are to read in *Siris* more than evidence of senility, we must overcome the obstacle of its disconcerting style and examine how and speculate why Berkeley turns to authorities:

---

[9] *Œuvres*, Vol. I, p. 286.
[10] *Essay* (IV.xvii.19), p. 686. Not surprisingly, Locke does not note here that he borrows his terminology from Aristotle (*Topica* 156b).

If we may credit Plutarch, Empedocles thought aether or heat to be Jupiter. Aether by the ancient philosophers was used to signify promiscuously sometimes fire and sometimes air. For they distinguished two sorts of air. Plato, in the *Timaeus*, speaking of air, saith there are two kinds, the one more fine and subtle, called aether, the other more gross, and replete with vapours. This aether or purer medium seems to have been the air or principle from which all things, according to Anaximenes, derived their birth, and into which they were back again resolved at their death. Hippocrates, in his treatise *De Diaeta*, speaketh of a fire pure and invisible; and this fire, according to him, is that which, stirring and giving movement to all things, causes them to appear, or, as he styles it, come into evidence, that is, to exist, every one in its time, and according to its destiny.

(V.87–8)

Notice first that Berkeley is careful to make us aware that he is quoting others. Indeed, he seems unnecessarily diligent in this, not only taking care to identify his source-texts, but also introducing qualifying clauses like 'according to him' or 'as he styles it'. And the whole passage is prefaced with 'if we may credit Plutarch', a shrewd reservation about the integrity of the *De placitis philosophorum* and one which warns us that some of Berkeley's material is second-hand to begin with. The effect of all this caution is to make it clear that in each case he is doing no more than reciting the opinion of another author. We are given no indication that Berkeley actually holds or even favours any of these views; instead it seems as if he is just recalling each opinion for consideration. Notice also the density of authorities here: four in this brief paragraph alone. In this extremely crowded forum, Berkeley's thinkers seem to lose any privileged status. It is as if he is not concerned about the quality so much as the quantity of opinions he can pack into his prose. Each thinker is handled tersely, sometimes only barely mentioned. Nor are they accompanied by any of that fulsome and uncritical veneration that so disgusted Malebranche about the scholastic commentators. At the same time Berkeley interprets his sources with caution. It only 'seems' that Anaximenes' 'air' is the same thing as Plato's 'aether'.

So on a closer examination of *Siris* we can find nothing of the authorial bullying or the magisterial tone that Locke and Malebranche attributed to the arguer who relies on authorities. In fact, while this paragraph cites four authorities, it fails to apply them – there is no explicit theme in support of which all this learning has been gathered. Berkeley himself does not venture on to the field, but leaves us to try to see the point, and the point is not particularly clear. True, Empedocles, Plato, Anaximenes and Hippocrates all seem to be talking about roughly the same thing, about some sort of fire/aether/air element. But is this aether Anaximenes' seminary of things, or Hippocrates' great cause, or even God, as Empedocles seems to suggest? Berkeley doesn't tell us. We are left puzzling as to what we are to make of these extremely speculative and suggestive, but ultimately unresolved statements. And as we read on in *Siris* no simple answer emerges. Berkeley simply proceeds to cite more authorities, to note what Aristotle and Galen and even Virgil say about aether, to recall what the ancient Egyptians thought, to show the importance of fiery aether in the holy books of the Chinese and the Persians, and finally to invoke Scripture itself, wherein 'God is more than once said to be a consuming fire' (V.94). And after many pages, Berkeley is only willing to make the following summary:

We have seen that in the most remote ages and countries, the vulgar as well as the learned, the institutions of lawgivers as well as the reasonings of philosophers, have ever considered the element of fire in a peculiar light, and treated it with more than common regard, as if it were something of a very singular and extra-ordinary nature. Nor are there wanting authors of principal account among the moderns who entertain like notions concerning fire, especially among those who are most conversant in that element, and should seem best acquainted with it.

(V.95)

Sure enough, Berkeley now proceeds to cite the views of numerous moderns, of Homberg and Boerhaave and Newton, on the nature of fiery aether, revealing that they too treat this element 'with more than common regard'.

In this accumulative process, Berkeley compiles the sayings of his authorities not as truths but as discrete and unassimilated pieces of evidence. He explains this himself at one point:

The displeasure of some readers may perhaps be incurred by surprising them into certain reflections and inquiries for which they have no curiosity. But perhaps some others may be pleased to find a dry subject varied by digressions, traced through remote inferences, and carried into ancient times, whose hoary maxims (Sects. 298, 301), scattered in this essay, are not proposed as principles, but barely as hints to awaken and exercise the inquisitive reader, on points not beneath the attention of the ablest men.   (V.157)

Here Berkeley casts his authorities as part of his essay's excursive and tentative project. *Siris* begins as a natural history, but as it moves from tar to metaphysics, its style and method do not change. Its authorities are presented impartially. Like his random facts on tar, they are intentionally undigested, the raw material of induction. Again the result is an extremely involving text, one that demands that we determine the order and meaning of the data that Berkeley scatters before us. It is up to us to weigh Empedocles against Plato, and decide how far, and in what ways, each is right. The effect of *Siris*'s teasing rhetoric proves to be quite the opposite of that deadening of the mind that Malebranche associates with the reading of ancient maxims. Berkeley intends that his authorities should 'awaken and exercise the inquisitive reader'.

The question still remains why Berkeley should have chosen to revive a type of argument so long outmoded and so vigorously rejected by his own philosophical tradition. And why, at the same time, does Berkeley transform this argument into something that neither Locke nor Malebranche seemed able to imagine: authorities that are not, apparently, authoritative? Part of the answer lies, perhaps, in the rhetoric of his earlier writings. Although he never bolstered his earlier arguments with learned authorities, Berkeley's early works do reflect a consciousness of the power and influence of the philosophical text. Each of his major writings invokes another text against which it can argue: the *Principles* sets itself against Locke's *Essay*, the *Three Dialogues* distinguishes its immaterialism from Malebranche's theory of seeing all things in God, and *Alciphron* attacks the writings of Shaftesbury, Mandeville and the free-thinkers. In each case Berkeley establishes some anti-authority, some mistaken book against which his own work stands as a much-needed corrective. One could in fact plot Berkeley's career as a personal battle of the books, wherein he tilts with the great body of deistical and materialist writing emerging in his generation. Moreover he was thoroughly aware that contemporary British philosophy, despite its abjuration of learned authority, was none the less setting up its own sages. Locke's *Essay*, for example, simply replaces Plato and Aristotle with Boyle and 'the admirable Mr. Newton'. The anti-Newtonianism which emerges in almost all Berkeley's writings is a reaction to the near-deification of that thinker by his contemporaries. In *De Motu* his attack on Newtonian physics begins with the warning that 'no one's authority ought to rank so high as to set a value on his words and terms unless they are found to be based on clear and certain fact' (IV.31). Likewise the *Analyst* warns against the 'undue authority' assumed by mathematicians in general, and Halley and Newton in particular. Berkeley's stated plan in this work is to question mathematics with that same freedom assumed by these mathematicians when they question religion, 'to the end that all men may see what right you have to lead, or what encouragement others have to follow you' (IV.65). In these writings Berkeley consciously aims at curbing the influence of the most powerful philosophical texts of his day.

Siris is a fitting conclusion to Berkeley's life-long challenge to modern authority, for it clarifies Berkeley's view of the role of philosophical literature, both ancient and modern, in learning. First, he makes it clear in *Siris* that by celebrating the ancients he is simply trying to restore a balance; we should attend to ancient and modern alike. Many of the authorities cited are modern. Berkeley repeatedly traces the genealogy of certain ideas from the very origins of literature, through the Egyptians and the Greeks, to his own day. Sydenham is shown to agree with Hippocrates. We even learn that there is much in Newton which is in concert with the central conceptions of Aristotle and Plato. If *Siris* as an essay denies us a direct and systematic proof, it does reveal a consensus of learned thought. It may not present us with a lucid definition of aether or a clear account of its place in nature, but we do learn that all ages and cultures agree in giving it a central role. Berkeley displays in *Siris* what Locke and Malebranche had denied, a tradition of truth.

By tracing the tradition of Western thought Berkeley is able to show that the atheistical materialism resurgent in his own day is an aberration. Moreover, he implies that this diversion from truth can be corrected by broader philosophical reading. In a passage near the end of *Siris*, Berkeley laments the decline of the study of ancient philosophy:

> It might very well be thought serious trifling to tell my readers that the greatest men had ever a high esteem for Plato; whose writings are the touchstone of a hasty and shallow mind; whose philosophy has been the admiration of ages; which supplied patriots, magistrates, and lawgivers to the most flourishing States, as well as fathers to the Church, and doctors to the Schools. Albeit in these days the depths of that old learning are rarely fathomed; and yet it were happy for these lands if our young nobility and gentry, instead of modern maxims, would imbibe the notions of the great men of antiquity. But, in these free-thinking times, many an empty head is shook at Aristotle and Plato, as well as at the Holy Scriptures. And the writings of those celebrated ancients are by most men treated on a foot with the dry and barbarous lucubrations of the Schoolmen.   (V.151)

Berkeley goes on to say that British politicians could do worse than turn to Plato to learn a little honest statecraft, and that there they might find an instructive image of a poorly-run nation. He then remarks 'whoever has a mind may see it in page 78 of the second tome of Aldus's edition of Plato's work' (V.152). If we reach for our Aldus we find Socrates' parable from the *Republic* of a ship without a pilot – a satiric image of Berkeley's England where party had come to mean more than integrity. Berkeley's suggestion here is as instructive as it is amusing. He sends us off to discover Plato at his most witty and pertinent, showing us truly how far Plato is from the 'dry and barbarous lucubrations of the Schoolmen'. More important, Berkeley encourages us here to do exactly what he has been advocating, to read the ancients. This amusing ploy reveals something of the implicit purposes of *Siris*. In its innumerable concise synopses of thinkers and their books, *Siris* is a great subject index to ancient and modern philosophy. Laying before us tantalizing snippets of books, it is constantly turning outwards to the texts it draws from, encouraging us to head for our library shelves and find out more.

In all this, Berkeley recognizes something that Locke and Malebranche missed in their attacks on learned authority, namely that the processes of reading are fundamental to learning. While *Siris* displays a mind exploring the world through analogy, so it shows that same mind sifting the books it has read for some guiding themes. While Berkeley had never appealed to authorities in his more didactic writings, he had always insisted on the importance of reading for the growth of the mind. In *Guardian* No. 62, which defends the universities, Berkeley insisted that ancient literature remain the core of the curriculum. And we have seen how at the end of *Alciphron* Crito reasserts the importance of the ancients in modern university education (III.329). In an age when most undergraduates still experienced learned texts largely through extracts read in lectures and synopses passed from student to student, Berkeley set a priority on building university libraries.[11] In 1733, when many of the subscribers to the Bermuda project refused Berkeley's offer to return their donations, he took the money and purchased a case of Latin quartos for Harvard library and 1,000 volumes for Yale (VIII.219–20). This latter gift included standard texts, both ancient and modern, in all the arts and sciences, and formed in itself the backbone of a good library. In 1748 Berkeley spent another fifty pounds on a gift to Harvard, this time of modern theological standards.[12] And when, in these last years, Berkeley discovered that his friend Johnson was founding King's College, later to become Columbia, he wrote 'Let the Greek and Latin classics be well taught. Be this the first care as to learning' (VIII.302).

Both Locke and Malebranche, with their emphases on meditation and sensory experience, were in danger of denying the role of literature in learning. Of course Berkeley concedes to Malebranche the importance of critical and reflective reading. In *Siris* his authorities are permitted only to provide the reader with 'hints'. And each text is carefully compared to other texts and so placed in the light of the larger tradition of learning in which it participates. But Berkeley recognizes at the same time that the mind mired in the 'vulgar habits of life' needs some 'tradition or teaching' which might excite the latent seeds of knowledge (V.154). As he was so fond of pointing out, free-thinking proved, more often than not, to be rambling and incoherent thinking. For Berkeley the philosophical text serves as a guide as well as a source, a focus for criticism and reflection, a 'touchstone' against arcane thought.

The *Three Dialogues* and *Alciphron* both insist on the importance of language in learning. In the *Three Dialogues* Hylas and Philonous ulti-

---

[11] See L. S. Sutherland, 'The Curriculum', in *The Eighteenth Century*, Vol. V. of *The History of the University of Oxford*, ed. L. S. Sutherland and L. G. Mitchell (Oxford: Clarendon Press, 1986), p. 475.

[12] Berkeley's charities to American universities are summarized by Edwin S. Gaustad, *George Berkeley in America* (London: Yale University Press, 1979), pp. 83–9. For a catalogue of Berkeley's gift to Yale see 'Bishop Berkeley's Gift of Books in 1733', *The Yale University Library Gazette*, 8 (1933), 9–26. In a letter of 7 September 1731, Berkeley entrusts Johnson with a box of his own books to be given 'to such lads as you think will make the best use of them in the College, or to the School at Newhaven' (VIII.312).

mately manage to reach a common ground through constant appeals to the rules of logic and language. It ends in concord with both parties content with what has been achieved. In *Alciphron*, by contrast, Berkeley portrays a contest in which Alciphron and Lysicles prove incapable of holding to the public standards of discourse. Appropriately the dialogue ends with the disintegration of a community; the free-thinkers simply abandon the debate for the pleasures of London. This emphasis on the role of community in learning is, I believe, just as important for *Siris* as for Berkeley's dialogues. The essay as much as the dialogue is a genre which illustrates as it teaches, exemplifying the processes of the attainment of knowledge. If we leave *Siris* with any clear impression, it is that we are not alone in our ruminations. Through his revival of the argument from authority, Berkeley insists that we compare our own thoughts with the sayings of thinkers of all nations and ages. The harmony that Berkeley encourages us to discover in *Siris*'s myriad voices substantiates his claim that learning is a communal enterprise with goals shared by all. For Berkeley both reading and logical disputation are essential to this task, because in both the mind grows through an exploration of language, the common repository of human knowledge.

Conclusion

The Introduction to the *Principles* shows Berkeley grappling with fundamental problems of the functions of words. This early interest in language did not fade: in the Seventh Dialogue of *Alciphron*, written twenty years later, he addresses the same problems in much the same way. There is, however, a striking change of emphasis in this later discussion. In the Introduction to the *Principles* a Lockian view of language had predominated. There Berkeley presented his book as one in which 'ideas' were to have priority over language. He ended the Introduction by establishing a pact between writer and reader, promising to make as little use of words as he possibly could and exhorting us to 'endeavour to attain the same train of thoughts in reading, that I had in writing' (II.40). In the Seventh Dialogue of *Alciphron* these sentiments reappear, but now they are put in the mouth of the minute philosopher. Alciphron argues that there is neither knowledge nor valid communication without distinct 'ideas': 'He who annexeth a clear idea to every word he makes use of speaks sense; but where such ideas are wanting, the speaker utters nonsense' (III.287). Alciphron tells Euphranor, as Berkeley once told us, that in ideal discourse language permits the reader or listener to have 'the same train of ideas in his which was in the mind of the speaker or writer' (III.288). He proceeds to advocate the analytic method which Berkeley had applied so successfully to the language of material substance in Part I of the *Principles*: 'it is an allowed method to expose any doctrine or tenet by stripping them of the words, and examining what ideas are underneath, or whether any ideas at all' (III.289). The point of Alciphron's learned and thorough representation of Locke's views on language becomes clear when he turns this 'allowed method' on the language of spirit:

What is the clear and distinct idea marked by the word *grace*? . . . At the request of a philosophical friend, I did cast an eye on the writings he shewed me of some divines, and talked with others on this subject, but after all I had read or heard could make nothing of it, having always found, whenever I laid aside the word *grace*, and looked into my own mind, a perfect vacuity or privation of all ideas. And, as I am apt to think men's minds and faculties are made much alike, I suspect that other men, if they examined what they call grace with the same exactness and indifference, would agree with me that there was nothing in it but an empty name.   (III.290)

Where in the *Principles* Berkeley seemed to promote this method of stripping away words as an essential tool for philosophical inquiry, here it becomes a pretext for the free-thinkers' final assault on the language of faith.

Berkeley had a specific reason for this apparent change of attitude. Alciphron is voicing here one of the most effective arguments made by Collins against the existence of God. In the Introduction to *A Philosophical Inquiry concerning Human Liberty* Collins continued the process, begun in his *Discourse of Free-Thinking*, of eroding the significance of the key terms of Christian discourse. With Locke as his authority, Collins called for 'clear and distinct ideas' in religious writing:

When we use the term God, the Idea signify'd thereby, ought to be as distinct and determinate in us, as the Idea of a triangle or a square is, when we discourse of either of them; otherwise the term God, is an empty sound.[1]

Collins knew, of course, that *God* is not like *triangle*, and that it conjures up no clear mental image. The unstated consequence of his argument is that all religious discourse is invalid. While in the *Principles* Berkeley had recognized the insufficiency of Locke's theory of language with regard to spirit, Collins's insidious argument alerted him to the real danger it posed to his central religious principles, indeed to Scripture itself. In *Alciphron* Berkeley has realized that Locke's ideation theory of language has become the grounds on which 'religious assent or faith can be evidently shown in its own nature to be impracticable, impossible, and absurd'. Alciphron claims that his argument for the emptiness of words like *grace* is 'the primary motive to infidelity' and the very 'citadel and fortress' of modern atheism (III.286).

I have argued that in the *Principles* Berkeley may have relied on Locke's ideas-for-words doctrine because it facilitated his own attack on the abstract terms *matter* and *substance*. I have also shown how Berkeley had conceded by the end of the *Principles* that Locke's view was limited in a number of ways: that it did not seem to apply to spirit words, and that general terms did not name distinct abstract ideas but had a multiple reference to a variety of particular ideas. In the Seventh Dialogue Euphranor raises these points again in answering Alciphron, but by far the most substantial part of his reply is an elaboration of the second, rhetorical theory of language that Berkeley had sketched in sections 19

[1] *A Philosophical Inquiry concerning Human Liberty* (London: R. Robinson, 1717), p. 4. John Toland had similarly relied on Locke's terminology and methodological strictures to substantiate his attack on mysteries; see *Christianity not Mysterious* (n.p., 1696).

and 20 of the Introduction to the *Principles*. Euphranor reasserts Berkeley's claim that Book III of Locke's *Essay* is far too narrow in its strictures:

there may be another use of words besides that of marking and suggesting distinct ideas, to wit, the influencing our conduct and actions, which may be done either by forming rules for us to act by, or by raising certain passions, dispositions, and emotions in our minds. A discourse, therefore, that directs how to act or excites to the doing or forebearance of an action may, it seems, be useful and significant, although the words whereof it is composed should not bring each a distinct idea into our minds.   (III.292)

Avrum Stroll has argued that Berkeley uses this theory of emotive meaning 'primarily as an epistemological weapon – to attack the doctrine of abstract ideas as formulated by Locke'.[2] While this may be the case in the *Principles*, it is not true of *Alciphron*, where the emotive and instrumental functions of words are given much more extensive treatment. Euphranor's response to Alciphron describes not only a more comprehensive view of language, but one which is, in many of its features, fundamentally opposed to Locke's theory.

In the course of this study I have tried to respect the autonomy of each of Berkeley's four major philosophical texts and treat each as a distinct effort with its own context, theme and purpose. What has emerged is ample evidence of Berkeley's versatility as a writer. In these four works his material ranges from epistemology to ethics and from religion to natural philosophy. He is as effective in satire as in demonstration, as adept at aggressive polemics as at candid, philosophical 'reflection and inquiry'. And these four works display his mastery of the major philosophical genres – the treatise, the dialogue, and the essay. Yet despite the diversity of Berkeley's writings, some salient and distinguishing features of his rhetoric emerge, features which reflect his own questioning of the workings of language. In Euphranor's probing discussion of words and meaning it is possible to trace some fundamental concerns which have shaped and directed Berkeley's writing.

In the Seventh Dialogue, Alciphron follows Collins in concentrating on the problem of the speaker who uses words without ideas. In replying Euphranor shifts the focus of the discussion to the experience of the interpreter of language. Much language is designed to stimulate emotions, dispositions, and intentions in the reader or listener, and Berkeley's consciousness of this potential is very much evident in his own rhetoric. His writings reveal a concern to establish an effective relationship with the reader through his tone. Even in his early notebooks we

---

[2] *The Emotive Theory of Ethics*, University of California Publications in Philosophy, 28, no. 1 (1954), p. 24. In fact, for the third edition of *Alciphron* (1752) Berkeley eliminates the three sections in which Euphranor attacks abstract general ideas, making his emotive theory the initial as well as the most thorough response to Alciphron's ideas on language.

find him plotting to 'speak positively' to encourage the reader to think before he censures. Likewise Berkeley displays an almost dramatic awareness of his philosophical *personae*. The *Principles* makes a concerted effort to establish a common-sense *ethos* so that Berkeley might distance himself from the popular perception of the philosopher as abstruse and sceptical. Even more impressive is his anticipation of the reader's reactions to his texts. In the *Principles*, with its *prolepsis*, use of the second person and extended section of refutations, Berkeley gives us a voice in the text through which we can express our doubts and confusions about his principle. Berkeley's subsequent adoption of dialogue meant that he could develop this voice into a full character. In the *Three Dialogues* Hylas becomes our surrogate, expressing our initial difficulties with immaterialism and then showing us how these doubts are overcome. Likewise, the characters of Crito and Euphranor in *Alciphron* serve as exemplary figures, patterns of the staunch and assured Christians that Berkeley's dialogue encourages us to become. Even *Siris*, which adopts a radically different technique from Berkeley's earlier philosophical writings, is clearly designed with the readers' responses in mind. Its extremely subdued and self-effacing *persona* encourages our sympathetic participation in the processes of reflection and inquiry portrayed by the text. Berkeley is encouraging us to become 'inquisitive readers' as we follow the wanderings of his essayist's mind (V.157). In each work Berkeley gives us a role in the text through which he may shape our responses to his themes.

In describing the experiences of the reader or listener, Euphranor seems to accept emotive meaning as a regular and valid component of language. He lists a variety of affective states that may be stimulated by words – not just 'passions' and 'emotions', but 'dispositions' and even 'habits of mind' (III.292 and 307). Both these latter terms imply a relation to a conceived object or an inclination to a conceived action in which the cognitive and emotive converge.[3] In his own writing Berkeley seems to recognize that there is a significant emotive increment even to philosophical words. The *Principles* and the *Three Dialogues*, I have argued, are both designed to undermine our emotional attachments to a world based on *material substance*. In the *Principles* Berkeley employs both a demonic portrait of the infidel philosopher and Scriptural exhortation as affective levers to free us from our irrational commitment to *matter*. And the *Principles* opens with a recognition of the pain and perturbation that can

---

[3] Olscamp, in arguing that Berkeley was not an emotivist in his ethics, is careful to point out that Euphranor is not insisting in the Seventh Dialogue that ethical language is devoid of cognitive content. Berkeley is simply arguing that we need not cash such words in terms of ideas to feel their full emotive impact; see *Moral Philosophy*, pp. 132–6. Likewise David Berman stresses that a rational theism is naturally antecedent to faith in Berkeley's view; see 'Cognitive Theology and Emotive Mysteries in Berkeley's *Alciphron*', *Proceedings of the Royal Irish Academy*, 81 (1981), section C, 219–29.

accompany the most rigorous forms of philosophical inquiry, which end, all too often, 'in a forlorn scepticism' (II.25). In the *Three Dialogues* Berkeley uses Philonous's radically sceptical line of questioning to create just such feelings of pain and dislocation in order to make us receptive to the difficult truths of immaterialism. But in *Alciphron* Berkeley displays a full range of methods – irony, parody, *exempla* and satire – in which the affective and the argumentative co-operate. Our resentment and fear are skilfully aroused as Berkeley depicts the free-thinkers as enemies to religion and reason whose schemes threaten even to destroy our families.

Emotive language is clearly not an end in itself for Berkeley. It is an instrument for 'influencing our conduct'. It 'excites us to the doing or forbearance of an action'. Euphranor illustrates this when he explains the 'significance' of the doctrine of the Trinity:

> a man may believe the doctrine of the Trinity, if he finds it revealed in Holy Scripture that the Father, the Son, and the Holy Ghost, are God, and that there is but one God, although he doth not frame in his mind any abstract or distinct ideas of trinity, substance, or personality; provided that this doctrine of a Creator, Redeemer, and Sanctifier makes proper impression on his mind, producing therein love, hope, gratitude, and obedience, and thereby becomes a lively operative principle, influencing his life and actions, agreeably to that notion of saving faith which is required in a Christian.   (III.297)

Emotive language is valid as it becomes 'operative' in the hearer or reader, affecting his will and so influencing his conduct. Again, this sort of pragmatic meaning is a regular feature of Berkeley's own writing. His occasional and social writings – *Advice to the Tories, An Essay towards preventing the Ruin of Great Britain, The Querist* – all put their emotive appeals to good purpose, leaving us in no doubt as to our immediate responsibilities. But there is a strong hortative quality in Berkeley's philosophical books as well, where he demands that we come to terms with his ideas and act upon them. The *Principles'* aggressive mode of discourse insisted that we weigh the evidence ourselves and come to a decision for or against immaterialism in full knowledge of the consequences of such a decision. In both *Alciphron* and *Siris*, by contrast, Berkeley uses the open-endedness of his texts to effect his pragmatic purposes. The one specifically encourages us to engage in public debate with atheists, the other to continue to 'exercise and bestir ourselves' in the search for God in nature.

Berkeley does, however, qualify his approbation of affective language when he explains the significance of the doctrine of the Trinity. A 'proper impression' of the words depends on the reader's having quite specific emotional responses – 'love, hope, gratitude, and obedience' – and then acting appropriately on these feelings – 'agreeably to the notion of saving faith'. Likewise the term *grace*, which Alciphron dismissed as empty, is shown by Euphranor to be valid because it is 'a principle destructive of evil habits and productive of good ones' (III.296). It seems that the argument from utility, which was the basis of the *Principles'* *a posteriori* proof of immaterialism and Crito's defence of Christianity in *Alciphron*, is a prevailing principle in Berkeley's theory of language as well. In summarizing his argument, Euphranor insists again that words

> have other uses besides barely standing for and exhibiting ideas, such as raising proper emotions, producing certain dispositions or habits of mind, and directing our actions in pursuit of that happiness which is the ultimate end and design, the primary spring and motive, that sets rational agents at work.   (III.307)

This insistence that pragmatic language must promote the general good is perhaps the strongest belief shaping Berkeley's rhetoric. When, in 1710, he deplored the 'uselessness' of the *New Theory of Vision*, he accepted that his primary task as a writer was 'to reduce men to the study of religion and things useful' (VIII.31). True to his word, throughout the rest of his career his philosophical priorities are inseparable from his responsibilities as priest and patriot. The conclusion of the *Principles* exhorts us to read Scripture and to meditate on the central Christian principles substantiated by his epistemology. There is nothing but sincerity in his claim here that 'the consideration of *God*, and our *duty* . . . was the main drift and design of my labours' (II.113). These unimpeachable ends justify Berkeley's rhetoric. Each of his philosophical writings directs us to the central truths of Christianity, truths which Berkeley called 'salutary' in the belief that the happiness of the individual and of society as a whole depended on them.

Berkeley also recognized that the pragmatic, ethical ends of language are not achieved solely through our emotions. Euphranor shows that language can 'direct' as well as 'excite', that it is capable of 'forming rules for us to act by'. He uses simple sign systems, such as numbers and gambling counters, to demonstrate how signs can function as intellectual tools, facilitating 'the disposition and management of our affairs' (III.293). In reply to Alciphron's doubts about the word *grace*, Euphranor reflects that even a tried scientific term like *force* is difficult to realize in determinate ideas, and yet that without *force* we should be deprived of many 'useful truths' in physics and mechanics (III.295). Moreover, his criticism of Locke's theory of abstract ideas argues that general words function as universals, their multiple reference helping us to exceed the particularity of our ideas. Drawing these thoughts together, Euphranor suggests that in the acquisition of knowledge 'the mind makes her progress . . . by an apposite choice and skilful management of signs' (III.304). Here Berkeley defends language as the means of inquiry, the very medium of thought. Alciphron, following Locke, had insisted on a rift between words and ideas and lamented the ways in which language fails to represent our thought. Euphranor corrects this misconception when he concludes

that the true end of speech, reason, science, faith, assent, in all its different degrees, is not merely, or principally, or always, the imparting or acquiring of ideas, but rather something of an active operative nature, tending to a conceived good.   (III.307)

Speech, reason and faith are not so easily distinguished as Locke would have us believe. For Berkeley, language is the vehicle of faith and reason, and the means of the attainment of truth.

This conviction informs a final salient feature of Berkeley's writing, its logical formalism. In all his books Berkeley draws our attention to his adherence to the established rules of logic, the rules by which the mind effects 'a skilful management of signs'. In his notebooks Berkeley reveals that he perceived his immaterialist argument as an unshakable logical demonstration. Appropriately, the *Principles* is the antithesis of Locke's informal discursive mode. It is concerted and often syllogistic in argument, and its rigorous forensic form is divided according to the logical distinction of *a priori* from *a posteriori*. And it celebrates above all the primacy of the metaphysical principle, the truth embodied in language from which the philosopher must proceed. In Berkeley's subsequent writings this self-conscious advertisement of the nature and integrity of his own method turns to the teaching of logic itself. In the *Three Dialogues* Philonous's elenchus is celebrated for its capacity to establish the meanings of words and expose fallacy. Likewise in *Alciphron* the elenchus is presented as a model rational inquiry beside the sophistical and insubstantial techniques of the free-thinkers. Even in *Siris*, which seems at first almost wayward in its progress, we find Berkeley immersing us in a specific method of reasoning – inductive analogy. Analogy is taught as a way of 'reading' nature; natural phenomena themselves may be manipulated like signs to discover far-reaching truths. Moreover, by blending empirical observation with the 'hoary maxims of the ancients', Berkeley challenges our Lockian preconceptions about the tension between word and idea. *Siris* is his final and most thorough elaboration of the metaphor that had informed his epistemology from the beginning: that the sensible world is God's language.

Berkeley's rhetoric puts into practice his discoveries about the power of words to stir emotions and ultimately spur the reader into action. But his work also testifies to a belief in the integrity of language as the medium of philosophical inquiry, and in this conviction Berkeley is true to his vocations as educator and priest. Berkeley's experiences as a fellow of Trinity College and his aspirations as the tireless projector of a college for America find expression everywhere in his writing. The *Three Dialogues'* dramatization of disputation; *Alciphron*'s defence of the universities against the new curricula of the coffee-houses; *Siris*'s reliance on the writings of the ancients – all these confirm Berkeley's allegiance to a traditional education where language was still revered as the key to learning. But Berkeley's linguistic theory and rhetorical practice also display the priorities of an Anglican divine. It is as an expositor and defender of Scripture that Berkeley comes to explore the non-cognitive functions of language. It is in puzzling over how we understand Paul's promise of 'good things' that he discovers, in the Introduction to the *Principles*, that some language is primarily emotive. And, of course, Collins's attack on the language of Scripture motivates Berkeley's further explanation of instrumental signs. Finally, Berkeley's work everywhere celebrates the truth and power of Scripture. Biblical images and phrases pervade his style, while the *Principles*, the *Three Dialogues* and *Siris* all conclude with a confirmation of his favourite text, that in God 'we live, and move, and have our being'. Berkeley's sensitivity to powers of language finds its most feeling expression when Euphranor defends the style of Scripture:

O Alciphron! If I durst follow my own judgment, I should be apt to think there are noble beauties in the style of the Holy Scripture: in the narrative parts a strain so simple and unaffected: in the devotional and prophetic so animated and sublime: and in the doctrinal parts such an air of dignity and authority as seems to speak their original divine.   (III.228)

In its varied tones and styles Scripture is the pattern and authority for a language in which truth becomes 'an operative principle' directing our lives.

Select bibliography

Primary sources

Addison, Joseph, *The Freeholder*, ed. James Leheny (Oxford: Clarendon Press, 1979)

The Miscellaneous Works of Joseph Addison, ed. A. C. Guthkelch, 2 vols (London: G. Bell, 1914)

Anti-Siris: or, English Wisdom Exemplifi'd by various Examples, but, particularly, The present general Demand for Tar Water, On so unexceptionable Authority as that of a R—t R—d Itinerant Schemist, and Graduate in Divinity and Metaphisicks (London: M. Cooper, 1744)

[Arnauld, Antoine, *et al.*] *Logick: or, the Art of Thinking*, 4th ed. (London: J. Taylor, 1702)

Bacon, Francis, *The Philosophical Works of Francis Bacon*, ed. James Spedding *et al.*, 5 vols (London: Longmans, 1857–8), Vols. I and IV

Bentley, Richard, *A Confutation of Atheism from the Origin and Frame of the World* (London: H. Mortlock, 1692)

Berkeley, Anne, Notes to 'George Berkeley', in 'Corrigenda and Addenda to the Second Volume', in *Biographia Britannica*, 2nd ed., 5 vols (London: W. and A. Strahan, *et al.*, 1778–93), Vol. III

[Berkeley, George] *The Ladies Library: Written by a Lady: Published by Mr. Steele*, 3 vols (London: J. Tonson, 1714)

The Works of George Berkeley D.D., ed. Alexander Fraser Campbell, 4 vols (Oxford: Clarendon Press, 1901)

The Works of George Berkeley, Bishop of Cloyne, ed. A. A. Luce and T. E. Jessop, 9 vols (London: Nelson 1948–57)

Blackwell, Thomas, *Memoirs of the Court of Augustus*, 3 vols (Edinburgh: Hamilton *et al.*, 1753–63)

Blair, Hugh, *Lectures on Rhetoric and Belles Lettres*, 2 vols (London: W. Strahan, 1783)

Bolton, Robert, *A Translation of the Charter and Statutes of Trinity-College, Dublin* (Dublin: R. Bolton, 1749)

Boswell, James, *Life of Johnson*, ed. George Birkbeck Hill and Rev. L. F. Powell, 6 vols (Oxford: Clarendon Press, 1934–64)

Boyle, Robert, *The Sceptical Chymist: or Chymo-Physical Doubts & Paradoxes* (London: F. Crooke, 1661)

A Discourse of Things above Reason: Inquiring whether a Philosopher should admit there are any such (London: J. Robinson, 1681)

Browne, Peter, *A Letter in Answer to a Book entitled* Christianity not Mysterious (Dublin: J. North, 1697)

The Procedure, Extent, and Limits of Human Understanding (London: W. Innys, 1728)

Browne, Thomas, *Pseudodoxia Epidemica: or, Enquiries into very many Received Tenets, and Commonly Presumed Truths*, 3rd ed. (London: N. Ekins, 1658)

Butler, Joseph, *The Analogy of Religion Natural and Revealed to the Constitution and Course of Nature* (London: J., J. and P. Knapton, 1736)

Chandler, Thomas B., *The Life of Samuel Johnson, D.D.* (New York: T. and J. Swords, 1805)

Charleton, Walter, *The Immortality of the Human Soul, Demonstrated by the Light of Nature: In Two Dialogues* (London: H. Herringman, 1657)

Cheyne, George, *Philosophical Principles of Religion: Natural and Revealed*, 2nd ed. (London: G. Strahan, 1715)

Coleridge, Samuel Taylor, *Collected Letters of Samuel Taylor Coleridge*, ed. Earl Leslie Griggs, 6 vols (Oxford: Clarendon Press, 1956–71)

[Collins, Anthony] *A Discourse of Free-Thinking, Occasion'd by the Rise and Growth of a Sect call'd Free-Thinkers* (London: n.p., 1713)

A Philosophical Inquiry concerning Human Liberty (London: R. Robinson, 1717)

A Discourse concerning Ridicule and Irony in Writing, in a Letter to the Reverend Dr. Nathanael Marshall (London: J. Brotherton, 1729)

Cudworth, Ralph, *The True Intellectual System of the Universe: The First Part; wherein, all the Reason and Philosophy of Atheism is Confuted; and its Impossibility Demonstrated* (London: R. Royston, 1678)

Dacier, André (ed.), *The Works of Plato Abridg'd*, 2 vols (London: A. Bell, 1701)

Derham, William, *Physico-Theology: or, a Demonstration of the Being and Attributes of God, from the Works of Creation*, 2nd ed. (London: W. Innys, 1716 [1714])

Descartes, René, *Œuvres de Descartes*, ed. Charles Adam and P. Tannery, 12 vols (Paris: J. Vrin, 1964–76)

Diogenes Laertius, *The Lives, Opinions, and Remarkable Sayings of the Most Famous Ancient Philosophers*, trans. T. Fetherstone *et al.* (London: E. Brewster, 1688)

Dryden, John, 'A Defense of an Essay of Dramatique Poesie', in *The Indian Emperor*, 2nd ed. (London: H. Herringman, 1668)

Of Dramatick Poesie, an Essay (London: H. Herringman, 1668)

The Poems of John Dryden, ed. James Kingsley, 4 vols (Oxford: Clarendon Press, 1958)

Eachard, John, *Mr. Hobb's State of Nature considered; In a Dialogue between Philautus and Timothy*, 2nd ed. (London: N. Brooke, 1672)

Flemyng, Malcolm, *A Proposal for the Improvement of the Practice of Medicine . . . [with] some Remarks on a Book entitled* Siris, 2nd ed. (Hull: G. Ferraby, 1748)

The Free-Thinker, 3 vols (London: n.p., 1722–3)

Glanvill, Joseph, *Scepsis Scientifica: or, Confest Ignorance, the Way to Science*, 2nd ed. [of the *Vanity of Dogmatizing*] (London: H. Eversden, 1665)

Saducismus Triumphatus: or, Full and Plain Evidence Concerning Witches and Apparitions, 2nd ed. (London: J. Collins and S. Lownds, 1681)

[Goldsmith, Oliver] 'Some Original Memoirs of the Late Famous Bishop of Cloyne', in *Collected Works of Oliver Goldsmith*, ed. Arthur Friedman, 6 vols (Oxford: Clarendon Press, 1966), Vol. III

Guardian, ed. John Calhoun Stevens (Lexington, Ken.: University of Kentucky Press, 1982)

Hales, Stephen, *Statical Essays: containing Vegetable Staticks*, 2nd ed., 2 vols (London, W. Innys *et al.*, 1731)

    An Account of Some Experiments and Observations on Tar-Water (London: R. Manby and H. S. Cox, 1745)

Hobbes, Thomas, *Leviathan or the Matter, Forme, and Power of a Commonwealth Ecclesiastical and Civil*, ed. Michael Oakeshott (Oxford: Blackwell, 1946)

Hume, David, *The Letters of David Hume*, ed. J. Y. T. Greig, 2 vols. (Oxford: Clarendon Press, 1932)

    Hume's Dialogues Concerning Natural Religion, ed. Norman Kemp Smith, 2nd ed. (1935; rpt. London: Nelson, 1947)

    Enquiries concerning Human Understanding and concerning the Principles of Morals, ed. L. A. Selby-Bigge, 3rd ed., rev. P. H. Nidditch (Oxford: Clarendon Press, 1975)

    A Treatise of Human Nature, ed. L. A. Selby-Bigge, 2nd ed., rev. P. H. Nidditch (Oxford: Clarendon Press, 1980)

Hurd, Richard, *Moral and Political Dialogues; with Letters on Chivalry and Romance*, 3rd ed., 3 vols (London: A. Millar *et al.*, 1765)

Hutcheson, Francis, *An Inquiry into the Original of Our Ideas of Beauty and Virtue*, 2nd ed., 2 vols (London: J. Darby, 1726), Vol. I

Johnson, Samuel, *A Dictionary of the English Language* (London: J. and P. Knapton *et al.*, 1755)

    The Rambler, ed. W. J. Bate and Albrecht B. Strauss, Vols. III–V of *The Yale Edition of the Works of Samuel Johnson* (New Haven: Yale University Press, 1969)

Johnson, Samuel, *Samuel Johnson, President of King's College: His Career and Writings*, ed. Herbert and Carol Schneider, 4 vols (New York: Columbia University Press, 1929)

[Jurin, James] *A Letter to the Right Reverend the Bishop of Cloyne, occasion'd by His Lordship's Treatise on the Virtues of Tar-Water* (London: J. Robinson, 1744)

LeClerc, Jean, *Logica: Sive, Ars Ratiocinandi* (London: A. Churchill, 1692)

    Monsieur Le Clerc's Extract and Judgment of the Characteristicks of Men, Manners, Opinions, Times, in Three Volumes (London: E. Sanger, 1712)

Leslie, Charles, *The Theological Works of the Reverend Charles Leslie*, 2 vols (London: W. Bowyer, 1721)

The Lives of the Ancient Philosophers (London: J. Nicholson and T. Newborough, 1702)

Locke, John, *A Paraphrase and Notes on the Epistles of Paul . . . to which is Prefix'd, An Essay for the Understanding of St. Paul's Epistles, by consulting St. Paul Himself* (London: A. and J. Churchill, 1707)

    Some Thoughts on the Conduct of the Understanding in Search of Truth ([England]: n.p., 1741)

    The Educational Writings of John Locke, ed. James L. Axtell (Cambridge: Cambridge University Press, 1968)

    Epistola de Tolerantia, ed. Raymond Klibansky, trans. J. W. Gough (Oxford: Clarendon Press, 1968)

    Two Treatises of Government, ed. Peter Laslett, 2nd ed. (Cambridge: Cambridge University Press, 1970)

An Essay concerning Human Understanding, ed. Peter H. Nidditch (Oxford: Clarendon Press, 1975)

Malebranche, Nicholas, *Christian Conferences: demonstrating the Truth of the Christian Religion and Morality . . . to which is Added His Meditations on Humility and Repentance* (London: J. Whitlock, 1695)

Father Malebranche His Treatise concerning the Search after Truth, trans. Thomas Taylor, 2nd ed. (London: W. Boyer, 1700)

Œuvres Complètes, ed. André Robinet *et al.*, 21 vols. (Paris: J. Vrin, 1958–70), Vols. I–IV

[Mandeville, Bernard] *The Fable of the Bees: or Private Vices Publick Benefits*, 2nd ed. (London: E. Parker, 1723)

A Letter to Dion, Occasion'd by his Book call'd Alciphron, or the Minute Philosopher (London: J. Roberts, 1732)

The Fable of the Bees, ed. F. B. Kaye, 2 vols (Oxford: Clarendon Press, 1924)

Milton, John, *The Poems of John Milton*, ed. John Carey and Alastair Fowler, 2nd ed. (London: Longmans, 1968)

Montaigne, *Les Essais de Michel Seigneur de Montaigne*, ed. Pierre Coste (London: J. Tonson and J. Watts, 1724)

More, Henry, *Divine Dialogues, Containing Sundry Disquisitions & Instructions concerning the Attributes and Providence of God* (London: J. Flesher, 1668)

Newton, Isaac, *Opticks: or, a Treatise of the Reflections, Refractions, Inflections and Colours of Light* (London: S. Smith and B. Walford, 1704)

Opticks: or, a Treatise of the Reflections, Refractions, Inflections and Colours of Light, 2nd ed. (London: W. and J. Innys, 1717)

The Mathematical Principles of Natural Philosophy, trans. Andrew Motte, 2 vols. (London: B. Motte, 1729)

Norris, John, *Cursory Reflections upon a Book call'd an* Essay concerning Human Understanding (London: S. Manship, 1690)

Pope, Alexander, *The Correspondence of Alexander Pope*, ed. George Sherburn, 5 vols (Oxford: Clarendon Press, 1956)

Rand, Benjamin, (ed.), *Berkeley and Percival* (Cambridge: Cambridge University Press, 1914)

Rapin, René, *The Whole Critical Works of Monsieur Rapin*, trans. Basil Kennet *et al.*, 2nd ed., 2 vols (London: R. Bonwicke *et al.*, 1716)

Shaftesbury, Antony Ashley Cooper 3rd Earl of, *Characteristicks of Men, Manners, Opinions, Times*, 2nd ed. ([England]: n.p., 1714)

preface, *Select Sermons of Dr. Whichcot* (London: A. and J. Churchill, 1698)

Second Characters or The Language of Forms, ed. Benjamin Rand (1914; rpt. New York: Greenwood, 1969)

The Spectator, ed. Donald F. Bond, 5 vols (Oxford: Clarendon Press, 1965)

Spence, Joseph, *Observations, Anecdotes, and Characters of Books and Men*, ed. James M. Osborn, 2 vols (Oxford: Clarendon Press, 1966)

Sprat, Thomas, *History of the Royal Society*, ed. Jackson I. Cope and Harold Whitmore Jones (London: Routledge, 1959)

Stanley, Thomas, *The History of Philosophy* (London: H. Moseley and T. Dring, 1655)

Stock, Joseph, *Memoirs of George Berkeley, D.D. Late Bishop of Cloyne in Ireland*, 2nd ed. (London: J. Murray and R. Fauldner, 1784)

Swift, Jonathan, *The Prose Works of Jonathan Swift*, ed. Herbert Davis, 16 vols (Oxford: Blackwell, 1939–74)

The Correspondence of Jonathan Swift, ed. Harold Williams, 5 vols (Oxford: Clarendon Press, 1963–5)

Sydenham, Floyer (trans.), *The Dialogues of Plato*, 3 vols (London: W. Sandby, 1767–79)

The Tatler, ed. George H. Aitken, 4 vols (London: Duckworth, 1898–9)

[Tindal, Matthew] *The Rights of the Christian Church Asserted* ([London]: n.p., 1706)

Toland, John, *Christianity not Mysterious* ([London]: n.p., 1696)

'A Vindication of Lord Shaftesbury's Writings and Character; against the Author of a Book, called, *Alciphron, or the Minute Philosopher*', *London Magazine*, nos. 676–7, 10 and 17 June 1732.

Walker, Obadiah, *Of Education: Especially of Young Gentlemen*, 6th ed. (London: R. Wellington, 1699)

Walpole, Horace, *The Yale Edition of Horace Walpole's Correspondence*, ed. W. S. Lewis *et al.*, 48 vols (London: Oxford University Press, 1937–83), Vol. XVIII

Ward, John, *A System of Oratory, Delivered in a Course of Lectures*, 2 vols (London: J. Ward, 1759)

Warton, Joseph, *An Essay on the Genius and Writings of Pope*, 4th ed., 2 vols (London: J. Dodsley, 1782)

Whiston, Williams, *Historical Memoirs of the Life of Dr. Samuel Clarke*, 2nd ed. (London: F. Gyles and J. Roberts, 1730)

Wilmot, John, *The Poems of John Wilmot, Earl of Rochester*, ed. Keith Walker (Oxford: Blackwell, 1984)

[Wishart, William] *A Vindication of the Reverend D— B—y, from the scandalous Imputation of Being Author of a late Book, intitled*, Alciphron or the minute Philosopher (London: A. Millar, 1734)

Secondary sources

Aaron, R. I., 'A Catalogue of Berkeley's Library', *Mind*, 41 (1932), 265–75

Acworth, Richard, 'Locke's First Reply to John Norris', *Locke Newsletter*, 2 (1971), 7–11

Adams, Robert Merrihew, 'Berkeley's "Notion" of Spiritual Substance', *Archiv für Geschichte der Philosophie*, 55 (1973), 47–69

Alexander, Peter, *Ideas, Qualities and Corpuscles: Locke and Boyle on the External World* (Cambridge: Cambridge University Press, 1985)

Ardley, Gavin, *Berkeley's Renovation of Philosophy* (The Hague: M. Nijhoff, 1968)

Armstrong, Robert L., 'Berkeley's Theory of Signification', *JHP*, 7 (1969), 163–74

Bambrough, Renford, 'Literature and Philosophy', in *Wisdom: Twelve Essays*, ed. Renford Bambrough (Oxford: Blackwell, 1974), pp. 274–92

Beal, M. W., 'Berkeley's Linguistic Criterion', *Personalist*, 52 (1971), 499–513

Belanger, Terry, 'Publishers and Writers in Eighteenth-Century England', in *Books and their Readers in Eighteenth-Century England*, ed. Isabel Rivers (Leicester: Leicester University Press, 1982), pp. 5–25

Belfrage, Bertil, 'A Clash on Semantics in Berkeley's Notebook A', In *George Berkeley: Essays and Replies* (Dublin: Irish Academic Press, 1985), pp. 117–26

Bennett, Jonathan, *Locke, Berkeley, Hume: Central Themes* (Oxford: Clarendon Press, 1971)

Berman, David, 'Anthony Collins and the Question of Atheism in the Early Part of the Eighteenth Century', *Proceedings of the Royal Irish Academy*, 75 (1975), section C, 85–102

'Berkeley's Letter to Lord Orrery', *Berkeley Newsletter*, 3 (1979), 12–13

'Berkeley's Philosophical Reception after America', *Archiv für Geschichte der Philosophie*, 62 (1980), 311–20

'Bishop Berkeley and the Fountains of Living Waters', *Hermathena*, 128 (Summer 1980), 21–31

'Cognitive Theology and Emotive Mysteries in Berkeley's *Alciphron*', *Proceedings of the Royal Irish Academy*, 81 (1981), section C, 219–29

Review of *The Guardian* edited by J. C. Stevens, *Berkeley Newsletter*, 7 (1984), 23–6

'Bishop Berkeley's Gift of Books in 1733', *The Yale University Library Gazette*, 8 (1933), 1–41

Black, Edwin, *Rhetorical Criticism: A Study in Method* (New York 1965; rpt. London: University of Wisconsin Press, 1978)

Bloom, Edward A., and Lillian D., 'The Satiric Mode of Feeling: A Theory of Intention', *Criticism*, 11 (1969), 115–39

Satire's Pervasive Voice (London: Cornell University Press, 1979)

Bowles, G., 'Physical, Human and Divine Attraction in the Life and Thought of George Cheyne', *Annals of Science*, 31 (1974), 474–88

Bracken, Harry M., *The Early Reception of Berkeley's Immaterialism 1710–1733*, rev. ed., International Archives of the History of Ideas, 10 (The Hague: M. Nijhoff, 1965)

Brett, R. L., *The Third Earl of Shaftesbury: A Study in Eighteenth-Century Literary Theory* (London: Hutchinson, 1951)

Browne, Joseph William, 'Berkeley and Scholasticism', *Modern Schoolman*, 49 (1971–2), 113–23

Brunet, Olivier, 'Le Sentiment Esthétique Chez Berkeley', in *Deuxième Congrès International D'Esthétique et de Science de L'Art* (Paris: Félix Alcan, 1937), Vol. II, pp. 29–32

Buchdahl, Gerd, *The Image of Newton and Locke in the Age of Reason*, Newman History and Philosophy of Science Series, 6 (London: Sheed and Ward, 1961)

Bynum, W. F., 'Health, Disease and Medical Care', in *The Ferment of Knowledge: Studies in the Historiography of Eighteenth-Century Science*, ed. G.S. Rousseau and Roy Porter (Cambridge: Cambridge University Press, 1980)

Cadbury, Henry J., 'Bishop Berkeley's Gifts to Harvard Library', *Harvard Library Bulletin*, 7 (1953), 73–87 and 196–207

Cantor, G.N., 'Two Letters Relating to Berkeley's Social Circle', *Berkeley Newsletter*, 4 (1980) 1–3

'The Theological Significance of Ethers', in *Conceptions of Ether: Studies in the History of Ether Theories 1740–1900*, ed. G. N. Cantor and M. J. S. Hodge (Cambridge: Cambridge University Press, 1981), pp. 135–55

Carr, Stephen Leo, 'The Rhetoric of Argument in Berkeley's *Siris*', *University of Toronto Quarterly*, 51 (1981), 47–60

Charlton, William, 'Is Philosophy a Form of Literature?', *British Journal of Aesthetics*, 14 (1974), 3–16

Colie, Rosalie, 'The Social Language of John Locke: A Study in the History of Ideas', *Journal of British Studies*, 4, No. 2 (1965), 9–51

'The Essayist in his *Essay*', in *John Locke: Problems and Perspectives*, ed. John W. Yolton (Cambridge: Cambridge University Press, 1969), pp. 234–61

Costello, William T., *The Scholastic Curriculum at Early Seventeenth-Century Cambridge* (Cambridge, Mass.: Harvard University Press, 1958)

Cragg, Gerald R., *Reason and Authority in the Eighteenth Century* (Cambridge: Cambridge University Press, 1964)

Cranston, Maurice William, *John Locke: A Biography* (London: Longman, 1957)

Croll, Morris W., *Style, Rhetoric, and Rhythm: Essays by Morris W. Croll*, ed. J. Max Patrick *et al.* (Princeton: Princeton University Press, 1966)

Davie, Donald, 'Berkeley's Style in *Siris*', *Cambridge Journal*, 4 (1950–1), 427–33

'Irony and Conciseness in Berkeley and Swift', *The Dublin Magazine*, 27 (1952), 20–9

'Berkeley and Philosophic Words', *Studies*, 44 (1955), 319–24

The Language of Science and the Language of Literature, 1700–40, Newman History and Philosophy of Science, 13 (London: Sheed and Ward, 1963)

'Berkeley and the Style of Dialogue', in *The English Mind: Studies of the English Moralists presented to Basil Willey*, ed. H. S. Davies and G. Watson (Cambridge: Cambridge University Press, 1964), pp. 90–106

'Yeats, Berkeley, and Romanticism', in *English Literature and British Philosophy*, ed. S. P. Rosenbaum (Chicago: University of Chicago Press, 1971), pp. 278–84

Dobrée, Bonamy, 'Berkeley as a Man of Letters', *Hermathena*, 82 (1953), 49–75

Downey, James, *The Eighteenth-Century Pulpit: A Study of the Sermons of Butler, Berkeley, Secker, Sterne, Whitfield and Wesley* (Oxford: Clarendon Press, 1969)

Edwards, Thomas R., 'Mandeville's Moral Prose', *ELH*, 31 (1964), 195–212

Ehrenpreis, Irvin, *Swift, The Man, His Works, and the Age*, 3 vols (London: Methuen, 1962–83)

Elkin, P. K., *The Augustan Defence of Satire* (Oxford: Clarendon Press, 1973)

Flage, Daniel E., *Berkeley's Doctrine of Notions: A Reconstruction based on his Theory of Meaning* (London: Croom Helm, 1987)

Flew, Anthony, *Hume's Philosophy of Belief: A Study of the First* Inquiry (London: Routledge, 1961)

Freimarck, Vincent, 'The Bible and Neo-Classical Views of Style', *JEGP*, 51 (1952), 507–26

Fuller, Henry M., 'Bishop Berkeley as a Benefactor of Yale', *The Yale University Library Gazette*, 29 (1953), 1–18

Furlong, E. J., 'How Much of Steele's *Guardian* No. 39 Did Berkeley Write?', *Hermathena*, 89 (1957), 76–88

Gaustad, Edwin S., *George Berkeley in America* (London: Yale University Press, 1979)

Grassi, Ernesto, *Rhetoric as Philosophy: The Humanist Tradition* (London: Pennsylvania State University Press, 1980)

Grayling, A. C., *Berkeley: The Central Arguments* (London: Duckworth, 1986)

Hacking, Ian, *Why Does Language Matter to Philosophy?* (Cambridge: Cambridge University Press, 1975)

Hall, Rupert A., 'English Scientific Literature in the Seventeenth Century', in *Scientific Literature in Sixteenth & Seventeenth Century England: Papers Delivered at the Sixth Clark Library Seminar* (Los Angeles: University of California Press, 1961), pp. 23–45

Harth, Philip, *Contexts of Dryden's Thought* (Chicago: University of Chicago Press, 1968)

Heimann, P. M., 'Ether and Imponderables', in *Conceptions of Ether: Studies in the History of Ether Theories 1740–1900*, ed. G.N. Cantor and M.J.S. Hodge (Cambridge: Cambridge University Press, 1981)

Hollingshead, Gregory, 'George Berkeley and English Literature of the Eighteenth Century' (unpublished Ph.D diss., University of London, 1974)

 'Bishop Berkeley and the Gloomy Clerk: Pope's Final Satire on Deism', *Durham University Journal*, 75 (1982–3), 19–27

Hone, J. M., and M. M. Rossi, *Bishop Berkeley: His Life, Writings, and Philosophy* (London: Faber, 1931)

Houghton, Walter E., 'The English Virtuoso in the Seventeenth Century', *JHI*, 3 (1942), 51– 73 and 190–219

Howell, Wilbur Samuel, *Eighteenth-Century British Logic and Rhetoric* (Princeton, N.J.: Princeton University Press, 1971)

Huizinga, J., *Homo Ludens; A Study of the Play-Element in Culture* (London: Routledge, 1949)

Jessop, T. E., *A Bibliography of George Berkeley*, International Archives of the History of Ideas, 66, 2nd ed. (The Hague: N. Nijhoff, 1973)

Jones, Richard Foster, *et al.*, 'The Background of the Attack on Science in the Age of Pope', in *Pope and His Contemporaries: Essays presented to George Sherburn*, ed. James L. Clifford and Louis A. Landa (Oxford: Clarendon Press, 1949), pp. 96–113

 The Seventeenth Century: Studies in the History of English Thought and Literature from Bacon to Pope (Stanford, Cal.: Stanford University Press, 1951)

Kaye, F. B., 'The Influence of Bernard Mandeville', *Studies in Philology*, 19 (1922), 83–108

Kennedy, George A., *Classical Rhetoric and Its Christian and Secular Tradition from Ancient to Modern Times* (London: Croom Helm, 1980)

Keynes, Geoffrey, *A Bibliography of George Berkeley Bishop of Cloyne*, Soho Bibliographies, 18 (Oxford: Clarendon Press, 1976)

King, Lester S., *The Philosophy of Medicine: The Early Eighteenth Century* (Cambridge, Mass.: Harvard University Press, 1978)

Kretzmann, Norman, 'The Main Thesis of Locke's Semantic Theory', *Philosophical Review*, 77 (1968), 175–96

Kuhn, Albert J., 'Glory or Gravity: Hutchinson vs. Newton', *JHI*, 22 (1961), 303–22

Lambert, Richard T., 'The Literal Intent of Berkeley's Dialogues', *Philosophy and Literature*, 6 (1982), 165–71

Land, Stephen K., *From Signs to Propositions: The Concept of Form in Eighteenth-Century Semantic Theory* (London: Longmans, 1974)

Lang, Berel, 'Space, Time and Philosophical Style', in *Philosophical Style: An Anthology about the Writing and Reading of Philosophy*, ed. Berel Lang (Chicago: Nelson-Hall, 1980), p.p. 144–72

Leary, David E., 'Berkeley's Social Theory: Context and Development', *JHI*, 38 (1977), 635–49

Levi, Albert William, 'Philosophy as Literature: The Dialogue', *Philosophy and Rhetoric*, 9 (1976), 1–20

Leyburn, Ellen Douglas, 'Bishop Berkeley: The Querist', *Proceedings of the Royal Irish Academy*, 44 (1937–8), section C, 75–98

'Bishop Berkeley, Metaphysician as Moralist', in *The Age of Johnson: Essays Presented to Chauncey Brewster Tinker* (New Haven: Yale University Press, 1949), pp. 319–28

Linnell, John, 'Berkeley's *Siris*', *Personalist*, 41 (1960), 5–12

Love, Rosaleen, 'Herman Boerhaave and the Element–Instrument Concept of Fire', *Annals of Science*, 31 (1974), 547–9

Luce, A. A., 'More Unpublished Berkeley Letters and New Berkeleiana', *Hermathena*, 48 (1933), 25–53

Berkeley and Malebranche: A Study in the Origins of Berkeley's Thought (London: Oxford University Press, 1934)

'Berkeley's Bermuda Project and His Benefactions to American Universities, with Unpublished Letters and Extracts from the Egmont Papers', *Proceedings of the Royal Irish Academy*, 42 (1934–5), section C, 97–120

'Berkeley's Essays in the *Guardian*', *Mind*, 52 (1943), 247–63

The Life of George Berkeley Bishop of Cloyne (London: Nelson, 1949)

The Dialectic of Immaterialism: An Account of the Making of Berkeley's Principles (London: Hodder & Stoughton, 1963)

March, W. W. S., 'Analogy, Aquinas and Bishop Berkeley', *Theology*, 44 (1942), 321–9

Maxwell, Constantia, *A History of Trinity College Dublin 1591–1892* (Dublin: University Press (Trinity College), 1946)

McCracken, Charles J., *Malebranche and British Philosophy* (Oxford: Clarendon Press, 1983)

McDowell, R. B., and D. A. Webb, *Trinity College Dublin 1592–1952: An Academic History* (Cambridge: Cambridge University Press, 1982)

McGowan, William H., 'George Berkeley's American Declaration of Independence', *Studies in Eighteenth-Century Culture*, 12 (1983), 105–13

Merrill, Elizabeth, *The Dialogue in English Literature*, Yale Studies in English, 42, ed. Albert S. Cook (New York: Henry Holt, 1911)

Morrisroe, Michael, 'Ciceronian, Platonic, and Neo-Classical Dialogues: Forms in Berkeley and Hume', *Enlightenment Essays*, 3 (1972), 147–59

Newton-Smith, W. H., 'Berkeley's Philosophy of Science', in *Essays on Berkeley*, ed. John Foster and Howard Robinson (Oxford: Clarendon Press, 1985), pp. 149–61

Nicolson, Marjorie, and G. B. Rousseau, 'Bishop Berkeley and Tar-Water', in *The Augustan Milieu: Essays presented to Louis A. Landa* (Oxford: Clarendon Press, 1970), pp. 102–37

Odom, Herbert H., 'The Estrangement of Celestial Mechanics and Religion', *JHI*, 27 (1966), 533–48

Oertel, Hans Joachim, *George Berkeley und die Englische Literatur*, Studien zur Englischen Philologie, 80 (Halle: M. Niemeyer, 1934)

O'Higgins, James, *Anthony Collins: The Man and His Works* (The Hague: M. Nijhoff, 1970)

Olscamp, Paul J., *The Moral Philosophy of George Berkeley*, International Archives of the History of Ideas, 33 (The Hague: M. Nijhoff, 1970)

Pahl, Gretchen Graf, 'John Locke as Literary Critic and Biblical Interpreter', in *Essays Critical and Historical Dedicated to Lily B. Campbell*, University of California Publications of English Studies, 1 (Berkeley: University of California Press, 1950), pp. 139–57

Parks, Stephen, 'George Berkeley, Sir Richard Steele and *The Ladies Library*', *Scriblerian*, 13 (1980), 1–2

Perelman, Ch., and L. Olbrects-Tyteca, *The New Rhetoric: A Treatise on Argumentation*, trans. John Wilkinson and Purcell Weaver (London: University of Notre Dame Press, 1969)

Piquet, Jean-Claude, 'Kunst und Philosophie', *Studi Internazionali di Filosophia*, 2 (1970), 49–63

Pitcher, George, *Berkeley*, The Arguments of the Philosophers, ed. Ted Honderick (London: Routledge, 1977)

Popkin, Richard H., 'Berkeley and Pyrrhonism', *Review of Metaphysics*, 5 (1951–2), 223–46

Porter, Roy, 'Laymen, Doctors and Medical Knowledge in the Eighteenth Century: The Evidence of the *Gentleman's Magazine*', in *Patients and Practitioners: Lay Perceptions of Medicine in Pre-Industrial Society*, ed. Roy Porter (Cambridge: Cambridge University Press, 1985), pp. 283–314

Preston, Thomas R., 'Biblical Criticism, Literature, and the Eighteenth-Century Reader', in *Books and their Readers in Eighteenth-Century England*, ed. Isabel Rivers (Leicester: Leicester University Press, 1982), pp. 97–126

Price, John Valdimir, 'The Reading of Philosophical Literature', in *Books and their Readers in Eighteenth-Century England*, ed. Isabel Rivers (Leicester: Leicester University Press, 1982), pp. 165–96

Purpus, Eugene R., 'The "Plain, Easy, and Familiar Way": The Dialogue in English Literature, 1660–1725', *ELH*, 17 (1950), 47–58

Rauter, Herbert, "The Veil of Words": Sprachauffassung und Dialogform bei George Berkeley', *Anglia*, 79 (1961), 378–404

Rée, Jonathan, 'Descartes' Comedy', *Philosophy and Literature*, 8 (1984), 151–66

Rendall, Stephen, 'Dialogue, Philosophy, and Rhetoric: The Example of Plato's *Gorgias*', *Philosophy and Rhetoric*, 10 (1977), 165–79

Richetti, John J., *Philosophical Writing: Locke, Berkeley, Hume* (Cambridge, Mass.: Harvard University Press, 1983)

Ritterbush, Philip C., *Overtures to Biology: The Speculations of Eighteenth-Century Naturalists* (London: Yale University Press, 1964)

Robinet, André, 'Leibniz: Lecture du *Treatise* de Berkeley', *Etudes Philosophiques*, 1983, 217–23.

Robinson, Richard, *Plato's Earlier Dialectic*, 2nd ed. (Oxford: Clarendon Press, 1953)

Rousseau, G. S., 'Science Books and Their Readers in the Eighteenth Century', in *Books and Their Readers in Eighteenth-Century England*, ed. Isabel Rivers (Leicester: Leicester University Press, 1982), pp. 197–255

Rudowski, Victor Anthony, 'The Theory of Signs in the Eighteenth Century', *JHI*, 35 (1974), 683–90

Ryle, Gilbert, 'John Locke on the Human Understanding', in *John Locke: Tercentenary Addresses* (London: Oxford University Press, 1933), pp. 15–38

Plato's Progress (Cambridge: Cambridge University Press, 1966)

Saintsbury, George, *A History of English Prose Rhythm* (London: Macmillan, 1912)

Schaffer, Simon, 'Natural Philosophy', in *The Ferment of Knowledge: Studies in the*

Historiography of Eighteenth-Century Science, ed. G. S. Rousseau and Roy Porter (Cambridge: Cambridge University Press, 1980), pp. 55–91

Seeskin, Kenneth, 'Socratic Philosophy and the Dialogue Form', *Philosophy and Literature*, 8 (1984), 181–93

Stephen, Leslie, *History of English Thought in the Eighteenth Century*, 3rd ed., 2 vols (1902; rpt. London: John Murray, 1927)

Stewart. M. A., 'Berkeley and the Rankenian Club', in *George Berkeley: Essays and Replies*, ed. David Berman (Dublin: Irish Academic Press, 1986), pp. 25–45

Stroll, Avrum, *The Emotive Theory of Ethics*, University of California Publications in Philosophy, 28, No. 1 (1954), 1–92

Stubbs, John William, *The History of the University of Dublin from its Foundations to the End of the Eighteenth Century* (Dublin: Hodges, 1889)

Suchting, W. A., 'Berkeley's Criticism of Newton on Space and Motion', *ISIS*, 58 (1967), 186–97

Sutherland, James R., 'Restoration Prose', in *Restoration and Augustan Prose* (Los Angeles: University of California, W. A. Clark Memorial Library, 1956), pp. 1–18

On English Prose (Toronto: University of Toronto Press, 1957)

Sutherland, L. S., 'The Curriculum', in *The Eighteenth Century*, Vol. V. of *The History of the University of Oxford*, ed. L. S. Sutherland and L. G. Mitchell (Oxford: Clarendon Press, 1986), pp. 469–91

Tipton, I. C., *Berkeley: The Philosophy of Immaterialism* (London: Methuen, 1974)

Turbayne, Colin Murray, *The Myth of Metaphor*, 2nd ed. (Columbia, S.C.: University of South Carolina Press, 1970)

Tuveson, Ernest, 'The Importance of Shaftesbury', *ELH*, 20 (1953), 267–99

Urmson, J. O., *Berkeley*, Past Masters (Oxford: Oxford University Press, 1982)

Warnock, G. J., *Berkeley* (Oxford: Blackwell, 1952)

Wasserman, Earl R., 'Nature Moralized: The Divine Analogy in the Eighteenth Century', *ELH*, 20 (1953), 39–76

Watt, Ian, 'The Ironic Tradition in Augustan Prose from Swift to Johnson', in *Restoration and Augustan Prose* (Los Angeles: University of California, W. A. Clark Memorial Library, 1956), pp. 19–46

Wheeler, K. M. 'Berkeley's Ironic Method in the *Three Dialogues*', *Philosophy and Literature*, 4 (1980), 18–32

Sources, Processes and Methods in Coleridge's Biographia Literaria (Cambridge: Cambridge University Press, 1980)

White, Alan R., 'A Linguistic Approach to Berkeley's Philosophy', *Philosophy and Phenomenological Research*, 16 (1955–6), 172–87

Wild, John, *George Berkeley: A Study of his Life and Philosophy* (Cambridge, Mass.: Harvard University Press, 1936)

Williamson, George, *The Senecan Amble: A Study in Prose from Bacon to Collier* (London: Faber, 1951)

Winkler, Kenneth P., 'The Authorship of *Guardian* 69', *Berkeley Newsletter*, 7 (1984), 1–6

Wisdom, John, *Philosophy and Psycho-Analaysis* (Oxford: Blackwell, 1953)

Wordsworth, Christopher, *Scholae Academicae: Some Account of Studies at the English Universities in the Eighteenth Century* (1877; rpt. London: Frank Cuss, 1968)

Woozley, A. D., 'Berkeley's Doctrine of Notions and Theory of Meaning', *Journal of the History of Philosophy*, 14 (1976), 427–35

Yolton, John W., *John Locke and the Way of Ideas*, Oxford Classical and Philosophical Monographs (Oxford: Oxford University Press, 1956)
  Locke and the Compass of Human Understanding: A Selective Commentary on the Essay (Cambridge: Cambridge University Press, 1970)

Index